Beating Autism

Beating Autism
How Alternative Medicine Cured My Child
A Personal Memoir

by
Anne M. Evans

West River Publishing

Copyright © 2015 by Anne M. Evans
All rights reserved. No part of this book may be reproduced in any form or by any means—electronic, mechanical, photocopying, scanning, or otherwise—without permission in writing from the publisher, except by a reviewer, who may quote brief passages in a review.
Published by West River Publishing (WRP), West River Maryland, USA

Medical illustrations by Ryan Conway M.D.

WRP Books are available at special discounts for bulk purchases. For more information visit http://www.westriverpublishing.com.

Hardcover ISBN: 978-0-692-37465-8
ebook ISBN: 978-0-692-374672

Library of Congress Cataloging-in-Publication Data
1. Autism Spectrum Disorders – Popular works
2. Asperger's Syndrome – Popular Works
3. Attention Deficit Hyperactivity Disorder – Popular works
4. Dyslexia – Popular works
5. Alternative Medicine – Healthcare
6. Food Additives – Toxicology
7. Energy Medicine – Popular works
8. Traditional Chinese Medicine – Healthcare
9. Mental Health – Popular works
10. Psychology – Popular works
11. Nabudripad's Allergy Elimination - Healthcare

Printed in the United States of America

*Dedicated
To my loving Sarah
who put up with the sickness, the suffering,
and the agony of recovery
to forge a path toward healing
for other children on the spectrum.*

Contents

Foreword		ix
Author's Preface		ixx
Acknowledgments		xxv
Commentary on Field Control Therapy®		xxvii
Part One—Sarah's Story		**31**
One	A Rude Awakening	33
Two	Daddy's Little Girl	37
Three	Feeling Like a Yo-Yo	41
Four	My Worst Nightmare	45
Five	Shopping Around	51
Six	Heaven Sent	57
Seven	Making the Decision to Use Energy Medicine	61
Part Two—The Journey Begins		**63**
Eight	The Tools We Used at Home	65
Nine	Food Elimination	75
Ten	Nutritional Supplements	97
Part Three—The Cure		**105**
Eleven	A Brief Explanation of Integrated Chinese Medicine or Energy Medicine (as I experienced it)	107
Twelve	Body Out of Balance	111
Thirteen	The Tickle Doctor	117
Fourteen	The Basic Treatments	123
Fifteen	The Vaccine Link	137
Sixteen	Customizing the Program	145
Seventeen	Unwelcome Guests	151
Eighteen	Returning to the Custom Program	159
Nineteen	Rebuilding the Central Nervous System	165
Twenty	Food, Supplements, and Concentration	169
Twenty-one	Chinese Emotions	175
Twenty-two	The Coil	177
Twenty-three	Unlocking Sarah's Organs	183
Twenty-four	Home-schooling and Epsom Salts	191
Twenty-five	More Unwanted Visitors	195
Twenty-six	Improving Concentration and Memory	199
Twenty-seven	Putting the Foods Back	205
Part Four—The Follow-Up		**207**
Twenty-eight	The Follow-Up	209

Appendices

Appendix A. Sarah's Total Recovery Protocol	211
Appendix B. Medical Test Results	213
Appendix C. Psychological Tests—Before and After	219
Appendix D. Sarah's Treatment List	227
Appendix E. How to Find a NAET or an FCT® Practitioner	238
Appendix F. Resources Used	240
Index	242

List of Tables and Illustrations

The Tools	66
A List of Sarah's Symptoms	77
Sarah's Short Food Elimination List	80
Sarah's Gluten-Free Flour Blend	85
Salicylate and Phenolic Foods Removed from Sarah's Diet	87
Sarah's Total Sensitivities	93
Foods Sarah Did Eat	94
Sarah's Specific Food Responses	95
A Summary of Sarah's Elimination Stage of Recovery	96
Marrow Bone Stock	103
Sarah's Supplements (May 2001)	103
Chinese Meridian System	110
Chalkboard Photos	133
Broca's Region	141
Optic Nerve and Visual Cortex	152
Toxoplasmosis-Filled Retina	153
Revised Supplement List	170
Hypothalamus	173
Sarah's Psychological Evaluation WISC III age 7	191
Sarah's Psychological Evaluation WISC III age 10	193
Post-treatment Retina	203

Foreword

As I wrote this foreword, many thoughts, regarding all aspects of treating a beautiful little girl named Sarah, who lived in a world we knew nothing of, stirred again in my mind. Her world had no normalcy as the average person would experience it. If I were to title this foreword, I would certainly call it "From Tears to Smiles." This book portrays the effects of Sarah's recovery from the emotional, physical, mental, and spiritual viewpoints experienced by Sarah, her parents, and myself; and assuredly friends and other people who interacted with her for various reasons.

I have to mention that Sarah's mother, Anne Evans, is a wonderful person who has a very deep and clear understanding of biological systems due to her education. She has knowledge and expertise beyond many of the professional dieticians I have had occasion to deal with. She had begun supplementation, food withholding, diet/food approaches that helped Sarah in many ways. She loves to help other people incorporate her findings and experience in their search to resolve problems. You will read the effects of specific foods in terms of signs and symptoms that Sarah had. Then, you will see Anne evolve to a point that could go no further, and she ran into a brick wall. Sarah was doing better with a dietary approach, but could not be really brought to normalcy. There is good reason for this. In my clinical experience, I have found that an offending food, an allergen, will leave a memory in the energetic body that dietary changes, supplements, and so forth cannot correct. Another approach must be used to edit, or delete, these memories once they are discovered and mapped into the system's brain functional areas.

I practice acupuncture, and I combine the aspects of traditional Chinese medicine, my electrical engineering and physics background, and Western medicine. I have had to put aside my scientific, Newtonian mind. I have found that many things related to the human biological system were more of a complicated quantum control system that associated with molecules, cells, cellular organization, organs, and communicative connectivities. In fact, I believe each cell is a holographic, multidimensional canvas that portrays all aspects of the whole body. I also believe that living biological formats (including humans) are capable of generating and receiving scalar energy that provides our information system with transport and control functions. This scalar system reacts with the holographic aspects of cells and cellular organization in the organs, brain, glands, and yet-to-be-defined pathways of the body. This scalar energy is difficult to measure. It does not fall off in intensity over long distances. Therefore, it does not diminish in intensity by one over the square of the distance between centers, as do other forms of electromagnetic radiation and fields. It is not a vectored radiation. In other words, it has no direction, like electricity. Scalar energy constitutes a new realm in terms of integrating the format into my energetic approach using detection equipment that I have designed and built.

Overview of the Technique

This book describes the diagnosis, treatment, and resolution of autism. I have had the profound privilege of setting a number of people on the spectrum free to a normal life. I have worked countless hours to perfect protocols in the use of a very important healing method called the *Nambudripad Allergy Elimination Technique* (NAET). NAET was discovered and systematized by my mentor and friend, Devi Nambudripad M.D. PhD. DC. Lac. and has been in use for more than twenty-five years. It uses fundamental acupuncture, acupressure, nutritional therapies, and concepts derived from ancient Chinese medicine. Another important technique is a testing format utilizing neuromuscular sensitivity (NST). This is a format of muscle strength determination associated with applied kinesiology, developed in 1960 by Dr. George Goodheart. It is also referred to as *muscle response testing* (MRT). Each practitioner must be re-certified for testing on a regular basis, and must stay current in various required advanced topics. MRT, NST, and Chinese pulses are used in combination for diagnosis. The points along the meridians are used to resonate and detoxify tissues, balance hormones, and boost the immune system. The cells of the body respond by opening portals in the cellular walls and releasing toxins into the lymphatic system for drainage from the body. Thus, whole systems are cleansed and are able to function normally again. While some individual techniques used in this therapy are ancient, the combination was derived by Dr. Nambudripad.

My work is not easy, as the person being treated is lost to the world, to their families, and to friends. There are human suffering and emotional aspects that are constantly in a dynamic that must be dealt with. People, of course, would like a single small, white pill to treat and cure autism, and they would like this to happen overnight. Naturally, that is not possible. Therefore, I often deal with other affairs of life surrounding the patient to make the change in lifestyle possible to encourage recovery. At times, I have to treat the mother or the father as each develops problems that need to be dealt with. This helps heal the entire family, increasing the health of the autistic child. Thus, I have watched many children mature over the last eighteen years as they grow into a young adults. In fact, many have graduated from college. Some were horribly aggressive and destructive. One, at the age of four, ate the wooden door framing of one of my treatment rooms; and yes, I get a smile now over this. In many cases, I had to figure out how to treat a child the parent could not hold. Sarah was difficult, but had no serious aggressiveness. Her difficulty was that there were too many systems, organs, offending foods, environmental influences that kept her in a non-developing state and world, with brain wiring problems.

Customized Therapy

I also point out that the therapy is a series of treatments based on the system diagnosis for each individual patient. The diagnosis changes and associated treatments are unique to each person based on their complex energetic physiology, symptoms, and sensitivities. Please note that this is a very sharp departure from current biomedicine, which gives a few prescriptions to try to reduce symptoms. The patient does not really get a tailor-made treatment and also deals with chemical side effects.

In addition, a lot of what I see does not really respond to current biomedicine. My cases require the use of supplements and other, more natural approaches. In fact, I often have to treat patients to get rid of sensitivities to some supplements, vitamins, and foods, so they are not bothered by them. All my cases have had supplement reviews. I determine sensitivities using the NAET protocols for any items that offend. I may recommend certain natural supplements to provide for a patient's specific needs. I test and dose the amount and determine the Chinese clock time for the supplement to be taken and specify how many days to administer. In many cases, I use Chinese food energetics to support body organs and systems. Supporting foods are determined by testing, removing sensitivities, dosing amounts, and then timing when to take the foods. This is common in failure-to-thrive patients who are weak and need custom food intake. Often, I test over two hundred items at intake, based on the patient's signs and symptoms. This type of research and discovery process is done in all cases, and lays the groundwork for my thinking and subsequent treatment.

My practice has a high density of people with substantial academic backgrounds, positions in the government and private corporations, lawyers, doctors, professors, engineers, architects, professional athletes, and people who simply have an intense desire to get relief from problems for themselves and their families. I really have to demonstrate testing and discuss studies with my patients to explain why they aren't getting better using conventional medicine. I am so pleased that, without exception, all have kept open minds and are pleasant to work with, even though they all have problems that could not be fixed by conventional medicine. We have extensive discussions about supplements, high-quality organic foods, diets, and so forth that they have tried. Yet, their problems have not resolved, or they were not improving, using conventional approaches. These patients can't find anyone who can work on the missing link to life, the energy and its associative processes. This is their reality, as they don't know the solution exists in the form of NAET and integrated Chinese medicine.

In some cases, foods contain chemicals that offend as an allergen, and eliminating these foods does not address the sensitivity since the chemicals may also be found in many other foods as well. In some cases, certain chemicals mime others when heated, and then become an allergen. Some foods offend when taken with another food; we call this a *combination*. In some cases, changes in seasons cause the chemical mix to change. For instance milk will exhibit hormonal changes when the season changes from summer to fall. I have found that most children on the spectrum, and adults, cannot tolerate today's supplements, as there may be an associated allergy or sensitivity. Plus, the supplements overload and cause toxicity and further problems, with signs and symptoms that are varied, unusual, and unique to each person. I feel that resultant toxins may be stored in fatty tissues and neural membranes and cells. I recommend Anne Evans's approach as the way to get started and to clean up and stabilize the patient as much as possible, and really serve as an effective tool to support the child and calm many issues.

At some point, specialized energetic treatments are needed to discover all offending items and maladaptations, which must be erased to make progress possible. This is depicted in the treatment notes for each encounter. There is also another aspect to this picture. A lot of patients exhibit a type 1, IgE antibody reaction or hypersensitivity. The IgE antibody reaction refers to immunoglobulin E. This is one of five major immune responses the body creates to fight invading antigens. The labels A, D, E, G, and M refer to the antibody binding sites on the receptors as well as the locale (tissue type) in the body where they function. Conventional medicine can only test for IgE – one type of immunoglobulin! NAET can test for ALL types, and treat them all. The E type may cause loss of airway use (anaphylaxis and death if not treated) and severe symptoms, such as hives, wheezing, foggy brain, and so forth. In Sarah's case, I had to watch carefully and diagnose the risk of the treatment, as she would start to develop features of a type 1 reaction that could potentially cause serious consequences. I could place an offending food or chemical in her energy field at a distance and her cheeks would turn red, Chinese pulses would show a decrease in energy level, and a fast pulse would occur. Fortunately, she did not have anaphylaxis in her medical history, but as an experienced practitioner, I knew the patient could eventually sensitize and develop severe life-threatening reactions, for which I needed to be prepared. I have sensitive patients wait in my office and treatment rooms longer, and make sure they are stable prior to release. I make sure they have someone with them when they leave the office. In some instances, I request that they get an EpiPen and learn how to use it. Sarah's treatments were never short; she always had an energetic "cool down," which I monitored. She would get reactions as her system re-programmed and eliminated toxin buildups. This is referred to as *retracing*.

Many of my protocols using NAET were developed resolving severe cases of multi-chemical sensitivity (MCS). So individualized, or customized, therapy resulted in protocols for multiple patients. Some protocols were developed to treat people with neurological and brain disorders that surfaced when they were in the vicinity of offending allergens. I tested and treated Sarah in a profoundly noninvasive and safe way, developed with my MCS practices and protocols.

Clinical Trials and Case Results

As I mentioned, NAET is used as the defining treatment methodology. As a matter of background, the reader may google NAET and go to its website. To portray NAET at this moment, there are more than twelve thousand medically licensed practitioners worldwide. Its foundation, Nambudripad's Allergy Research Foundation (NARF) is actively pursuing research funding and initiating studies to effectively maintain the medical use of NAET and to portray the results of NAET from the viewpoint of scientific validation using evidence-based studies as well as fully registered trials.

I am often asked if there are a scientific studies of the random controlled trial format (a gold standard) used for pharmaceuticals. My response is simple: our work is based on case history, and associated evidence of validity and results. Trials are expensive, but are slowly being done. I do offer and discuss examples of trials, and also clinical treatment summaries. While clinical results harvested from the research of patients have been found, they are expensive in terms of manpower. In fact, a review of 150 milk-intolerant patients (treated in my practice) required about three hundred man-hours of effort and intense supervision due to multiple factors that have to be summarized. This is worthwhile, as the analysis helps people see results in the form of symptoms relieved, number of treatments, associated allergens treated, and so forth, but it is a burden for a practice that should be treating patients and relieving human suffering; it also requires private funding.

The power of NAET is in the case results of thousands of practitioners who represent successful resolutions of a substantial number of problems and diseases. The results have attracted many thousands of patients only through word of mouth from successful cases. This is a ground-level evolution. Few referrals are made from the conventional medical community, yet a number of insurance plans will pay for treatment. Most patients have been referred to NAET clinics by other patients who have had substantial benefits in resolving serious problems through NAET. (More information on NAET is located in appendix F.)

Typical results of NAET milk-intolerant patients in my clinic demonstrate the resolution of problems in fewer than twelve treatments. One hundred percent of patients with anaphylactic allergies (type 1, IgE severe reactions) to bee stings were resolved (no longer anaphylactic or allergic) within 14 treatments. We reviewed speech problems in 20 patients in 1999 that showed 9 started talking in 10 visits, and 12 within 20 visits.[1] (For various reasons 2 children failed to gain the ability to speak.) This review occurred during a discussion setting at a NAET symposium and is summarized on the NAET website.

Of current interest is a peanut allergy study.[2] In this study, patients with peanut allergies were treated using NAET. Prior to treatment their blood was tested for peanut-specific IgE and IgG levels. Blood levels were retaken to determine any measurable biomedical response to treatment. This allergy is well-known and affects people who eat, touch, and smell peanuts. Cascade reactions are known to be severe. The study shows that the treatments are effective, as evidenced by a peanut-ingestion challenge.

The IgE and IgG responses did not change in the short-term. The tryptase levels, in addition, did not elevate, which indicates that the IgE reaction is not the best marker as tryptase levels usually increase in the short term (for a time period of 15 to 120 minutes) with an allergic reaction. I have found IgE will modulate down over time and through re-treatment. This study does not have a control group that was treated using a placebo to determine its effects. The treatment methodology NAET uses does not easily lend itself to placebo treatments. Points that are treated, for instance, may respond with minor effects of touch and so forth. Some reactions may be strong, but short-term. In addition, the treatments show effectiveness upon an ingestion challenge. Therefore, there is little likelihood of a placebo effect to be valid should that be designed and tested. Another problem is that the patients are frightened of ingestion challenges; this would rule out any participants for a placebo study.

There is a need to further establish the mechanisms of reaction in peanut allergy cases. This has been elusive to current medical practices. I like this study, as it depicts the NAET modulation of the immune system reaction to achieve a very beneficial effect, and it also demonstrates that mechanisms are involved that are not well understood (this is the domain of energy medicine). We take the results and run, so to speak, and they are exquisitely powerful and repeatable.

Another study of value is the current autism pilot study,[3] which was published in *Integrative Medicine* in 2011. This study depicts the use of NAET desensitization to multiple allergens to treat autism. Pharmaceutical treatment options produce only limited success. Furthermore, it was found that there was decreased severity of autism after treating with NAET for nutritional, toxin-related problems and infections that may be associated with autism. The study is a worthwhile document to read to gain an understanding of the NAET approach and effectiveness. A total of sixty participants, who each had a valid diagnosis of autism, were enrolled.

Outcome measurements of the effectiveness of treatment were determined by analyzing the improvement of scores on the Autism Research Institute Autism Treatment Checklist (ARI-ATEC). This has four sub-scales, of speech/language/communications; sociability; sensory/cognitive awareness; and health/physical/behavior. The score for each sub-scale was provided by questioning parents or primary caretakers. Other ratings were also used to provide a framework for analysis. After a year of treatment, the randomly selected control group, which were not treated showed no improvement and their scores remained in the severe range. They were free to do any other treatment modality. The treated group showed statistically significant decreases in mean severity scores for all four of the ARI-ATEC subtests. Speech and language difficulties decreased 82.1 percent, sociability difficulties decreased 64.7 percent, sensory/cognitive awareness difficulties decreased 63.5 percent, and health/physical/behavior difficulties decreased 66.0 percent. The decrease in the four categories was 68.4 percent. (Confidence levels are calculated for all the referenced scores, and the study has a substantial amount of statistical power. Most importantly, it depicts the ability to relieve the underlying cause autism and its symptoms.) It should be noted here that in the treated group of thirty, twenty-three were improved to the extent that they could function in regular school classes. I point out that the complete program for autism treatment with NAET requires seventy-five to one hundred office visits. I also note from the study that resolving severe difficulty with communications showed improvement in fifteen to twenty treatments.

In my clinic, I have had patients with many symptoms. There were some who only screamed; others had a high-pitched screams with actual words embedded. Many were mute. One patient cried loudly for over five years without ceasing, except when he fell asleep. Others talked backward, mixed words, and so forth. NAET works on all these problems, and I must say, the treatments are tailored for each of them. I have been amazed at the number of symptoms that some children exhibit. Their lives change when severe problems become a thing of the past.

I profoundly congratulate Sarah for having so much spirit and an intellect that eventually allowed her to understand where she had been and how she was healed. She is happy about where she is now, and her quest for deeper knowledge is now within her grasp. Anne Evans has really expertly recorded an amazing history in layman's vernacular that has clarity and can serve as an approach for parents and caretakers in their own endeavors with autistic children. This writing can serve as a guidebook for mothers and fathers of autistic children and can be handed to physicians who are dealing with cases in their practices. Sarah's original pediatrician had pointed out that even if a cause were found, there would be no treatment, as medicines would not go beyond the blood-brain barrier. Now there is a treatment.

Let's turn tears into smiles.
Ross J. Stark D.Ac.

Ross J. Stark left this world to join the Lord on September 22, 2014. He is sorely missed by the Annapolis community who knew him. May he rest in peace.

Notes

1. *Results of 10-Year-Survey of the NAET Clinic Patients*, NAET website, http://www.naet.com/pdfs/NAET_Booklet_new.pdf, accessed October 13, 2014.

2. Brady Vincent. *Biomedical Analyses of a Holistic Peanut Allergy Treatment: NAET*. Proceedings of the National Conference on Undergraduate Research (NCUR), Ithaca College, New York, March 31–April 2, 2011, https://www.naet.com/pdfs/peanutAllergy.pdf.

3. Jacob Teitelbaum et al. *"Improving Communication Skills in Children with Allergy-Related Autism Using Nambudripad's Allergy Elimination Techniques: A Pilot Study,"* Integrative Medicine 10, no. 5 (October/November 2011): 37–43, http://www.naet.com/pdfs/Autism-NAET-full-study-IMCJ_10_5_Teitelbaum-Published.pdf.

Author's Preface

Autism is an unusual disorder. It manifests differently in every person. This makes it difficult to diagnose and treat. There exists a basic group of symptoms which are peculiar to autism. They revolve around impaired social interaction and lack of emotional response. They include poor communication skills, repetitive behaviors, limited eye contact, and failure to respond to others. A seemingly normal infant who is healthy at birth, sits up at six months, crawls at eight months, walks by one year, and in many cases, develops speech, suddenly, for no obvious reason, begins to degenerate. The toddler may lose speech, suddenly begin to limp or toe-walk, cease to make eye contact, and lose all social skills. Eventually, he departs from reality into a world of his own.

The autistic do not necessarily have a low I.Q. Many can be surprisingly intelligent and gifted, as was the case with our daughter. Yet, there are a plethora of physical symptoms, which may or may not appear, or may even come and go. Some symptoms appear early in life in one child, yet may not appear until after puberty in another. My husband, Norm, and I discovered the signs in our daughter, Sarah, in preschool. We had to remove her, and I home-schooled. Yet, I have spoken with many parents whose children were mainstream through the elementary and middle school years, only to have their child diagnosed on the spectrum in high school.

It is important to state that this story of healing and the creation of this book took place over the course of several years. During that time, the American Psychiatric Association's *Diagnostic and Statistical Manual of Mental Disorders* (DSM) was updated. Volume IV of the DSM listed autism, Asperger's, and attention deficit disorder as individual diseases. Volume 5 now recognizes a spectrum of disorders and refers to the set of symptoms as *autism spectrum disorder* (ASD). I certainly concur with this term, as my husband and I witnessed a very broad range of behaviors in our child. There were days when no one would ever recognize her as sick, yet there were also days when I feared she would be permanently institutionalized at age eighteen.

Sarah's preschool teacher reported that she had autism. Another teacher labeled it attention deficit disorder with dyslexia. Two competent physicians denied she had anything wrong with her. One specialist stated that there was nothing he could do because he had no tests to adequately diagnose her symptoms. Following a year and a half of confusion, her pediatrician told me in words that she was autistic, yet recorded "delayed development" on her medical file. In other words, despite a laundry list of very severe symptoms, there was no usable diagnosis for the underlying cause of the symptoms from the conventional medical community. We were not alone. We shared this unresolved situation with thousands of other parents worldwide, and that is one of the reasons I decided to pen this book.

We were not alone in another way. I had always seen how God protected and guided me through life. I knew I could count on Him. Jesus' divine presence made itself apparent through each step of the recovery process, pointing the way from nutritionists to doctors, from diet therapy to energy medicine. I want to share with the reader everything He led me toward.

The current state of mental disorders in the United States is alarming. The National Institute of Mental Health (NIMH) in Washington, D.C., reports that 18.6 percent of all US adults have some form of mental illness.[1] This is close to 44 million people. It is much more than the disease burden of all cancers combined.[2] Close to one in five adults suffers from a diagnosable mental disorder.[3] How many more go undiagnosed, and how many more are children? Here I would like to state that I do not, personally, view autism as a mental illness. Children with autism are perfectly normal children who suffer with reactions to toxins, allergens, pathogens, and the ensuing neural inflammation. I state this to differentiate them from individuals who have genetically abnormal brain or neural tissues.

In the 1960s, autism was so rare that there was not even a name for it. For decades the Centers for Disease Control (CDC) reported only one case in 10,000 people.[3] Over the last few decades, the number of cases has skyrocketed. *Time* magazine ran an article in their May 6, 2002 issue, titled "The Secrets of Autism", which reported one case per 150 people.[4] It stated that as many as 300,000 children may have autism. In a little over a decade, this figure has exploded. The CDC indicates, on their Data & Statistics website, that one in 68 children is diagnosed with some symptoms of autism.[5] They go on to report a 30 percent increase in just 2012 and 2013. There is definitely an epidemic in the United States. (This argues for an environmental, not a genetic, cause.)

On the same spectrum of mental disorders lies *attention deficit disorder* (ADD), sometimes called *attention deficit/hyperactivity disorder* (ADHD). The main symptoms are an inability to maintain concentration and to complete tasks. Memory recall and coordination may be affected, with impulsive hyperactivity, uncontrollable temper outbursts, and risk-taking behavior. Sometimes social skills are impaired.

The NIMH website reports that nine percent of the nation's children ages thirteen to eighteen have attention deficit disorder.[6] The CDC reports that 11 percent of children ages four to seventeen have been diagnosed with ADHD as of 2011.[7]

Dyslexia is a term used to describe a variety of visual and reading disorders caused by mental processing problems. They include *dyscalculia* (inability to perform mathematical functions) and *dysgraphia* (inability to write within a defined space) as well. Though estimates of prevalence depend on the particular definition of dyslexia used in a given study, according to Linda S. Seigel, PhD, writing in the journal *Paediatrics & Child Health*, 5 to 10 percent of the population is considered to have it.[8]

Symptoms of all of these disorders listed above, autism, ADHD, and dyslexia manifested themselves in Sarah from her birth to about age seven and a half, with autism being the strongest consistent symptom. In spite of all these symptoms, it was very difficult to get a specific diagnosis. The conventional medical community is hesitant to diagnose very young children on the belief that they may out-grow many of the symptoms. They also refuse to diagnose very young children because the only protocol available to treat autism is behavior modification, and that doesn't begin until the child is school age. If the symptoms lean more toward ADHD, the protocol is drug therapy, and no doctor is eager to drug preschool children. Hence, children may go for years without being diagnosed.

In fact, the conventional medical community has no real tests to diagnose the underlying cause of autism. In Sarah's case it was obvious that she responded differently to each type of food she ate. There were individual mental and behavioral responses to individual food items. Yet, when I consulted the leading pediatric allergist at John Hopkins Medical Center in Baltimore, Maryland, he told me there were no tests to determine which foods would cause such effects. In fact, there are no physical tests to diagnose the underlying causes of any mental disorders. Doctors have no way to ascertain which toxins cross the blood-brain barrier. A variety of lengthy psychological examinations are available to document the symptoms. Then, labels are applied depending on the behavioral symptoms identified. However, there is no true diagnosis for any mental illness.

In conventional American medicine, we have a tendency to think of one disease, one pathogen. For example, if we have a sore throat, we get a culture for streptococcus, or strep., one symptom, one pathogen; then we are provided one antibiotic. The truth is, there are literally hundreds of pathogens that cause illness in the body, especially with mental illness. The current clinical situation for mental illness is not as cut-and-dried as it is for physical illness.

Early in my years of studying microbiology, I learned that the human body is host to a myriad of viruses, bacteria, and protozoa. Many are parasites. For the most part, they are not a problem in a healthy host's body. The immune system keeps them under control. Some are even welcome in a symbiotic relationship, producing vitamins or minerals. Yet in our modern, heavily polluted world, the human body becomes weakened. Organ tissues are infected with chemicals, such as lead, mercury, aluminum, chlorine, pesticides, herbicides, solvents, and fluoride, to name a few. Nutritional elements are replaced by toxins. Tissues, such as the brain, become starved. In weakened tissues, these otherwise harmless bacteria and viruses start to colonize and dwell in the tissues. They use up vitamins and minerals the human body requires and give off toxins that enter the bloodstream and pass across the blood-brain barrier into the mind. Some even colonize the brain itself. The child's symptoms depend on which organs the pathogens and toxins reside in, which pathogens have grown out of control, and which tissues have grown so inflamed that they can no longer function normally.

In Sarah's case, as stated earlier, her pediatrician had told me verbally that she was autistic, yet he wrote "delayed development" on her medical file. A psychologist had written "adjustment disorder." Neither practitioner had ever outlined a plan for recovery. Having exhausted all earthly, conventional, medical possibilities, I turned to Heaven. There I found guidance, reassurance, confidence, and a cure. My husband and I traveled down the road of alternative medicine, and we found a protocol more sophisticated than anything ever dreamt of in the conventional world: integrated Chinese medicine (ICM). I was so happy that God had instilled the confidence in me to know that this was our path, and I never looked back. I never regretted leaving our pediatrician behind. As a Christian woman I initially had a problem using a therapy when I didn't fully understand the source, and its history was from the Far East. There was a limited fear that it might lead away from God. As I grew to know the practitioner, who was a Catholic, he assured me that his practices were well grounded in physics. I also knew that God had created the energy of the universe, the same way He created everything else. Norm supported me in this path.

The only disadvantage to the world of alternative medicine is that most insurance companies will not cover the therapy. We used Norm's flex benefits, from his job, to make the weekly payments. It was manageable and worth every penny to watch our child recover. We paid between $15,000 and $20,000 dollars to bring Sarah to complete wellness. The cost of her supplements is an ongoing, personal expense. We felt that this was very reasonable since many families rely on their state's autism waiver, which can begin at $30,000 per year for the life of the child. This runs into millions of tax dollars per state. For a fraction of one year on the waiver, our child was healed. Any child can be healed the same way that Sarah was.

What Norm and I discovered through ICM was that it does not rely on pharmaceuticals, Applied Behavior Analysis (ABA), pivotal response testing, or anything of the kind. ICM is based on high-resonance energy frequencies. Using these frequencies, the patient's body is relieved of toxins, heavy metals, parasites, and inflammation. Hormones can be balanced. The immune system can be boosted to fight off pathogens without antibiotics. There were no drugs, nor surgeries, nothing invasive that could harm a small child. The doctor we used identified pathogens that conventional doctors had no method of locating, and he removed all of them. The condition of Sarah's brain was reviewed one tissue type at a time: hypothalamus, pituitary, cerebrum, cerebellum, corpus callosum, amygdala, and brain stem. A pathogen, *Toxoplasma gondii*, was identified in the retina of Sarah's eyes, along the optic nerve, and into the visual cortex of her brain. Her diet was altered to diminish many of the symptoms of autism, but more importantly, it was altered to starve the pathogen and to nourish the child. Once the pathogen was starved, Sarah's normal personality began to shine through. This is true healing from the inside out. We documented as much as we possibly could with before-and-after blood tests, retinal scans, urine analysis, and psychological testing. All the tests are recorded in the appendices of this book.

The therapy was so successful and we were rewarded with such a healthy daughter that I could not keep silent. I need to share this therapy with the world to encourage and guide other parents in how to seek out and find qualified alternative practitioners that can help everyone have the success we did.

Notes

1. National Institute of Mental Health, "Any Mental Illness (AMI) Among Adults," NIH, Health & Education, accessed November 24, 2014, www.nimh.nih.gov/health/statistics/prevalence/any-mental-illness-ami-among-adults.shtml.

2. Centers for Disease Control and Prevention, "CDC Mental Illness Surveillance: Fact Sheet," http://www.cdc.gov/mentalhealthsurveillance/fact_sheet.html, last reviewed December 2, 2011.

3. Mental Illness, "Mental Disorders in America," MedicineNet.com, accessed November 24, 2014. http://www.medicinenet.com/script/main/art.asp?articlekey=21466.

4. J. Madeleine Nash, "The Secrets of Autism," *Time*, May 6, 2002, 46.

5. Centers for Disease Control and Prevention, "Autism Spectrum Disorder: Data & Statistics," http://www.cdc.gov/ncbddd/autism/data.html, upd. March 24, 2014.

6. National Institute of Mental Health, "Attention Deficit Hyperactivity Disorder Among Children," http://www.nimh.nih.gov/health/statistics/prevalence/attention-deficit-hyperactivity-disorder-among-children.shtml.

7. Centers for Disease Control and Prevention, "Attention-Deficit / Hyperactivity Disorder (ADHD): Data & Statistics," http://www.cdc.gov/ncbddd/adhd/data.html, upd. September 29, 2014.

8. Linda S. Siegel, "Perspectives on dyslexia," *Paediatrics & Child Health* 11, no. 9 (November 2006): 581–87, http://www.ncbi.nlm.nih.gov/pmc/articles/PMC2528651/.

Acknowledgments

There are so many people without whose help Sarah would never have been healed. It is difficult to mention all of you, but I will try. If I have left anyone out, please forgive me.

Firstly, I extend a special debt of gratitude to Ross Stark and his family, who took more than a professional interest in Sarah's recovery. They took a genuine interest of true friends. Thank you all so much. Secondly, I want to extend warm and loving thanks to my husband, Norman D. Evans, who was willing to leave the conventional medical community and support our child's recovery financially. His famous words "I'll pay for results," should mark a new trend in healthcare. Those words inspired other fathers to look for alternative assistance for their own children.

Next, I would like to thank all of my friends who I pestered to read and proof copies of the drafts. They include nutritionist and radio talk-show host Dana Laake, US Naval Academy chemistry professor Deb Dilner, child therapist and educator Ann Gibbs, private tutor and educator Karen Heuer, and former corporate executive Frances Jensen. You are true friends.

I would also like to thank all of the friends who listened to me "belly-ache" during Sarah's recovery. Throughout the dark times, when it looked as though things were not working, when I feared she would never be normal, you lent me your ears. You were supportive, and you never stopped saying, "How's the book coming along?" You are to be commended. Because of you, a message of healing has made it out to the world. You are: Elizabeth Finkle, Marilyn Roper, Pat and Jerry Reed, Elizabeth Kinney, Dian Vandemark, Dale Smith, Heather Strang, Brenda Jackson, and Becky Hutchison.

In addition, I would like to thank Lynn and Gerry Miller, Sarah's first grade teacher and our church pastor respectively, along with Margy Wolf, the school principal. They were patient and willing to work with us through the first year of Sarah's recovery program.

Lastly, I would like to thank all the doctors and laboratories, who gave me permission to use their names, including Dr. Zoltan Rona; Great Plains in Lenexa, Kansas; MetaMetrix in Duluth, Georgia; and Doctor's Data in St. Charles, Illinois.

Most importantly, I would like to thank Dr. Devi Nambudripad for developing NAET and sharing it with the world. God bless you all.

What and Why is Field Control Therapy?

Field Control Therapy (FCT) is not some magic, healing, medical machine but, rather, a medical theory with its corresponding diagnostic and therapeutic means with the goal of effectively addressing the most crucial obstacle in medicine.

This obstacle is the inability to determine exact causes of all chronic diseases, including autism, ADHD, and a 1,000 other chronic diseases. Here is one of many quotes from reputable scientists which make this message quite clear, Colin J. Alexander, MD, former professor of medicine at the Auckland University School of Medicine states, "Medicine has failed in the care of chronic diseases. None of the types of research or clinical trials have made a difference because we have not identified a cause." The reason for this is inadequate diagnostic means, which automatically lead to further disability, and the inability to judge well the final and actual results of all medical treatments, whether conventional or alternative. Inevitably, the purported benefits of all these treatments fall into the spectacular land of, "take my word for it". To give a more specific example, while all of medicine cites hundreds of thousands of scientific references concerning abnormal immune function and neurotransmitters, leaky gut, food allergies, and nutritional, metabolic, energetic, lymphatic, or other imbalances, the fact remains that none of these are the direct causes of chronic diseases, but only the symptoms. That is why all of these abnormalities are only secondary in both general and medical importance, because all of these originate from their corresponding primary and more fundamental sources – dysfunctional organs and tissues. However, the best kept secret in medicine is that none of the commonly used medical tests can determine most (e.g. 99%) of these dysfunctional organs and tissues and as importantly, the real causes of these dysfunctions. I, in my own medical practice, hit this wall many years ago until I accidently came across an obscure article, *Future Medicine Based on Controlled Energy Fields*[1], by the former chairman of materials science, Professor Emeritus of Stanford University, William A. Tiller, PhD. Since materials science is a subspecialty of physics, with the latter being the preeminent science of all, it also is the one that ultimately explains properties of all matter, including living cells. Professor Tiller explained the deeper properties of human organs and tissues. In this article, he specifically emphasized the facts that:

a) Since due to their fundamental role, energetic fields determine and regulate chemical properties, once these fields become abnormal they can cause all other body chemistry and related abnormalities and pathologies.
b) These fields are accessible to noninvasive energetic diagnostic screening, such as muscle testing in applied kinesiology and others.
c) These fields are amenable to energetic therapeutics, such as homeopathy, in order to correct these disease causing and sustaining fields.

However, not being a medical doctor, Professor Tiller could not be more specific in how to diagnose the main cause of disease using applied kinesiology or other related bio-resonance testing methods, or homeopathy, in order to produce the best results. And, the facts are that all of these methods have been and continue to be used for decades. While these methods have thousands of different combinations and ways to be utilized, including mixed treatments, all of them have provided only inconsistent results in clinical practice.

In the 1980's, under the kind, private tutorship in physics of Professor Tiller, I initiated having energetic conversations with the organs and tissues, directly through bio-resonance testing or applied kinesiology, based on my conventional medical knowledge while adding and screening for their true merit, many alternative treatments and ideas. This conversation was based on the well-known phenomena in physics, the matter-energy duality and resonance. While the former states that *all the substances in the universe, poisons or living tissues, possess their corresponding, unique energy fields or fingerprints, like IDs*, the latter allows for *two similar energy fields to enter into resonance communication*. The test is conducted in the following way. An adult or child lies on his back on an examining table while holding a metal rod that is connected by a cable to a metal testing platform on which I place homeopathic vials, which are prepared from internal organs and tissues, and numerous morbid agents such as mercury, lead, and other environmental pollutants, or infectious agents like parasites, bacteria, yeasts, viruses, vaccines, and electromagnetic radiation. Only rarely, are foods (like gluten or dairy) or environmental allergens tested since these are just symptoms, not the primary cause of illness.

When a patient is sensing, via conductive circuit (the rod, table, and platform), a corresponding energy field of a vial placed on the platform, he responds to this vial of malfunctioning, stressed organ or tissue with a stress reaction. Such a reaction is manifested by an involuntary muscle reflex whereby he tightens one of his leg muscles, which I detect by holding my hand over his ankle. Following such a stress reaction, we continue the energetic conversation with that organ or tissue by subjecting it to another question through other vials, or by asking, "Why are you sick?" by placing potential causes of stress, one at a time, on the platform. Among these, as I previously mentioned, are environmental, infectious and electromagnetic agents, vaccines, and, also, medications or nutritional supplements, many of which have side effects. After identifying all of the malfunctioning or stressed organs and their corresponding morbid causes, both the strictly individualized homeopathic treatment and proper life-style guidance concerning electromagnetic radiation and healthy diet, are offered.

In the beginning, I was looking for the primary causes of illness, for the identified dysfunctional organs and tissues. Following my findings, I treated these causes using no other treatments or special diets, besides homeopathy, so as not to confuse the picture of why a patient has or has not positively responded to the treatment. Even with homeopathy, I had to use and test its different approaches one at a time. Yet, I have found most of them unsatisfactory. So, I had to evolve my own homeopathic approach based on up-to-date, modern-day, medical knowledge inclusive of conventional medicine, toxicological, electromagnetic and other important environmental factors. This has finally proved to be the most successful. Likewise, with the help of Professor Tiller's work, I was able to evolve greatly and deepen the diagnostic yield of bio-resonance testing that, unlike its counterparts in alternative medicine, became capable of indicating multiple layers of morbid causes of disease, whether in the brain or other organs. Failure to identify these multiple layers, akin to a facial tissue box where one layer or cause removed reveals the next one under it to treat, not only leads to therapeutic failures, but side effects and, even, long-lasting damage. Following the scientific enhancement of this system over many years, and its universal application to all chronic diseases, not just to autism, FCT has been able to achieve clinical outcomes which remain unparalleled in medicine today.[2,3]

Likewise, based on years of long experience both in bio-resonance testing and its based treatment, FCT seeks and addresses only the most important causes of disease, not just the first abnormality in sight. By so doing, Field Control Therapy leads not only to far superior results in the shortest time possible, but also to substantial cost containment and reprieve from many unnecessary tests and other treatments in both conventional and alternative medicine.

Savely Yurkovsky M.D.

Notes
1. *Future Medical Therapeutics Based Upon Controlled Energy Fields*; Proceedings of the Association for Research and Enlightenment's Medical Symposium, Phoenix, AZ, January 1976. and *Towards a Future Medicine Based on Controlled Energy Fields*, Phoenix 1, no. 1, 5 (1977).

2. For more details concerning the scientific basis of bio-resonance testing and homeopathy refer to *The Power of Digital Medicine* by Savely Yurkovsky, MD. http://www.yurkovsky.com/

3. Dr. Yurkovsky's webinar program, besides his DVDs, presents numerous reversals of chronic diseases, besides autism, which have been documented by conventional medical tests and specialists. http://www.yurkovsky.com/webinar-001/

part one
Sarah's Story

one
A Rude Awakening

From her birth in October 1995, Sarah had been a beautiful, healthy, and strong baby with big, blue eyes and golden - blonde hair. She was a large baby who nursed well and slept long. She crawled, walked, and spoke at the normal ages. She was extremely bright, with an uncanny ability to listen and pick up on everything she heard. By age three, she was reading at the first grade level. She attracted enormous amounts of attention everywhere we went. Strangers commented on her beauty, intelligence, and adult speech. One of the most frequent comments was on her rosy complexion. The slightest bit of exertion sent a flush to her cheeks that complemented her brilliant blue eyes. Little did I know the charming, rosy flush was the herald of a slowly growing nightmare.

In fall 1999, when Sarah was just turning four, Norm and I placed her in a private preschool affiliated with our church. Within the first few weeks, I was asked by the teacher to take my daughter to the pediatrician to examine her gait. Compared to the other children in her class, her steps were uneven as she walked. The pediatrician said there was nothing wrong with her, at least not that he could see. I didn't challenge him even though in my heart I agreed there was a problem with her gait. I wanted to believe she would outgrow it. I knew she wasn't running up and down stairs like other children. She only climbed one step at a time. Nor could she pedal her tricycle. She had no strength in her right leg. In fact, it was as if her right leg were "turned off."

A few weeks after the doctor's visit, I was in my kitchen when the telephone rang. It was Sarah's teacher. In a very prying, meddlesome tone, she asked about a bandage on Sarah's leg. I told her that a bee had stung Sarah. She wanted to know what the pediatrician had said about it. I thought that very intrusive on her part, but I replied that I was to give her an antihistamine for children and watch the sting for twenty-four hours. She seemed very unsatisfied and huffed as she hung up.

I was left alone with my thoughts. The more I recalled the bee sting incident, the more I realized there had been a peculiar element to it.

It was not an ordinary honeybee; it was a yellow jacket. The day before, it had attached itself to Sarah's leg and was gnawing a small hole above her ankle. Sarah had walked into the house from the front yard and entered the kitchen very calmly, not shedding a tear, not screaming, but peacefully stating,

"Mom, there's a bug on my leg."

Any other four-year-old would have run in screaming, but not Sarah. I realized that she had felt no pain! I quickly plastered the wound with baking soda and water to draw out the venom, cleaned it, and put on a bandage. Through the whole ordeal, she remained stoic, a true little preschool brave heart. However, I remained confused as to why she felt no pain. I knew that pain is a gift given for a purpose. Without it, we do not know when we are in danger of being hurt. We do not know when we are ill. We do not know when to cease a potentially dangerous activity, or when we need a physician. Sarah needed to have that ability. A mild angst settled in my heart.

A few more weeks had passed when I received a third telephone call from Sarah's teacher. This time she was clearly frustrated even angry.

"Mrs. Evans," she cried, "it is absolutely impossible to teach your child anything at all!" She went on tell me that Sarah simply could not participate with the group, and got up to run around whenever she pleased.

She expected both Norm and me to come to the school immediately just to talk to her. Her irate behavior caused me to believe she was fairly incompetent. So, I asked what the children were working on in class. She replied that they were learning the letters of the alphabet. I told her that Sarah already knew her alphabet and had been reading for a year. She was probably bored and just wanted to make her own fun. She was indignant at this and hung up the phone.

Several more weeks passed, and it was late fall and time for the first preschool report cards. When I received Sarah's, I noticed her teacher had written several comments about a repetitive speech pattern. I knew that was simply Sarah's way of memorizing things. She had an incredible auditory memory. The teacher was unsatisfied with my explanation and insisted that my husband and I come in for a conference.

In December 1999, just before the Christmas holiday, the two of us entered her office and had a closed-door discussion. It was a very tense meeting for me. I was glad Norm was with me. His presence kept me calm. We sat across the desk from her. She turned on a device that created artificial nature sounds. She said it was to keep our conversation private from anyone within earshot. The atmosphere was strained enough without her contributing this affectation of secrecy about our child.

The teacher proceeded to describe a child to us that I did not know and had never seen, one who was so easily distracted that she couldn't remember to go to the bathroom. She said Sarah didn't play with other children, never knew the topic of conversation, and lived in her own dream world. Once again, the teacher broached the subject of Sarah's repetitive speech pattern. Growing impatient with this comment, I blurted out,

"Do you think this is symptomatic of something?"

I had no idea how those words entered my head or what prompted me to ask them, but they became pivotal in Sarah's recovery.

The teacher very purposefully laid her hands upon her desk, lowered her head, leaned forward and glared sternly at the two of us and intonated in a slow, deliberate voice,

"Well," she sighed, "have you ever seen the movie *Rain Man*?"

I couldn't believe it! This was *my* child she was talking about. I wanted to leap over the desk and throttle the woman, but I remained calmly seated. Norm and I stared at each other in disbelief. But that wasn't all.

"Well," the teacher concluded, "I see no reason to call Child and Family Services at this point—as long as you discuss it with your pediatrician."

What?!? Sarah could memorize whole books and videos and perform math functions years ahead of her grade level! Now this teacher was threatening to call in a government agency if we did not act at her behest? And, was she suggesting that my child was autistic?

In the end, the teacher finally agreed to test Sarah. Norm and I left the school in a state of shock.

two
Daddy's Little Girl

Following the emotional meeting with Sarah's teacher, my memory was sparked, and I became mildly aware of something irregular in Sarah's ability to build relationships from toddler days. It was very subtle at first, but it was slowly growing worse.

My husband and I were older parents and were very happy when Sarah came along. The day she was born, Norm clutched her to him and wouldn't let go until he had to put her in the car seat to take her home. Those first nights, while adjusting to her new world, he held her in his arms so I could sleep. In the evenings, he sat with her in front of the computer, singing the Beach Boy's "Little Surfer Girl," while he surfed the Internet, and she stared up at him with great, wondering eyes. Their relationship grew and progressed into peek-a-boo and trips to the park.

When Sarah was about eighteen months old, Norm received an exciting business contract. This meant he had to make frequent trips to California from our home in Maryland, one week each month, for a year and a half. During this time, a strange transformation took place in their relationship. It slowly began to deteriorate.

He flew out on Sunday evenings, spent the week in California, and returned with jet-lag around midnight the following Friday night. He would sleep long into Saturday morning to catch up on rest. During this time, Sarah took no interest in him. She instead became absorbed in her stuffed animals. Upon waking, Norm would go to great lengths to regain her affection by bouncing her on his knee, tossing her in the air, or singing little songs. Frequently, these efforts only ended in tears and more distancing. Sometimes, it would take the entire weekend for him to reestablish a rapport with her. We simply attributed the problem to his traveling. Her relationship with me continued as normal.

When Sarah was about two, I joined a church prayer group that met on Saturday mornings. When my meeting fell on the same weekend as my husband's return from California, disaster would strike. I would leave the house early for the meeting before Sarah arose; and when I returned from my meeting, Sarah would be crying inconsolably. Norm would be frustrated to no end. Upon seeing me, she would find her composure again.

To rebuild the relationship, Norm decided he would plan special outings on the weekends to be with her. If Sarah heard the offer of a trip to the park or the shopping mall, she would jump at the opportunity to go. I always relished a few hours to myself; the arrangement was wonderful for me. Yet invariably, they would return home with Sarah in fits of screaming and crying. Often she was simply hungry. At times her hunger pangs were so great and so painful she would misread her own body's messages and push food away. I would have to catch her unaware, while screaming, with a spoonful of yogurt or pudding and pop it into her mouth. More times than not, however, Sarah's fits of screaming and crying were caused by her own inability to cope with too much outside stimulation.

One day, when Sarah was still around age two, while reading a book that taught opposites, my husband came across the combined pair of "loud" and "soft." Sarah appeared not to understand the terms. To demonstrate the word "soft," Norm began to whisper to her. She found this intriguing. Then to demonstrate "loud," he shouted out across the room, "LOUD." Sarah was awestruck. Her face froze and her eyes fixed upon her daddy. He repeatedly whispered, "soft" and she developed a trancelike gaze. The first few times they played the game of "loud-n-soft," I simply assumed she was intrigued by volume. I wasn't aware that anything else was going on.

Over time, Sarah grew more and more sensitive to loud sounds. She refused to watch television. She wouldn't sit in movie theaters. Neither Norm nor I realized that there was any relationship between her sensitivity to sound and her fabulous talent for memorizing everything she heard.

Before too long her sensitivity to sound became overwhelming. After a while, even the sound of her father's voice caused her to run away. He learned to speak more softly around her. When he hugged her, the strength of his arms was overwhelming to her sensibilities. She learned to say, "Gentle, Daddy" so he wouldn't hug her quite so tightly and cause her pain. Their relationship continued shakily from this point forward.

Her sensations were a paradox of opposites. Though she felt little or no pain, she did not want to be hugged too tightly, and hated wearing clothes. She could not tolerate loud noises, yet she had this tremendous memorization capacity. In addition, dyslexia was beginning to make itself apparent, but she could add and subtract numbers in the hundreds with no difficulty. Her sense of smell was out of sorts, and absolutely nothing smelled good to her, yet she showed signs of craving certain foods. Hindsight has taught me that all five senses were severely affected, but we had not yet been hit with the full impact of the disease.

three
Feeling Like a Yo-Yo

Christmas vacation 1999 had begun immediately following the conversation with Sarah's preschool teacher. We had planned an exciting holiday. It was the millennial celebration, and we had been on a waiting list for three years to attend the colonial Williamsburg celebration for New Year's Eve. Yet, prior to our Christmas and New Year holiday, I had to make one more trip to the pediatrician.

We had a good rapport with Sarah's pediatrician. He was quite likable, British of Indian decent, and he had a tranquilizing effect on me. We developed our relationship over the course of the fall while dealing with Sarah's recurring bladder infections. I always appreciated the fact that rather than placing her on antibiotics, he recommended a more holistic approach. He had me bathe her three times a day and supplement her diet with *acidophilus* and *bifidous*, two naturally occurring bacteria that aid digestion. This treatment was quite successful. (Little did I know that recurring infections—ear, nose, throat, or bladder—are potential symptoms of a much more serious metabolic breakdown.)

I recounted the story of *Rain Man* to him. He closed his eyes and shook his head. The first words out of his mouth were,

"I hate it when teachers practice medicine." He continued, "She's not autistic; she's one of the brightest children in my practice."

His words were comforting. They were just the words I wanted to hear. They allowed me to continue living peacefully in a state of denial. He recorded our conversation in his records to avoid any problems should the teacher call in a government agency.

I left his office feeling reassured, vindicated, and confident. The angst and worry dissipated. It was easy to believe the teacher had a problem, but not my beautiful Sarah. However, hindsight is 20/20. I now look back with an understanding of why my pediatrician said what he said. He didn't want to alarm me. He wanted his patient, my child, to have a home life that was free of worry and as comfortable as it could be. I can't fault him for that. Today, hindsight tells me the pediatrician had probably known of Sarah's disorder from around age eighteen months.

Feeling reassured, I was able to look forward to the holidays with excitement. We packed up our car and drove to colonial Williamsburg. We were greeted at the Williamsburg Inn with trays of drinks and hors d'oeuvres. The first event scheduled on our agenda was dinner at one of the taverns. We returned to our bedroom to find a bottle of champagne and chocolates on the beds. The entire weekend continued like this; one exquisite meal after another, as Sarah's personality quickly deteriorated. Her mood swung like a pendulum. We dubbed her the child that went from zero to fussy in 2.5 seconds. By Saturday night, January 1, 2000, she appeared to have the flu, but with no fever—simply muscle aches and an upset stomach. By noon on Sunday, she was vomiting. We drove home exhausted and slept for a day. At the time, flu was the only explanation that entered my mind for the illness.

Through the winter, Sarah missed much of her preschool class. There were a lot of snow days, but she was also struggling on and off with what I believed to be the flu and bladder infections. She missed school most of the month of January. Finally, however, the pediatrician decided to put her on her first antibiotic—Zithromax.

With antibiotics in hand and her temperament returning to normal, I thought it was time to send her back to school. The next morning after breakfast, I bundled her up in winter clothes and buckled her into her car seat. We were half-way to school in bumper-to-bumper traffic when I heard a retching sound in the back seat. I targeted the rearview mirror on Sarah. My beautiful, four-year-old angel was vomiting up blood all down the front of her snowsuit. I was stricken with horror. I tried not to panic. I was surrounded by vehicles, which were moving at a snail's pace. I changed lanes and pulled onto the shoulder. I hit the emergency light switch on the dash, shifted the car into reverse, and backed up against the traffic a quarter of a mile to the last intersection. Fortunately, we were only a mile from the pediatrician's office. I wasted no time getting there. A new doctor on staff was fairly quick to assert that Sarah was allergic to the antibiotic she had been given. We took her off the antibiotic. I bundled up my angel and took her home. She missed a few more days of school.

After a few weeks, when things were calming back down to normal, Norm and I decided to have a Saturday night out alone. I called Sarah's babysitter and bought tickets to a local theater production.

I set the girls up with dinner. There were plenty of snacks and juice, including some apple cider, if they wanted it. I told the sitter where we would be, gave her my cell phone number, and we went out the door.

Shortly after we were settled in the theater and the lights were dimmed, an announcement was made to turn off all cell phones and pagers. I wasn't the least bit concerned. Sarah was fine. The sitter was mature, and her mother was three doors away. My husband and I relaxed, sat back, and enjoyed a light comedy.

After the show, in the car on the way home, I pulled the cell phone from my purse and called the house to let the sitter know we were on the way. I was greeted with resounding excitement and frustration!

"I tried to call you," the sitter said excitedly.

"We had to turn off the cell phones in the theater," I replied.

"It was awful," she continued, "Sarah was vomiting all over the place. I didn't know what to do because I couldn't reach you. I called my mother and she came with my little brother. My mom tried to give her a bath to clean her up, but she kept throwing up. My brother was making silly faces to cheer her up, but nothing worked."

"We're twenty minutes away and will be home soon," I answered.

We hung up and I described the situation to Norm. It sounded like a three-ring circus in the bathroom, and Sarah had been center stage.

By the time we arrived home, all was calm. The sitter was exhausted and Sarah was asleep in bed with fresh pajamas. Evidence of the preceding drama, a set of soiled pajamas, lay on the bathroom floor. Norm paid the distraught sitter and drove her home. It had been a long night for her.

The following morning, Sarah awoke looking hung-over. She had horrific, dark circles under her eyes, contrasting against her pallor. A check with the thermometer revealed no fever, so I thought she must be dehydrated from the preceding night's event. We headed to the refrigerator for some juice. She wanted apple cider, so I gave her a small cup. Within minutes she was vomiting again. I believed that it was another virus. At any rate, it was becoming apparent that I had a very sick child.

I was struggling in my heart to come to grips with the fact that Sarah was weaker and less coordinated than other children her age. She did seem to be sick a great deal. Yet, I knew that children grew at wildly different rates, and my doctor was telling me that she was fine. He said there was nothing wrong with Sarah, but the schoolteacher had surmised autism. Sarah was caught in the middle, and my feelings were being jerked back and forth. I felt like a yo-yo.

four
My Worst Nightmare

In the midst of our family chaos, a memory from my school days arose in my mind of a friend who had had a dream so real that when she woke she thought the events of the dream had actually occurred. Occasionally, dreams can be so real that they alter our perspective. For many, however, dreams are bizarre illusions, and waking from them is a comfort, an assurance of the reality of our lives. Yet, for me the reverse occurred.

Sarah's favorite pastime and art form was, and still is, dance. All she wanted to be was a ballerina. In June 2000, at age four and a half, I registered her in the Royal Academy of Ballet at our local hall for the performing arts. It was a short, four-week summer session to find out how she liked it before the lengthy, expensive fall session would start. We immensely enjoyed shopping together for the official academy leotard and the correct slippers. She was so excited.

We arrived the first day to meet other three-, four-, and five-year-olds putting on tights for the class. The mothers were buzzing, same as the kids were. All the moms waited outside the studio as the children filed in and the dance instructor closed the studio door. Customarily, the mothers passed time in the café next door during the ballet lessons. Together we chatted of job changes, redecorating, visiting in-laws, and, of course, our kids.

The first couple of weeks of this new ritual passed by without a hitch. About the third week, though, the ballet teacher, Eileen Razzetti, proprietor of the Academy Ballet School of Annapolis, poked her head out the studio door and motioned for me to come over. She stated very politely and gently that she wanted me to see something and invited me into the studio to watch.

There were about ten little girls lined up in two rows facing a wall of mirrors. Sarah was on the end of the back row. Ms Razzetti was in front, facing the girls, with her back to the mirror. I positioned myself to watch. The instructor pushed a button on her CD player's remote control. The music began. The instructor made a gesture; the girls followed. She added a second gesture; the girls followed, but Sarah had trouble. She made a third gesture, and the girls followed. Sarah lost all control and began racing around the room in circles. The instructor, very sweetly and patiently, stopped the music, walked over to Sarah, took her hand, and led her back to her spot in line, smiling all the while. She returned to the front, pushed the button on her remote control, and started the music. Ms Razetti stepped right. The girls stepped right. Sarah stepped left. Ms Razzetti stepped back. The girls stepped back. Sarah stepped forward. Ms Razetti went up on her toes with her hands above her head. The girls followed, going up on their toes with their hands above their heads, while Sarah bent at the waist and tried to turn upside down. Then, the teacher pirouetted. The girls pirouetted. Sarah spun in a circle, lost all control, and began racing around the room again. Once more, Ms Razetti stopped the entire class, very obligingly, went over to Sarah and took her gently by the hand, and guided her back to her spot in line. Sarah was so exhausted she lay down on the floor and didn't want to move. She finally got up and came to sit in my lap and we watched the last few minutes of class together.

After class, the instructor came to me and gently asked if I knew what I was witnessing. I said I thought she was simply immature and uncoordinated, and perhaps in a year or so she would grow into the class. Ms Razzetti gently observed that Sarah could follow two or three movements and then would lose her ability to maintain attention. She felt there was a possibility that Sarah had attention deficit disorder. She continued stating that Sarah was not a bad child and was not in need of discipline. She genuinely wanted to please the teacher. She was just physically unable to carry out the motions.

I was so stunned; I must have looked like a block of ice. Ms Razzetti continued talking about doctors and medicines and how lucky I was to find out early, but I wasn't listening; I was absorbing the shock. I felt as if I had been hit by a truck. I walked away and packed up Sarah's things and we went home. I didn't know what to believe anymore. The pediatrician had said she was fine. I had written off the schoolteacher as a nut and put her out of my mind. Now, I was being hit with it again. No one had ever said the words "attention deficit disorder" to me before.

Once at home, I flew into a tailspin. I needed to share my thoughts and feelings with someone, yet there was no one for me to talk to. My husband was in California. I called the pediatrician. He was on vacation for two weeks. My family all lived very far away in other states. There was no one for me to lean on. I was completely alone. I was afraid to call any of my local friends for the pity I would hear and the shame I would feel. I hadn't spoken to a doctor so I didn't have a real diagnosis. So there was nothing I could tell a friend. I was in complete limbo and isolation.

It dawned on me that I had the computer and could at least obtain information if nothing else. (Of course, the Internet was still very new at this time.) An Internet search revealed thousands of websites for attention deficit disorder. There was a cesspool of information, and I didn't begin to know where to wade through it. A glimpse at a few sites revealed lists of symptoms and stories of coping with the illness. As I read the monitor, I gradually began to identify symptoms characteristic of my Sarah. A picture slowly began to emerge and crystallize in my mind of a very sick child who was not responsible for her own behavior—a permanent state that she would never outgrow. I woke up from my state of denial to find that my reality was a permanent nightmare.

I looked at the symptoms and they read exactly like Sarah's personality—four or five little projects going at once, none of them ever completed, inconsolable mood swings, chronic fatigue, fearfulness, lack of willingness to participate in activities, living solely in her imagination, and chronic fidgetiness. But Sarah had physical symptoms as well, including dark circles under the eyes and mosquito bites that turned into enormous, oozing welts that took months to heal, extremely dry skin, insensitivity to pain, extra sensitivity to light and sound, and recurring bloody noses and bladder infections.

As I sat alone in our guest bedroom, peering at the computer screen, I broke down and wept. There was no way to deny it or hide from it. My beautiful angel was a broken child that may never be fixed. I knew I had two weeks to wait until the pediatrician returned. They were two of the longest weeks of my life.

I would watch Sarah playing in the corner of the living room with her toys, leaving our reality for a world filled with angels, ballerinas, and butterflies. Sometimes she wouldn't return to my world for the entire day. Sometimes she would bring her characters back into my reality, hallucinating them into existence. I knew I was rapidly losing her. Presently, a new child entered our home, a little boy who was older than Sarah. They played together. They spoke to one another. They shared her toys. But I never heard him or saw him. He was quite invisible to me, but to Sarah he was as real as the grass and the trees. Within days she was playing only with him. Eventually, she ceased to make eye contact with me. I felt desperate and panicked. I had to arrest this disease before it grew any worse. What was worse was that I felt so alone, as if there were no help for us.

To relax one afternoon, Sarah and I went for a swim in our pool. Within minutes, large, red, blotchy hives erupted over the entire surface of her body. Horrified, I scooped her up in a panic, rushed into the house, and put her in the bath to wash off the chlorine. In a few minutes the blotches subsided, along with my fears. As we got dressed, I was wondering the entire time what was causing this disorder and what was going to happen next. I was fearful of every second that passed because I could see before my eyes that the disease was growing worse.

After the swimming pool incident, we drove to town to run some errands: the bank, post office, grocery. It was a bright, hot summer day. I had promised Sarah an ice cream, so we stopped at an ice cream parlor and she had a scoop of rainbow ice cream. It was intensely colorful. She had a lot of fun with it. By the time we left the shop, she was hiccuping intensely, as if she were drunk, and couldn't stop. As I buckled her into her car seat, I saw that she was breaking out in hives again. This time I couldn't rinse them away. By the time we arrived home, she was leaving reality, hallucinating in her own little world. We ate an early dinner, just the two of us, because my husband was still in California; then I put her to bed, hoping that sleep would ease some of the problem.

The next morning she awoke covered with hives, a pale, ghostly white face with dark rings around her eyes, like a child from a horror movie. She started vomiting up everything she had eaten the night before. I could see her entire body beginning to self-destruct. My child was disintegrating before my very eyes. I ran to the kitchen and got a large stainless-steel mixing bowl to keep by the bed for her to throw up in. (To this day we comment on the big silver bowl.)

What was I to do? A call to the pediatrician was futile. The nurse only said, "Keep her in bed and watch her. It's just the flu, and it will pass." She didn't understand the progression of the disease because she wasn't in my shoes.

The disease was certainly progressing. Other creatures were being hallucinated into existence. Sarah now owned a purple cat named Ronny Jones, who lived in the pyramids of Egypt. There was a tiny girl who lived on the tip of Sarah's little finger. She had long pink hair, and her name was Elizabeth. No one could hear her wee, small voice except Sarah. The space shuttle *Columbia* made frequent landings in our living room. And, at age five, Sarah had her own ten-year-old daughter, who bought her gifts, played with her, and performed all sorts of activities that Sarah was not able to do. This was much more than the vivid imagination of an only child. Sarah believed these things to be real.

A feeling of fear, panic, and isolation was closing in on me. How could I call any of my friends or family and tell them my child was going insane? Besides, they couldn't help—no one could fix this. Her pediatrician had said there was nothing wrong, nothing to fix. I had at last come to the realization that I was completely powerless over the nightmare that was consuming my daylight hours. There was nothing I could do and nothing her pediatrician was willing to admit to. My mother's wisdom would not cure this. My girlfriends' understanding wouldn't either. Where could I possibly turn? At long last I realized there was only one thing left to do. I should have done it first. It always takes me so long to admit that I am not in control, that I am defeated. I fell to my knees and I gave my suffering to Jesus Christ. I found it ironic that my child felt no pain and, therefore, didn't know to cry out for help. Yet, due to my emotional pain, I cried out to the Ultimate Physician.

There was an immediate response to my prayer. I discovered that I was not alone at that moment in that room, nor had I ever been alone. His Presence entered my heart, melted my suffering, and guided me down a path of healing that no doctor, no pediatrician, not the specialists at Johns Hopkins, nor any psychologists ever talked to me about, because none of them could duplicate it. Because I had built a relationship with Jesus over the years, I knew how to listen to His divine guidance. The gift of healing, that He gave my child, is the gift I pass on to you.

five
Shopping Around

While I was struggling to come to grips with Sarah's developing illness, I was keenly aware of her gifted intelligence. I was enraged that her teacher wanted me to hold her back a year in school. It was true that Sarah had a fall birthday and was the youngest in her class, and that her social development lagged as much as a year behind the other students'. She tended to play more in parallel, rather than in a group, with other children. She didn't build relationships with the other kids in class either. In fact, some of her excessive laughter or crying even alienated them. Many of them avoided her. It broke my heart to watch the other children exclude her. From the teacher's perspective, there was a reason to hold her back one year.

However, in my mind, it simply would have been denying her incredible intelligence. The pediatrician said it would be criminal to hold her back and that she needed a better school. Norm insisted that it would be academic disaster to hold her back. They were both certainly right. I had watched Sarah memorize and recite the text of entire videos after one viewing. I had watched her recite whole books, page by page, after one reading. At two and a half, she knew the Lord's Prayer, the Beatitudes, and the Twenty-third Psalm, plus several dozen Mother Goose rhymes simply by having listened to them. She was an auditory learner with incredibly keen ears. It was part of the magic of Sarah. By two and three quarters she knew all of the phonemes of the alphabet, and by three she was reading like a six-year-old. I found it odd that the teacher never caught on to this aspect of my daughter's intelligence. After all, wasn't it her job to bring out the best in my child?

After years of studying this disorder, I have learned that many children on the spectrum display unique gifts and talents. There exists a fear in the autism community that if our children are healed, these abilities will disappear. Nothing could be further from the truth. Children continue to nurture their gifts and use them to advantage due to their recovery.

Finally, in February, Sarah's teacher invited me into her office once again. She explained that she had tested Sarah as we had discussed prior to Christmas break. (Somehow, I believed she would inform before testing Sarah.) She had used the American Guidance System test, which was given to all new, incoming students for placement. It turned out to be very helpful. In every area - cognitive, verbal, and analytical - Sarah scored two and a half years ahead of her age level. Sarah was absorbing information at an enormous rate, but she was not demonstrating this knowledge in the classroom. Her teacher could not offer any solutions to help her excel. Fortunately, I had foreseen this and had already begun the search for another school in January 2000.

Shopping around for schools turned out to be quite an amazing experience. I discovered that there are as many philosophies about how to educate children, as there are children in the world. There were Christian schools, secular schools, classical Christian schools, Montessori schools, skills-based curricula, experimental curricula, and more. A person has to become an expert in education just to figure it all out.

Sarah was much more relaxed and confident about the school search than I was. She tested at half a dozen schools, consistently scoring two and a half years ahead of her age level. Everyone who tested her was quite surprised and complimentary. Norm and I finally narrowed our school choices.

The school we ultimately chose, after much consideration, was neither elitist nor exceptional. The curriculum was conventional, but it had something else—an overpowering amount of love and excellent communication skills, just the two things we needed to get Sarah through her sickest years. Her teacher was fabulous beyond my dreams. She was patient, aware of Sarah's illness, and she kept me informed daily of the symptoms she observed in the classroom. She detailed all of the objects or events that triggered Sarah's sensitivities. She took a personal interest in Sarah. So a little prayer and shopping around for schools paid off.

The next thing that paid off was shopping for doctors. Sarah reached her absolute sickest in June and July of 2000. Once we saw the pediatrician, following the horrendous vomiting and his return from vacation, it became apparent that he was concerned with the behavioral aspects of Sarah's disorder. I kept asking about the vomiting, the hives, and the allergic shiners under her eyes. He said he would give her a "little something" to help her focus in class and something else for the hives. I requested tests for allergies; he kept saying she was young, and we would do them later. He sent me off with directions to take Sarah to a local child psychologist. I couldn't understand any doctor who addressed only one aspect of this horrendous disorder. While I am certain he was concerned about Sarah's overall health, it appeared to me that he was focused on the behavioral aspects alone. I wanted him to address her whole body. Was he completely neglecting the vomiting and other allergic reactions? I felt it was time to go shopping around.

It was quite apparent that Sarah had food sensitivities, so I struck out on my own, leaving my pediatrician behind. I removed all of the foods from her diet that I suspected were causing difficulties: gluten, dairy, sugar, artificial colors and flavors, preservatives, pesticides, and *Ash* herbicides. We went entirely organic. Her behavior dramatically improved. Within four days she was more focused. She was entering my world, and her speech had improved. In the meantime, I called the pediatric allergy division of Johns Hopkins Medical Center in Baltimore, and made an appointment with their leading pediatric allergist. After the fact, I wrote a letter to my pediatrician and told him about the appointment. He called me into his office immediately and wrote out request forms for RAST (radioallergosorbent) testing. (RAST tests measure the amount of immunoglobulin E antibodies in the patient's blood serum for a given allergen.) With Sarah, one vial of blood was used to test between eighty and a hundred different allergens—all the foods she reacted to.

RAST testing is extremely limited. It does not test for any artificial ingredients (which are obviously dangerous to children with autism). It only tests for proteins; therefore, the very problematic groups of phenols, aromatic aldehydes, and salicylates go unrepresented. (More on these groups in chapter Nine, "Food Elimination.") In addition, it only tests one of the five possible immune antibody response types, immunoglobulin E—ignoring types A, D, G and M. Lastly, it can cause fear in small children because it means drawing blood.

Taking Sarah to the phlebotomist was an experience in itself. The receptionist and I, working together, spent an entire hour looking up the codes for the one hundred tests in the catalogues to load into the computer. Then we walked back to the lab where the blood was to be drawn. Sarah really did not know what was coming. She was quite brave and did not scream when jabbed with the needle. The phlebotomist took two vials of blood. But as she swung around to put Sarah's tubes in the test tube stand behind her, one slipped and she accidentally dropped it. It hit the hard tile floor at Sarah's feet and smashed, sending brilliant crimson blood spewing all over the furniture, filing cabinets, and shoes. I don't know what it did to Sarah to see her own blood smashed all over the floor, but I was appalled! To me, it was just one more sign that conventional medicine was not the route to true healing for my child. I bundled her up and got her out of the lab as quickly as possible.

In November 2000, we made the long trip to Johns Hopkins in Baltimore with the results of our RAST test in hand. They indicated that Sarah had no allergies at all. Seeing the specialist was yet another disappointment. When he entered the exam room, I handed the list of Sarah's symptoms to him. He leaned back quietly in his chair and absorbed the words on the page. His eyebrows rose as he read: hallucinations, vomiting, recurrent bladder infections, and so forth. Then I handed him the RAST results. He said he could have told us the results of the test would be negative. I told him about the elimination diet I had her on, and the transformation in her behavior. He replied that it worked for some and not for others. He then said there was nothing he could do for a special child like Sarah because there were no tests to identify food chemicals that passed the blood-brain barrier. We departed and he followed up with a letter to our pediatrician, stating that there was nothing he could do for Sarah. The letter remains in her medical file today.

Oddly enough, I was actually relieved. I was afraid we would have to perform or jump through hoops or that they would give drugs to my child! Instead however, I felt as if we had been set free of the conventional medical community. Norm and I were free to launch wholeheartedly into the nutrition solution for our child. In fact, the nutrition solution worked so well that three months later, at the time of our first visit with the psychologist, he claimed that he could find nothing to test her for.

I must admit he didn't look very hard. We were told the clinic where he worked was the finest in the area, and this psychologist came with extremely good references. When I arrived in October 2000, I found the clinic overburdened with children who were seen on a conveyor-belt basis. The psychologist listened to me for an hour, then denied everything I'd said about nutrition and the dietary restrictions I had placed on Sarah because it was not supported by the research studies he was familiar with. I showed him writing samples of Sarah's name when her diet was clean, and again when she had eaten something detrimental to her. He was surprised by this evidence, yet unconvinced. The following week he saw Sarah for one hour and played Pick Up sticks with her. Then he spoke to her kindergarten teacher on the phone. He never entered the classroom to watch her rocking in the corner by herself, or visited the playground to see her awkward gait, or heard her joke and tease with other children to discover her mental agony while searching for words. On the basis of Pick Up sticks and one teacher conversation, he diagnosed her with "adjustment disorder," which was a far cry from the seriously disturbed child she had been the preceding summer. Since he had no further recommendations, and with no referrals to any other practitioner, he dismissed her as a patient. I knew Sarah was being shipwrecked and abandoned, yet once again, I felt strangely relieved and set free of the conventional medical community.

Sarah's normal four-year-old signature when her diet was clean.

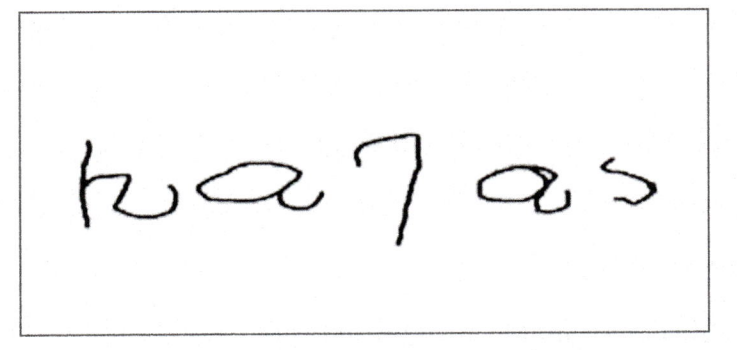

Sarah's signature twenty minutes after eating one bowl of dairy-free, vanilla ice cream containing corn syrup. These are the actual signature sizes.

There remained one symptom I had not pushed the doctors to investigate. Sarah had an extremely low basal body temperature. I had been recording it every morning for weeks with a brand new oral digital thermometer. It was 95.5 degrees Fahrenheit through fall 2000. Coupling this with her poor coordination and repeated bladder infections, I surmised that there might be a thyroid condition. In January 2001, we made one more trip to the pediatrician and requested blood tests for thyroid. He just shook his head. He told me I would make myself crazy if I continued to follow this path; that is to say, for a cure that didn't exist. He wrote up the order for the blood test anyway. I took the opportunity to question him about some materials I had read on the Internet about viral colonization in the lining of the intestine and asked if he knew any pediatric gastroenterologist who could biopsy her. He told me that there were many types of experimental techniques going on and that he was not up on the latest among them. Then he turned and looked me squarely in the eyes and said, *"Besides, you don't want anyone to experiment with your child, now, do you? Even if you do find something, then what? There is no way to remove it."*

At last, he finally confessed that Sarah was "slightly autistic." In addition, he gave me the names and phone numbers of another psychiatrist, and the director of our local school for the learning disabled. He wrote "delayed development" on Sarah's file, closed it, and walked out the door.

❧ ❧ ❧

At that moment, I learned the limits of the system. Together, Norm and I learned who could offer true help and who could not. We discovered places of safety and love for our small child. Shopping around for schools, doctors, and additional medical information paid off, and would continue paying, because the journey didn't end here.

six
Heaven Sent

Many months passed using the nutrition solution. Each day was a struggle to maintain balance and to be sure Sarah would not become "triggered." As many mothers know, the disease grows worse with time, and Sarah was reaching the point where nearly any trigger food would cause vomiting. I floundered searching for a more permanent solution. In time, we found it, and I'll share it in the rest of this book. I hope it will save you some floundering.

There is a very old joke that floats around certain circles. It goes like this:

> A man lives in a house in a flood zone. One day, there are torrential rains, and the water is rising. It covers the first floor, so he climbs to the second. It covers the second, so he climbs out onto the roof, where he begins to pray to God to rescue him.
>
> In a short while, a boat speeds up to him and the driver shouts, "Hop in." The man on the roof replies, "No thanks. God will rescue me." The driver shrugs his shoulders and the boat speeds away.
>
> Time passes. A second boat speeds up to his perch and the driver shouts. "Hop in. I'll take you to safety." The man on the roof replies. "No thanks. God will rescue me." The driver shrugs his shoulders and the second boat speeds away. Time ticks on. Finally a search helicopter passes overhead and lowers a ladder down to the man on the roof. The man shouts up to the helicopter. "No thank you. God will rescue me." The helicopter flies away.

More time passes. The man grows discouraged. He cries out to God, "Lord, Lord! Why haven't you rescued me?" Immediately, a great voice booms from above, "I SENT YOU TWO BOATS AND A HELICOPTER. WHAT MORE DO YOU WANT?"

For quite a long time I was the man on the roof. Hints for cures to Sarah's disorder were laid before me by well-meaning friends and I did not recognize them until someone spoke directly to my face. Fortunately, we did not miss the helicopter.

During the first few months of Sarah's recovery, those well-meaning friends recommended a variety of books and therapies. One cousin handed me all of her nutrition books. Some I read and used; some I read and thought useless. Most of the books were about diets and living and coping with illness. Many of them were about allergies. The author of one book was so strange and outlandish that I could not possibly fall prey to her ridiculous ideas. Her book was about healing through, of all things, energy, so I gleaned the allergy information and shelved the book. The first boat went by and I missed it.

All the while, Sarah was improving. The repetitive speech pattern diminished. She began to keep up with the other children in the park. Her peculiar gait was less noticeable. She was moving into my world at home and she was reading and writing with the other children in kindergarten. She could almost follow her ballet teacher. In fact, in spring 2001, we stopped at a toy store for a birthday gift for a classmate. Sarah, who had never ridden a tricycle, saw a two-wheeler bike, hopped on uninitiated, and rode it around the store effortlessly. It seemed that, with the exception of a few social quirks, she was becoming a fairly healthy girl.

She was quite simply an average girl who didn't eat wheat, corn, rye, barley, oats, oranges, apples, peaches, plums, strawberries, blueberries, raspberries, tomatoes, apricots, tangerines, grapes, raisins, herbs, spices, candy, cakes, cookies, milk, cheese, butter or ice cream. She was taking approximately twenty pills a day in the form of nutritional supplements to maintain her attention level. But, Norm, and I were happy. Who cared about the lifestyle change? The vomiting stopped and we had our girl back from the brink of potential loss. We were very satisfied, especially when the kindergarten teacher assured us she would pass on to the first grade in spite of the few social quirks she displayed. Norm and I may have been completely satisfied with Sarah and her transformation, but God was not. He had another plan.

Throughout the winter of 2001, while Sarah was in kindergarten, I repeatedly ran into a woman named Carla. I knew her, but not well. We had attended the same church, but we had never worked together on any projects or committees, so we were not close. I had learned through the prayer chain that she had suffered from cancer and had undergone surgery and chemotherapy. Yet, every time I saw her, she looked more radiant than the last, and she had never lost her hair. I couldn't figure it out. Friends said that she was practicing some form of alternative therapy. By the third or fourth time I saw her in public, I felt God's tug. I went home and wrote her a letter, knowing that she would understand the tug of God. The letter immediately resulted in a phone call. We talked about God, the church, Christian study classes, and the fact that we each knew the other, but had never been formally introduced. We never got around to discussing her alternative medicine. I felt it would be too impolite to pry. We said our "good-byes" and hung up. The second boat had just sped away.

Nine months passed. There was an enormous amount of healing with Sarah's nutrition routine; yet, it was a balancing act, and there were still periodic temper outbursts, hypersensitive reactions, and a certain lack of awareness and motivation she still needed to come out of. One afternoon, I was shopping in the local whole foods store and ran into a friend I hadn't seen in a year. I had always liked her. We hugged and said something trivial and parted. But in that one week, I ran into her three times at the same store. I thought to myself, *"Bingo! I haven't seen her in a year, and now I've run into her three times in one week?"* God's tug was undeniable.

The third time I saw her, I grabbed her arm and said,
"Do you have time for lunch?"
"Yeah!" she replied enthusiastically.
We parked ourselves in the store's café. Then I asked,
"So how are you doing?"
Her oldest child, who was also on the spectrum, was in third or fourth grade. Completely unsolicited, she replied, "We are doing fine and we are Ritalin-free." I knew her son had been off of corn derivatives and dairy, but I never knew any details.

I mentioned that we were using the nutrition solution, had removed gluten, dairy and some other foods, and were giving Sarah supplements that benefitted the various symptoms.

"That stuff's all fine," she replied, "but it only deals with the symptoms. She can be cured." Her voice was emphatic and it held the promise I had been waiting for God to send.

"We're doing ICM and you can't believe the difference," she continued. "My son's composing music, his bed-wetting has stopped, his grades have gone straight up, and he's eating corn and dairy again."

I knew exactly what she was talking about. I had read about it in the book, donated by the well-meaning cousin, written by the author of the "outlandish" energy techniques. It remained shelved at home. I felt safe around my friend after she had confessed all this, so I volunteered everything about Sarah—the autism, the attention deficit, the dyslexia, the vomiting and skin problems, the diet, the supplements. My Sarah had been far sicker that her son.

It was not just a coincidence that she had an extra business card from the ICM practitioner in her wallet. She told me the rates, and they didn't seem very expensive for the results that were promised.

"So your son's really healed?" I inquired again, to reassure myself.

"He's eating pizza with his classmates again, even with the dextrose in the sauce and the cheese on top."

I took the card home and prayed. Then, I pulled the "outlandish" energy book, by Ellen Cutler, down from the shelf. It was titled *Winning the War against Immune Disorders and Allergies*. I reread the section on the allergy elimination technique. As it turns out, the therapy is not so outlandish. In fact, it is quite commonplace in some parts of the world. It was something akin to acupuncture—or acupressure for small children—while holding on to a vial of the item to which one is sensitive. I was really frightened of what this unfamiliar therapy was all about; but I also knew that I was sitting on the roof of a flooded house, and two boats had sped away, leaving my child behind. So now I was ready to grab her and climb into the helicopter. I picked up the phone and called the NAET practitioner.

seven
Making the Decision to Use Energy Medicine

There is a stigma in the United States about using unconventional medicine. Non-Western physicians are labeled at best unscientific and at worst quacks and crackpots. Conventional medical libraries do not contain any information about Eastern statistics or protocols. They only contain information to support Western techniques. After all, the doctors and psychologists were always telling me that Western medicine is based on one hundred years of clinical trials. How could Norm and I consider doing something with our child that was unconventional or even "experimental," as the pediatrician had put it?

Being a microbiologist, I knew that the issue of a hundred years of clinical trials was an enormous fallacy. Clinical trials are only indicated when a new and potentially harmful drug or vaccine is being introduced to the population. There are no clinical trials for new surgical techniques. Modern chemical medicine is fewer than two hundred years old, so there is not very much history supporting it. Most clinical trials are conducted by exhausted, overworked graduate and doctoral students who want to complete their dissertations and get their degrees. These students have grown up in the system and have no reason to question or explore anything outside of the system. It would never occur to them that there may be another method of obtaining the results they are looking for. In addition, many of these trials are poorly set up and operated, including the Michael McGee cancer vaccine research study in 2000 at St. John Medical Center in Tulsa, Oklahoma the Johns Hopkins asthma and allergy trial that killed Ellen Roche in 1999; the hepatitis vaccine given to mentally retarded children at Willowbrook State School in New York back in the 1950s; and the 1999 University of Pennsylvania gene trial that killed eighteen-year-old Jesse Gelsinger. Of course there is no system in place for tracking medical studies that are not federally funded. So, private pharmaceutical companies that want to launch new products can experiment without supervision on anyone they please just by paying them money. So from my past experience inside the medical community, the fallacy of using only "safe," clinically-tested methods to heal my child had already been debunked.

With energy medicine, I would not be introducing any chemicals to my child. There would be no surgery. There was nothing invasive of any kind. So the entire "clinical trials" argument was irrelevant. Also, I understood that energy medicine had been practiced by billions of people in the Far East for more than two thousand years—over ten times longer than Western medicine. Energy medicine didn't need to pass laboratory tests because it had already passed the test of time.

Next, I had already discovered the limits of conventional medicine where mental health was concerned. They had nothing to offer us. They had told us there were no tests to explore what was going on beyond the blood-brain barrier. I was told I would make myself crazy if I continued my search. Many of the doctors I spoke with were not up on the latest techniques in autism recovery. None of them even knew how to speak with me about diagnosing the cause of the problem. Besides, my friend had already used this energy doctor and had had good results, so why should I listen to conventional doctors who had nothing to offer me?

The last remaining sticking point that I could see in our decision to use alternative medicine wasn't scientific at all. It was societal conventions. For some reason, in the United States, energy medicine is not promoted in a scientific package, although there is a great deal of physics behind it. It seems to be wrapped up in a spiritual or "new age" package. Many people do not know what to do with this, and it alarms them. As I continue through this book, it will become very clear that the energy is not a spirit, but a real measurable, tangible, series of frequencies or wavelengths that can be scientifically manipulated to gain extraordinary medical results.

At only fifty dollars per treatment (in 2001) and no chance of introducing a harmful agent to our child, we launched into energy medicine as a cure for Sarah's autism.

part two
The Journey Begins

eight
The Tools We Used at Home

This section is an account of how we functioned the first year Sarah was diagnosed, before we found our energy doctor. I have included a list of the tools I used initially, before beginning energy medicine, to bring Sarah out of autism, to end hyperactivity, and to lift dyslexia. I will also explain how I experienced each tool.

One of the most important things to bear in mind is that each child is an individual. What works for one may take additional experimentation for another. Older children take longer to heal than preschoolers. Experimentation for us caused some temporary setbacks. But all in all, there was a positive move toward recovery. I've known many children who were healed simply by removing the first item on the elimination list. Sarah was not that fortunate. I know far more children who were never healed because no one ever tried. Today Sarah is happy, vital, and progressing normally.

This tool list lays the groundwork and provides continuity and balance during the period of energy medicine therapy. The nutrition solution and the energy work together. Energy medicine removes the underlying causes and rebalances the metabolic disorders. Looking back, I understand that God moved Sarah and me through this nutrition portion of the journey to get her to a drug-free, steady state in preparation for ICM, NAET and FCT®.

As we progressed through this portion of her recovery, Sarah's behavior migrated through an entire spectrum of disorders. It was fascinating to note which foods induced the hallucinogenic behaviors, which the savant behavior, which the dyslexic behavior. (This will be covered in detail in chapter 9, "Food Elimination.")

The Tools
The skill of living in the present moment
The Internet, with discernment
A bound composition journal
Three textbooks
Food ingredient labels
A good organic food store
Nutritional supplements

I took great care to fully utilize all of these tools and follow the authors' directions to the letter. I wrote each tool very methodically so as not to leave one out. To forget one meant regression. Yet, I found no regression to be permanent. Any food that Sarah accidentally ingested which triggered unwanted behaviors left the body in about three days and the healthy child returned to me. Likewise, if I inadvertently noticed unusual behavior in my child, I could return to the tool list to find out how to correct the situation.

The Skill of Living in the Present Moment

A mother telephoned me one day having heard that I had healed my child. She wanted to learn how to heal her own child. I told her about food elimination. Her reply was, "I just knew you were going to say that. I just knew it!" She hung up and never called again. Another mother I know very well was asked at a dinner party if she had tried the nutrition solution for her two ADD children. Her terse reply was, "I read the list of foods you have to give up and it was too many." The topic was dropped immediately. I thought to myself, "*If my child had a broken leg, wouldn't I get her a cast?*" A person wears a cast only as long as the leg is healing; it is temporary. If a child has autism, the cure is to sacrifice a few foods temporarily. I would make any sacrifice for my child.

These stories are examples of people who are unable to live in the present moment. The human mind has the incredible ability to leap from one small suggestion to a grandiose generalization such as, "I will never again be able to eat any of the foods I like for the rest of my life." This is a fallacy. We cannot live in the future and the present simultaneously. We cannot anticipate what foods are being served next month, or next week, or even tomorrow. Anticipating food that isn't present is a waste of time.

Yesterday is a memory, and tomorrow isn't here yet. The only moment we hold any power or control over is this moment. This moment is the only moment in which we, as parents, can act to heal our children. For this moment, we can choose to serve our children food that will heal them and not add to their disorders. Tomorrow will take care of itself.

As for the number of food eliminations, think of the enormous abundance of food in this world. My Sarah is certainly not deprived, and neither are the other children I know on this program. Most of the food eliminated is "junk" or "non-food," which has little or no nutritional value anyway. If a child is ill and eating a food that is complicating the illness, then that food is a danger to the child. Why risk the danger? Every child is different. For many it is not necessary to remove every offending food suggested. Besides, the food elimination is only temporary until the metabolism is restored using energy medicine. Then the foods can be returned slowly, one at a time.

Therefore, the path to success in healing these children with autism begins with simply focusing on the food available at a given moment in time. Tomorrow will take care of itself.

The Internet

We are truly fortunate to live in an age in which we have access to so much information at our fingertips. The Internet was an incredibly valuable tool to me. I'm quite sure Sarah would not be healed if it had not been for the Internet. I found books on nutrition and dealing with the disorder. I found online drugstores that carried her supplements. I found support groups that linked me to additional sources for healing. All of the government sources for the latest information on therapies are accessible, with opportunities for study. Research databases are also available. Many of the resources I found are located in appendix F.

Shamefully, the Centers for Disease Control and the National Institutes of Health offer very little in support for these disorders. They do not recognize a cure, nor do they recognize alternative therapies. The Food and Drug Administration is at least honest about mercury toxicity in the environment.

The websites I used were launch points for Sarah's journey toward healing. They were not the end result. All of these sites are well linked and supported. However, I did find a plethora of unusable information on the web as well. Searches on autism and attention deficit disorder bring up tens of thousands of websites at a time. A lot of it was muck, so I put on my hip waders and climbed in. Discernment was never more needed than now. Immediately, anything that sounded like popular psychology or soft science therapies that worked with the illness, such as play therapies, audio therapies, or behavior modification, I excluded. Likewise, anything that spoke to numbing the symptoms, such as cocaine-based psycho stimulants, like Adderall, Ritalin, or Dexedrine, I also excluded. There were support groups; some, however, were advocacy groups that lobbied Congress to change school regulations to accommodate their sick children or to offer their children for chemical research. I found only a couple that support actual research toward discovering a cause and a cure. The best I found I have listed in appendix F, Resources. Most, I ignored. I only paid attention to those sites that addressed the underlying cause of the problem and led to a true cure.

Composition Journal

I personally used a plain black, speckled, bound composition book. If I were doing things over again from scratch, I would get a three-ring binder with pockets. I picked up so much material along my journey that I needed a place to store it all. The journal was the most important of all my tools.

I kept the journal on the kitchen counter. As I prepared Sarah's meals, I wrote down what she ate, and I wrote the date at the top of the page. I wrote each meal and what went into her snack box for school. I dated everything. I kept it simple. I didn't jump to conclusions. I didn't feel that I would have to do this every day for the rest of her life. It was a tool that set Sarah free from the foods that were harming her.

Why was this useful? In autism spectrum disorders, foods act as a trigger to behavior, which is caused by the underlying metabolic breakdown. Certain foods aggravate the disorder terribly. All of the symptoms can be dramatically reduced by the control of those foods. Many people already know this trick and are well aware of which foods are problematic for them. Often, doctors have told their patients which foods to avoid. Yet many families still are not having success. Our family has had success, and the journal is one of the reasons why. It allowed me to document foods and then to record Sarah's behaviors. I could easily see if there was a cause and effect. It was a painless practice for me, yet a huge step on the road to Sarah's recovery.

Following the food elimination stage, I found that Sarah's diet was pretty meager. I wanted to reintroduce a few foods to broaden her choices. They must be reintroduced one at a time, as with a new baby. Four days had to pass between each food trial; therefore, I had to remember to date the journal accurately. I used the journal to record Sarah's reaction to each food tested. Chapter 9, "Food Elimination," will provide more information on this topic.

The journal was also a great place to store new recipes. As I discovered new things that Sarah could eat, I experimented with them, creating new recipes—some good, some not so good. But all in all, Sarah and I had a lot of fun together in the kitchen.

The last, and most important, use I found for the food journal was as a medical record during the years that we progressed through her healing treatments. I recorded food, her treatments, supplements, bathroom habits, and reactions to her treatments that the practitioner could refer to. During each appointment I took the journal with me and read back the symptoms to the doctor. He could better judge in which direction to go for her treatment that day. It helped to customize her treatment and guide her recovery. The journal was indispensable.

Three Textbooks

Three specific books launched Sarah's journey toward healing. I would not have known how to get started without them. They are very descriptive of the disorders on the spectrum and how children react to given stimuli. Once on the road to recovery, however, we far surpassed anything in any one of these books. The books are:

Why Is Your Child Hyperactive?, by Ben F. Feingold, MD (Random House, 1985)
The ADD Nutrition Solution, by Marcia Zimmerman, CN (Holt Paperbacks, 1999)
Childhood Illness and the Allergy Connection, by Zoltan Rona, MD (Prima Lifestyles, 1996)

Dr. Feingold's book is thirty years old and was difficult to find, but I didn't give up. It is a must-have. Dr. Feingold was the chief of the Department of Allergy at Kaiser Permanente in San Francisco for years. He died in 1982. He was the first to document that when certain food allergens were removed from the diet, often dramatic behavioral changes occurred. He was also the first to report that artificial additives caused hyperactivity. And he was the first to demand responsible ingredient labels on food packages, which of course is the linchpin of this tool list. His understanding of salicylic acid and other chemical reactions between food and the body is dated, yet the book is not without merit. He opened the door to discussions about salicylate sensitivity. (More on salicylates and phenols and aromatic aldehydes in chapter 9.)

Marcia Zimmerman's book, *The ADD Nutrition Solution a 30-Day Plan*, is exceptional in its approach to this disorder. Zimmerman does not approach ADD as a psychological or neurological disorder, but as a digestive disorder, and that is absolutely where it all begins. With all due respect to the well-meaning physicians who do all they can to help, none of them have ever had so much as one course in nutrition in medical school. It's simply not taught. Zimmerman is a nutritionist. Her research is extremely thorough. She documents every inch of her recommendations. She explains the level of malnutrition from which these children suffer and provides descriptions, as well as age-appropriate dosages of the nutritional supplements that heal them. This book is essential for the supplement chapter. However, it is far more than a thirty-day plan. In thirty days, a dramatic improvement is seen. The result is a sick child who is symptom-free due to food restrictions. Marcia Zimmerman's book is excellent at helping to control symptoms and restoring nutrition. For Sarah, total healing took two and a half years, to find the cause and cure her of it.

Dr. Zoltan Rona is an interesting man. He is Canadian of eastern European descent. I found his book, *Childhood Illness and the Allergy Connection*, extremely useful because so many books focus on a single illness and treatment. Yet often, in children on the spectrum, and certainly in Sarah's case, there were multiple conditions. Rona addresses this. He was the only one who explained to me the problems of gluten and casein. Many authors speak of reducing these substances, but they don't explain why. He did. And notably, he did not speak in terms of reduction, which would have been the sure road to disaster for Sarah. He spoke of *total elimination*, which is the path to healing. In fact, we found it necessary to temporarily remove nearly all carbohydrates.

Food Ingredient Labels

Without food ingredient labels, Sarah's recovery would have taken much longer than it did. Listing ingredients on package labels is required by the Food and Drug Administration. Food packagers are required to list the chemical names of the ingredients. Most of us do not have the expertise to know the meanings of many chemical names. A lot of them are listed in Marcia Zimmerman's book. I had to completely let go of the old notion of purchasing by brand name. Without understanding the ingredients, recovery would have been severely compromised.

When I first began shopping by ingredient labels, it took a very long time to get through the store. I had to shop while Sarah was in school so I could study each label free of interruptions. Exploring our area's whole food stores became an adventure. The ingredient labels read quite differently from the food labels in our conventional grocery stores. Within a few months, I found enough "safe" products to stock our kitchen shelves. Once I became familiar with the new brand names we were using, my usual speedy grocery routine was back in place and shopping became a less rigorous experience.

The most important thing I noted about all packaging labels is that they are very deceptive. Of course, the idea is to entice you with what is written on the front label in hopes that you will not read the back label, where the ingredients are listed. I learned never to trust what was written on the front label. Companies often use sales language such as "all natural," "whole grain," or "stone ground." All of these marketing buzzwords were meaningless where Sarah's illness was concerned. High fructose corn syrup was natural, but it would also send her through the roof. Anything "whole grain" implied that it was loaded with gluten. None of these sales "buzz" words indicated that the product was organic. That was the key. Sarah's foods would need to be organic from here on out. We later found that her tissues were loaded with pesticides, herbicides, and antibiotics. I also found out that genetically modified organisms (GMOs) were very dangerous for her as well. By looking on the back label, under the word *ingredients*, I could discover whether or not the product really was organic. If it was not, I did not purchase it.

What else was I looking for on these ingredient labels? I looked for artificial colorings, preservatives, and any of the items Sarah was allergic to, which was nearly every natural and all artificial flavorings. I will explain in detail the foods I eliminated and why in chapter 9.

GMOs are growing into heated political battles in a few states. Some states are now attempting to require GMO labeling by law. While GMOs were dangerous, they were not yet a big issue when Sarah was young. They are now. Ingredient labels yield no information about GMOs. However, a new organization, the Non-GMO Project, provides labeling information for voluntary food producers, restaurants, and retailers. You can find them online at: http://www.nongmoproject.org/.

A Good Organic Foods Store

In 1980, as a student at the University of Texas in Austin, I had been a member of the original Whole Foods Co-op. At that time, it was just a fad. I had no idea what was going to occur over the next thirty years. There has been an explosion in the whole foods industry. Organic food stores of many types exist nationwide.

I had greatly feared the nutrition solution for Sarah's healing because it was nearly impossible to find ingredient labels that were free of the offending ingredients. In my local grocery store, everything was processed, except the foods along the outside aisles, and even those were not organic. The greatest problem stemmed from sheer volume of goods. There was so much food I was overwhelmed at the prospect of reading all those ingredient labels just to find new, "safe" brands. Out of fatigue, I would be tempted to buy what was convenient and easy rather than nutritious. I knew what I needed to do.

After putting Sarah in school one day, I drove ten miles beyond our usual grocery store to seek out the nearest organic foods store. It was another answer to a prayer. I discovered that thousands of people had walked this path before me. The store was smaller. The volume of products was manageable. Everything was clearly marked "organic" or "conventional." The ingredient labels had words I could pronounce. The package labels matched up with the books I was using. The employees understood my needs when I spoke to them. I wasn't alone anymore.

There were just a couple of drawbacks to whole foods shopping. The lack of pesticides and preservatives is an open invitation to parasites. All foods must be thoroughly washed and cooked. Raw vegetables must be soaked and peeled. Grains must be refrigerated. Parasites are a very real problem for children on the spectrum. In many cases they are the cause of the problem.

The other drawback was the expense. How could I justify paying those prices for food? How could I justify leaving my child in sickness, knowing there was a cure? Was it really all that expensive? Which was more expensive, paying the prices of the whole foods store or raising a child who would never support herself because she couldn't complete an education? We developed a new household budget that was uncomfortable, but it worked. I drove the additional ten miles for my routine shopping. The whole house benefitted from healthier foods, and Sarah recovered.

Nutritional Supplements

One acquaintance who knew Sarah's plight was also a child psychologist. Early in the journey she told me, quite emphatically, not to purchase any nutritional supplements because I might harm my child. I was so glad I was guided by Marcia Zimmerman's book, or I might have listened to her and Sarah would still be ill. The supplements are absolutely critical to the child's recovery. Zimmerman's book is an excellent beginning. The need for the supplements lies in the fact that children on the spectrum cannot absorb the necessary nutrients from food due to digestive disturbances and other imbalances. Because the microvilli in the intestine are damaged, they do not recognize and "uptake" nutrients into the body. Therefore, children with autism require additional supplementation. Providing the necessary nutrients to Sarah laid the groundwork for the energy medicine that permitted her body to permanently identify and "uptake" the nutrients. In addition, since Sarah was dairy-free, she needed calcium and vitamin D for her bones to grow. Since she was grain-free, she needed B vitamins for her central nervous system to work. (This is fully covered in chapter 10, "Nutritional Supplements").

The nutritionist we found specialized in treating disturbed children. Since our pediatrician's office refused to give us the name of a nutritionist, we had to find one on our own. I wasn't shy to leave the safe surroundings of the pediatrician's office and shop around for assistance. It really paid off for our family.

But it didn't come without a cost. The bulk of my grocery budget went toward supplements during the months of stabilization. We averaged two hundred dollars per month in supplements in 2001. Thankfully, after Sarah's cure was complete, it was no longer necessary to spend that kind of money on supplements. Even after seven months of energy therapy treatments, Sarah's body was able to uptake nutrients from her food naturally, and her supplement load was re-dosed by the physician and cut by two-thirds.

nine
Food Elimination

The elimination step in autism recovery is enormously powerful and little understood by most medical doctors and psychologists. Sarah's pediatrician told me that food elimination would reduce the symptoms but it would not make them go away entirely. How little he obviously understood the foods we eat. Elimination is important because it brings an immediate halt to the destruction of the patient's intestinal lining. The causative agents of autism act in a progressive manner. Frequently, symptoms grow worse with time. Eliminating certain foods stops the progression. I wish my doctor would have informed me of this step the minute he suspected a problem.

Within the digestive system lie many different digestive enzymes as well as neurotransmitter receptor sites, each of which is a perfect "handprint" for the food it is intended to digest or absorb. These receptor sites comprise an identification system. If there is interference with the makeup of these enzymes or the neurotransmitter sites and their specific handprints, then a wide array of undesired responses may result; they certainly did in Sarah. Remember, autism is not a mental disorder, but a symptom of metabolic breakdowns. Food elimination became necessary for us simply because Sarah could not metabolize so many things.

Elimination is the stage at which I saw with my own eyes how so many different disorders all stemmed from one condition. The metabolic breakdown causes a continuum of disease. Psychologists call it a spectrum of disorders. I went to my local library and read the DSM-IV, the Diagnostic and Statistical Manual of Mental Disorders, which is the psychologists' and psychiatrists' reference manual for diagnosing behavioral and mental illness. (The DSM-5 is now available.) It contains a section on pervasive development disorders, which covers autistic disorders, Rett's disorder, childhood disintegrative disorder, Asperger's, and pervasive development disorder. For each of these disorders, diagnostic features and recording procedures are listed.

Oddly, the DSM-IV only lists social, academic, and occupational behaviors. Few other symptoms are listed, unless there is severe retardation. Physical symptoms, such as allergies, food sensitivities, skin and bowel disorders, and the like, are nowhere to be found. To me, that is completely unscientific. Apparently, the American Psychiatric Association does not seem to mind that entire categories of symptoms go unobserved. They may assume that the primary physician is treating these disorders, yet that assumption completely isolates and alienates the treatment of the patient. It assumes there is no link between the physical and mental symptoms. In Sarah, I observed a definite and dramatic link.

Food elimination helped to clarify for me which aspects of Sarah's metabolism were not functioning correctly. Symptoms all depend on which foods the individual is sensitive to and exposed to, as well as when the withdrawal occurs. (Schizophrenia is often included on this continuum very near autism, but it was not one of Sarah's conditions. Schizophrenics, like Asperger's patients, lack the ability to recognize nonverbal social cues. This same program may also be beneficial to them.)

I wish to make one thing very clear. The food was not Sarah's enemy. Many nutrition gurus give the impression that there is something inherently wrong with today's food. Yes, there are many problems, but Sarah's disorder was not caused entirely by foods. It was caused by various metabolic, digestive, and immune system breakdowns and the resulting toxicity. There has been a systematic assault on individuals' immune systems in the last few decades. Once the immune system is righted, the disorders go away. At that point, foods can be reintroduced, one item at time, back into the diet. The elimination diet is only temporary until all the metabolic systems are balanced and restored. This is the story of how that restoration takes place.

> *Elimination is the stage at which I saw with my own eyes how so many different disorders all stemmed from one condition.*

A List of Sarah's Symptoms
Mid-July 2000

Autism Symptoms
- Diverted gaze (onset 18 months)
- Abnormal responses to sensory stimuli
- Lack of awareness of others
- Inability to make friends
- Repetitive speech pattern/echolalia
- Distress over environmental changes
- Inability to feel pain
- Imaginary brother she insisted was real
- Daydreams/hallucinations
- Gifted hearing/savant tendencies
- Auditory hallucinations

ADD Symptoms
- Lack of inhibitions
- Incessant chattering (with echolalia)
- Poor motor skills/uncoordinated
- Total loss of focus during physical activity
- Clingy
- Night activity/insomnia
- Short-term memory loss
- Inability to stay on task or complete tasks

Allergic Symptoms
- Dark circles under eyes
- Hives
- Vomiting
- Flushed cheeks and ears
- Recurring bladder infections

Additional Symptoms
- Occasional Bleeding
- Dyslexia/ Visual idiosyncrasies
- Delayed wound healing (months for a small bug bite)
- Severe Dehydration
- Undigested food in stool/yellow stool
- Low basal body temperature 95.5°F

So, if foods are not the problem, why did I eliminate them? Firstly, they were triggering the symptoms and making Sarah violently ill as well as destroying the lining of her intestine. Secondly, eliminating these foods helps to reestablish a balance in the body and alleviate the switching and hallucinating in the brain that many children with autism experience. Balance is the key to the entire program of healing. Thirdly, it eliminates or dramatically reduces the need for chemical medications, which only place an additional burden on the body, complicating the energy therapy and the immune system correction. Sarah was never on any medications for behavior. Finally, the foods we removed were of the type that nurtured the pathogens we wanted to kill. The idea was to starve the pathogens and to feed the child. All of these are very good reasons to eliminate grains, sugars, dairy products, artificial ingredients, preservatives, pesticides, herbicides, antibiotics, and GMOs.

Withdrawals—3-Day Rule

Once I made the decision to begin eliminating foods from Sarah's diet, I was not prepared for what came next. Most of the nutritionists and health gurus I was reading did not adequately explain about the withdrawal effects. Sarah's body was so accustomed to having these foods, they were like a drug to her precious little system, and removing them caused her to go haywire. For three days there were screaming fits, tears, heightened pain, and sensitivities. Her cravings for her "sick" foods were horrendous. She crawled on the floor like an animal and barked and meowed. She ran away from bright posters, colors, and imagery. Her clothing was painful, and she removed it at every available moment. Because she was only four, any observer would have thought she was acting out as a spoiled child. I alone knew the truth. At the end of three days, there was such a transformation that it was worth all of my suffering to watch her. She began speaking to me directly, making eye contact, as if nothing had ever happened. The month-old scrapes and oozing mosquito bites on her legs began to heal. The red flush mellowed, the vomiting stopped, and the repetitive speech pattern started to clear up. She did continue, however, to limp and search her mind for words. It's extremely difficult to watch your own child go through this three-day period. Yet, learning the three-day rule actually turned out to be a great asset. It explained a lot of behavioral problems. Many parents see immediate reactions to food exposures, yet are not aware of the mood swing or temper tantrum that's waiting for them three days later. It can come as quite a shock.

After one year of working with Sarah and observing the three-day rule, I learned that the offending foods would leave the body, yet a "memory" of them was left behind, imprinted in the compromised tissues. (In some people this memory can cause food cravings, nausea, or even mental disturbances upon future exposures.) Once her immune and metabolic systems were rebalanced using energy medicine, the "memories" of the offending foods caused no further reactions.

Knowing What to Eliminate

How did I know what to eliminate? For me there was an obvious distinction between those foods that are naturally occurring and those that he body is never likely to run into in nature, such as preservatives and artificial colorings. These substances are unfamiliar to our bodies and may not be metabolized at all. The healthy body passes such compounds to the liver or kidneys for elimination. As a family, our first step was to switch to organic foods. The second step was to talk to family members, looking for their reactions to foods. Many family members claim to have none, but a little gentle interrogation reveals a wealth of information. The last step was to observe my child's own symptoms that indicated specific foods to eliminate. A few of the nutrition books I have listed in the tools section provide specific symptoms and the causative foods.

Product labels can also be a huge asset for determining what to eliminate from the diet. Reading product labels can be a bit like studying a foreign language. The Food and Drug Administration requires the complete chemical name in many instances for compounds that are naturally occurring. In Sarah's case, she was sensitive to many compounds that are completely natural. But, first let's explore all the symptoms that can be revealed by family relations.

Family Relations

I became the family food detective. Since my own father had become ill and died when I was only fourteen, I had to interview my mother about my father's eating habits. The year before he died, he was forced to give up many acidic foods, including his beloved tomatoes. Couple that with my husband's sensitivity to aspirin and my mother-in-law's hive reaction to apples, and a picture begins to emerge—salicylate sensitivity.

I had long known that, even though I was not classified as a diabetic or a hypoglycemic, I had a problem with sugar and all refined carbohydrates. When Sarah had her bladder infections, even though there was no sugar in the urine, I was suspicious. The detective in me went into action. I called my mother. She reminded me of the bladder and kidney infections I had suffered between the ages of six and seven, with sugar in my urine. She also reported her own childhood years of bladder infections with sugar in both her urine and blood, plus the restricted diet she was forced to live on as a child in the 1930s.

Therefore, being the family food detective paid off for Sarah. I knew immediately to remove salicylates and all refined sugars and starches from her diet. However, I wish to make it clear that hyperactivity is not caused by sugar, as the popular myth suggests. In Sarah, it was caused by salicylates, phenols, aromatic aldehydes, and much more.

Sarah's Short Food Elimination List

Non natural ingredients (hidden food additives)
Pesticides, herbicides, GMOs, radiated foods
All grain products (except whole-grain organic brown rice)
Dairy products
Phenols,* aromatic aldehydes, and salicylates
Nightshades
Legumes
Hydrogenated fats

* Phenols include most fruits, some vegetables, herbs, spices, and many over-the-counter hygienic products and medications.

Reading Product Labels

As stated earlier, reading product labels is a bit like studying a foreign language; it can be deceptive if you do not know all of the idiomatic expressions. The fronts of package labels contain marketing information the producer uses to sell the product. It is not useful in determining food sensitivity. The reverse side contains the ingredients in fine print. They are usually written using their chemical names, following FDA regulations. This often leads to confusion because many natural compounds have chemical names as difficult to interpret as the man-made compounds, which the body would never come into contact with naturally. I learned to automatically pick up a package and turn it over to scan the ingredient list. Invariably, there would be three to four different types of sugars listed in all packaged products. For our household, that would be enough not to make the purchase. In addition, there may be, at the end of the list, a string of chemical names. These are often the preservatives and artificial colorings I will discuss in greater detail on the following pages. After months of tedious label reading, I found it much easier to shop only for fresh foods without labels— fresh fruits, vegetables, free-range meats, and whole grain rice—all grown by California's organic produce standards.

The first ingredient on the label exists in the largest quantity in the product. Subsequent ingredients are listed in the order of the amount present. If a person is sensitive to something and it is the third or fourth item on the label, it may be safe to eat the product. This was simply not true for Sarah. Eating reduced or smaller quantities was not an option. If any ingredient she was sensitive to were present in any amount, it would trigger the craving for more and set her up for failure in her diet. As stated earlier, the body holds a memory of a substance. There is a cumulative effect. Even small amounts of "trigger foods" caused Sarah dramatic problems. (In fact, for me, even the presence of certain items in the house could cause dizziness.) The reason for this is the stored, cellular memory. I will explain this in greater detail in the next section.

Naturally Occurring versus Non-naturally Occurring Ingredients

Many ingredients with lengthy chemical names can be completely naturally occurring and can be either from a plant source or a man-made source, such as citric acid, disodium inosinate, and disodium guanylate, to name a few. A compromised body, such as Sarah's, however, can be highly sensitive to completely natural compounds as well as artificial ones.

On the other hand, compounds that are not found in nature, such as preservatives, some food colorings, and modifiers, including FD&C Blue no. 2, FD&C Red no. 40, FD&C Yellow no. 5, MSG, ADA, BHA, BHT, and TBHQ, are theoretically, eliminated by a healthy body through the kidneys, liver, and intestine. Sarah's body, being compromised, did not know how to react to these compounds, and she would have an immediate and violent reaction, usually vomiting. We removed all of these things from Sarah's diet.

Following is a brief description of a few compounds that can create reactions in many sensitive people. Many more are listed in Marcia Zimmerman's book *The ADD Nutrition Solution*.

ADA stands for azodicarbonamide, a bleach that is used to make flour white. It causes asthma, coughing, wheezing, and rashes.

BHA and BHT stand for butylated hydroxyanisole and butylated hydroxytoluene, respectively. They are antioxidant preservatives. The World Health Organization has labeled them as carcinogens. TBHQ is tertiary butylhydroquinone and is another type of antioxidant made from petroleum-derived butane. It can cause vomiting, delirium, and collapse.

Citric acid may be artificially made or naturally occurring. It is a bleach, conditioner, and preservative. For Sarah, the source of the acid was irrelevant; she was unable to handle citric acid from any source. It caused severe hyperactivity and savant behavior. It is known to causes rashes, gastrointestinal symptoms, hyperactivity, and attention deficit.

DSI, DSG, and MSG stand for disodium inosinate, disodium guanylate, and monosodium glutamate. All of these are flavor enhancers. They provoke headaches, migraines, and asthma in some people. In children on the spectrum, they can cause extreme hypersensitivity, attention deficit, and intestinal dysfunction. Today, any product from Senomyx should be added to this list. Those concerned should research this company.

FD&C Blue no. 2, indigotine, is an artificial coloring. Many of the sulfates in dyes were originally used to help them bind tightly into fabrics, such as silk and wool. It's no wonder they cause ulcers in sensitive people.

FD&C Red no. 40 contains p-credine, which the National Cancer Institute has reported to be carcinogenic. I've seen it cause vomiting, bladder infections, and mood swings in some of Sarah's friends. The mothers never understood why their children threw up every time they ate hot dogs. This color would cause Sarah to vomit blood.

FD&C Yellow no. 5, tartrazine, resembles acetyl salicylic acid in chemical structure and is cross reactive in aspirin-sensitive people. It causes severe hyperactivity and recurrent hives. In addition, like salicylates, the chemical structure resembles neurotransmitters and will bind neural synapse receptor sites in both the digestive tract and the brain, causing extremely aberrant behavior from migraine headaches to severe bleeding.

How to Identify Sugar in Labels

The Food and Drug Administration requires food packagers to label each ingredient very specifically. Since there are many different types of sugars, mostly from grain sources, the chemical names are used to identify them. Some of the monikers for sugar include: glucose, maltose, sucrose, maltodextrin, modified food starch, barley malt, hydrolyzed corn syrup, dextrose, corn syrup, high fructose corn syrup, and rice syrup. High fructose corn syrup is a double threat due to the fact that mercury is used during processing.

Often ingredient labels carry as many as three of these names in a row. For Sarah, to eat any of these would mean a severe mood swing or uncontrollable temper tantrum. She could, however, eat maple syrup, which is not from a grain source, without demonstrating any symptoms. Therefore, I was sure it was not the sugar that caused the problem. Grain, in any form, from any source, was the problem for Sarah.

Dairy Sensitivity

I had taken Sarah off dairy products because my doctor had taken me off of them. I knew that anything I was sensitive to, she was sensitive to tenfold. (See chapter 10 to learn how I replaced Sarah's calcium.) I had no idea when I did it just how fortuitous this action was. Zoltan Rona told me that the protein in dairy products, called casein, was digested in the compromised intestines of children with autism into a morphine-like, opioid compound that acts as a hallucinogen. (See chapter 12, "Body out of Balance," for an explanation of the compromised intestine.) The new compound is, in fact, called casomorphin. No wonder Sarah had been hallucinating and making up people who weren't there. She never missed milk, but she did miss cheese. I tried to make up for it by providing a soy substitute. (She refused soy beverages, which I later found out was a blessing.) She soon became addicted to the cheese substitute. She begged for it and would eat little else. Of course, any addictive behavior is suspicious, so I read the label and found the troubling words, "emulsified with the dairy protein casein." I removed it from her diet. She had severe temper tantrums for three days as she struggled through withdrawals.

(Lactose in dairy products creates problems for many individuals as well. It causes an increase in mucus production, contributing to recurring sinus infections, asthma, as well as digestive problems.)

Again, I want to make it clear that dairy products themselves are not harmful. The trouble is in the way the diseased body perceives the dairy. Once the body is permanently healed, dairy can be consumed without problems.

Gluten

I had heard the word gluten buzzing around whole foods circles for years and didn't really know what it was. But knowing that Sarah's health was at stake, I had to find out. Once again, Dr. Rona came to the rescue. Gluten is a protein found in the seed coat of all grasses: wheat, corn, rye, barley, oats, rice, spelt, millet, and kamut. It provides elasticity during baking, giving rise to marvelous breads. Unfortunately, in the compromised guts of children with autism, it is digested into a substance called gliadorphin (also gluteomorphin) and, like casomorphin, is an opioid hallucinogen.

In Sarah, it caused amazing effects. She became quite intoxicated. She also started to draw remarkably well for a preschooler. Her pictures were very three-dimensional. I'm sure it was caused by the hallucinogens. However, her inability to digest grains, indicated by the undigested food in her stool, made it necessary to eliminate them from her diet. We did retain organic whole-grain brown rice because its gluten has a different chemical structure, making it more hypoallergenic. Following the three-day withdrawal period (we eliminated gluten and dairy simultaneously), the hallucinations ended and Sarah began to enter our world.

It is almost impossible to remove all gluten; it is ubiquitous. Since the body holds a memory of every compound that has ever passed through it, gluten remains long after we've stopped ingesting it. This has been noted through urine samples taken from autistic patients and is discussed in chapter 16, Customizing the Program, under Treatment 20. Once the immune and metabolic systems are rebalanced, all the remaining gluten in the body will pass out normally. All future gluten will be processed normally and after energy therapy, grains can be eaten again.

So if we did not eat gluten, what did we eat? Rice became our predominant grain. Organic rice pasta, if cooked with enough salt and olive oil, is an acceptable substitute for wheat pasta. Organic rice cakes became our snack food. For bread and other baked goods, I discovered a flour mix that replaces wheat flour quite nicely.

For baked goods that do not require a shape, such as pancakes, I add two teaspoons of gluten-free baking powder. For baked goods that require more shape, such as muffins, I add one teaspoon of xanthan gum per one cup of gluten-free flour blend.

---

from the kitchen of Sarah Evans

Recipe for: **Gluten-Free Flour Blend***

One part tapioca starch
Two parts potato starch
Two parts rice flour

* Use caution when introducing this blend into your child's diet, because potatoes may cause severe emotional symptoms in some children.

Phenols, Salicylates, and Aromatic Aldehydes

The literature on this topic is so patchy it took me a long time to come to an understanding that I could accept (although Sarah's energy doctor understood it very well) following is what I saw in Sarah and how I've come to understand it. None of the nutritionists, naturopaths, psychologists, or allergists I've met or read have discussed this, but here is my observation.

After Sarah had been on her elimination diet about four months and was beginning to make progress, I found her diet to be very limited. So I decided to try some food challenges to see whether or not we could return a few foods to her diet. (The challenge concept is presented later in this chapter.) In December 2000, we challenged Sarah with a six-ounce glass of orange juice. Within thirty minutes of drinking it, she got an adrenaline rush the likes of which I had yet to see. She was bouncing on the sofa, darting from room to room, chattering incessantly, and playing numbers games like Einstein. She had become a hyperactive savant. It lasted for two days. On the third day she experienced withdrawals causing short-term memory loss. What provoked this behavior? Was it the salicylic acid in the orange juice, or could it have been citric acid or the sudden influx of sugar?

Feingold had said it was salicylic acid (which is the major component in aspirin). The liquid form is calcium salicylate—a natural painkiller. No wonder Sarah had a limited or no reaction to pain!

She had reactions to many other aromatic foods as well. On the morning before Christmas 2000, I added cinnamon to a breakfast treat. All other foods in the breakfast remained constant. Within thirty minutes, Sarah's father complained of a headache while at the same moment I caught Sarah writing backwards on her little chalkboard— dyslexia. Cinnamon is an aromatic aldehyde. Toothpaste also became a real burden. Mint flavorings all contain forms of salicylates. All toothpastes made her mouth swell and turn red. All of the herbs and spices used in regional cuisines brought on the hyperactive adrenaline surge as well.

I could not figure out why, if Feingold had said the problem was salicylates, all of these other foods were causing problems too. I began to search, and what I discovered boggled my mind. My understanding is, of course, extremely simplistic. I am not a research chemist, but what I found helped with my child's needs and indicated what to remove from her diet.

There are several groups of compounds all containing what is called a benzene ring, which is a ring of six carbon atoms. It is often called an aromatic ring. Various carbon molecule arrangements extend from the ring, giving rise to phenols, salicylates, and aldehydes. Why do these compounds bring on a hyperactive adrenaline surge in some children on the spectrum? This is definitely an area of study for scientists in the field of autism research.

> *Sensitivities are due to stagnation and a build-up of compounds in the body's tissues. Energy medicine can relieve stagnation, thereby eliminating sensitivities.*

Following is the list of aromatic, phenolic, and salicylate laden foods that I removed from Sarah's diet. Please be reminded that the removal of these foods was only temporary until we had her system cleared energetically and rebalanced. Today she eats like a normal young lady.

Salicylate and Phenolic Foods Removed from Sarah's Diet
All artificial colors, flavors, preservatives, pesticides, and herbicides
Milk (contains at least 14 phenols)
Apples, apple juice, apple cider, apple cider vinegar Grapes, grape juice, all vinegars, raisins, and currants Peaches, apricots, nectarines, plums, prunes, cherries All berries: strawberries, blueberries, raspberries, blackberries Citrus: oranges, grapefruit, lemon, lime, tangerines
Vanilla extract, both natural and artificial
All vinegars, therefore, all condiments: mayonnaise, mustard, pickles, meat sauces, salad dressings, relish
Tomatoes, tomato sauce, tomato ketchup. (Ketchup is horrible. In addition to tomatoes it contains vinegar and high fructose corn syrup. Some children are so addicted they drink it straight from the bottle.)
Red and green bell peppers, chili peppers
Mushrooms, all fungi
All nuts and some seeds (almonds are the worst)
All mints and herbs, including peppermint, spearmint, wintergreen, bay, basil, oregano, thyme, marjoram, sage, and rosemary
All spices, including nutmeg, cinnamon, clove, ginger root, caraway, cardamom, allspice, mace, turmeric, and saffron
Deli meats, which are laden with spices and dyes

This list may appear to be a lot of foods to give up initially; however, we never felt we were giving anything up. Instead, we felt as though we had been set free from a horrendous disorder that was destroying our child's life. Dyslexia and hyperactivity ceased once these items were out of her system. Sarah slept through the night. She began completing tasks. She still had a few problems maintaining a long attention span and concentration; however, there was a tremendous improvement. I knew her body was in better shape for having eliminated offending foods as opposed to continuing the foods and providing her with psycho-stimulants.

As a family, we never felt deprived. There is an abundance of food in this world. Sarah continued to delight in pears, bananas, and pineapple, as well as broccoli trees. (Birthday parties were difficult; I packed a snack box for her.) All in all, we took things one day at a time and rejoiced in recovery.

Is Sugar Really the Problem?

Another theory concerning hyperactivity that Zimmerman proposes in her book, The ADD Nutrition Solution, indicates that huge amounts of processed sugar can be the problem. All mothers know their children function better without large doses of processed sugar, but Zimmerman explains why. During the post-digestive process, insulin diverts glucose away from the brain. Normal people experience fatigue after sugary treats or especially following a sugary breakfast cereal on an empty stomach. The brain compensates for lowered glucose by activating norepinephrine, which halts the flow of glucose away from the brain. Since the brain requires glucose to function, the body pumps up more norepinephrine out of the muscle tissues. Natural movement, hyperactivity, is the result to raise the level of norepinephrine. The entire time, the brain is struggling to concentrate. Many thanks to Marcia Zimmerman for simplifying this otherwise complex picture.

Neurotransmitters and Cross Reactions

But what made Sarah special? Why did she react so violently to these foods? It was not the food. It was something in her body and how it viewed the food. At the opening of the chapter, I stated that neurotransmitter receptor sites line the intestine. Each site is like a perfect handprint for the neurotransmitter that it is supposed to receive.

When a healthy site receives its expected neurotransmitter, it is like a hand fitting into a glove. Once the neurotransmitter's receptor site is engaged, the molecule will change its shape. This causes a message to be emitted to the nervous system or the immune system, as required, and a chain reaction of responses takes place. The same is true for digestive enzymes in the gut. For example, if a healthy individual takes an aspirin, the receptor sites within that individual's gut receive and identify some portion of the acetylsalicylic acid molecule; then a fourfold chain reaction ensues, addressing pain, fever, inflammatory response, and anticlotting agents. What happens in the individual who is not healthy? What if the neurotransmitter receptor sites have been compromised, for example, by a virus? The receptor sites may have lost their shape, or their ability to donate electronic charge. They, in turn, behave like gloves missing a couple of fingers. Only two or three of the fingers of the hand need to slip into the receptor sites to trigger some response, and the response may be horribly distorted. This is, in fact, what happened to Sarah. The fever-reducing reaction resulted in average body temperatures below 96 degrees Fahrenheit. The anticlotting reactions resulted in severe bloody noses and the vomiting of blood. The pain reduction reactions resulted in a child that could feel no pain at all, even when stung by a yellow jacket. The anti-inflammatory reaction resulted in wounds that would not heal. How did the lining of Sarah's intestine become so badly compromised? I will address the destruction of the lining of the intestine in greater detail in chapter 12, Body Out of Balance. For now, I rejoice in the fact that we found a cure—energy medicine.

Saturated and Hydrogenated Fats

Hydrogenated fats versus *non-hydrogenated fats* are more buzzwords we hear floating around in society, and most of us don't have a clue what they mean. Yet, for Sarah, they held one of the keys to an enormous part of her recovery.

We have all been frightened by the words "saturated fat" because we've been trained to believe they equal cholesterol, which means heart disease. Most of us have learned that saturated fat is solid at room temperature and unsaturated fat is liquid at room temperature. Yet, what is a saturated fat, really? It is a chain of twelve or more carbon atoms with another molecule at one end. Each carbon atom has two hydrogen atoms bonded to it as well. Therefore, the carbons are saturated with hydrogens, thus the name saturated fat. It's the long carbon chains that cause them to solidify. The molecular chains lie on top of one another, like a stack of pancakes, and build up in layers, causing the chains to become solid.

We have been told not to eat animal fat and dairy products because they contribute to heart disease. Instead, over the years, we've substituted tubs of margarine, which are liquid oils that have been hydrogenated; in other words, hydrogen has been forced into the carbon molecule to make them solid at room temperatures. A typical oil has fewer hydrogen atoms than a solid fat.

Due to all of the double-bonded carbon atoms, the molecules cannot lie on top of one another, forming a hard stack, so they remain an oil. But margarine in sticks and tubs is a solid. The chemical process of hydrogenation breaks the carbon-carbon double bond and forces hydrogens to attach where they would not otherwise be, thus creating an artificially saturated fat.

How did all this relate to Sarah? And why are these fats on the elimination list? Sarah's skin was so dry it frequently cracked. She would even get the "winter itch" and would scream, cry, and beat and scratch her legs from the dryness. She only found relief in warm oil baths. Many more children on the spectrum, and otherwise, suffer a variety of dermatitis conditions.

Further, neurons and brain cells are composed largely of liquid oils. Liquid oils are the building blocks of many tissues. If the body is being continually filled with saturated and hydrogenated fats, and not being supplied with the correct liquid oils, then the skin, brain, and neural tissues will never form properly.

So in our home, we eliminated all of the hydrogenated fats. I had to be very careful to READ INGREDIENT LABELS because hydrogenated oils are in nearly all packaged processed foods, cookies, cakes, and crackers. If the word hydrogenated was on the label, I didn't purchase the product.

Removing hydrogenated fats made room for the liquid oils that Sarah's body was so desperately starving for. Those fats are either monounsaturated fats or omega-3 oils. I will explain those in detail in chapter 10, Nutritional Supplements. For cooking, we switched to olive oil (omega-3) and organic sunflower seed oil (omega-6), both of which remain liquid when refrigerated and hold their chemical chains even at high temperatures. In addition, we supplemented daily with a tablespoon of cod liver oil (omega-3) as well.

Hidden Food Additives

Many foods have hidden additives that are extremely harmful to children on the spectrum. Here are a few that were sheer poison to Sarah.

- Eggs—the yellow dye tartrazine is fed to the chickens to make egg yolks more intensely yellow. Today we eat only organic eggs.
- Cured and processed luncheon meats, hot dogs, and hams—these are filled with red dye and spices, which caused vomiting, hyperactivity, loss of concentration, and savant behavior in Sarah.
- Fish is one of the most baffling foods that people are concerned over. There are reports of mercury in all fish. However, if the lining of the intestine is healthy, ingested mercury will pass right through the alimentary canal without any disturbance to the body. We did and still do eat Atlantic, cold-water fish.
- I feared beef and poultry because of feeding practices and the excessive use of antibiotics and hormones. We switched to fresh, free-range beef, poultry, and pork.

Food Challenges

When Sarah had been dairy-free, gluten-free, phenol and salicylate-free, and free of refined sugars and artificial ingredients for about four months, we wanted to see if we could expand her diet in any way.

I had read about rotation diets from many authors. They were based on the three-day rule I explained earlier in the chapter. The theory is that a person can eat a small quantity of a "trigger" food on day one, and by day four it will be out of the system so another trigger food may be ingested again in a small quantity. This concept is flawed and simply does not work. Because the body holds a memory of what has been consumed, there is a cumulative effect, causing food compounds to build up and trigger the body. The other great disadvantage to rotation diets is that they trigger cravings and a desire for more of the very food that is contributing to the illness. In short, rotation diets, in our experience, were worthless as a form of food challenge. Sarah required something much more formal and structured.

Marcia Zimmerman presented a solution. She provided specific symptoms to look for and a method for introducing a test food to children.

This is how we adapted it in our home for Sarah. I made a chart on the computer with the date and hour, the food being challenged, the body temperature before eating the food, the body temperature after the food challenge, a small writing sample taken before eating and a post-challenge writing sample, and a place to record symptoms.

We always challenged food on Fridays after kindergarten so I had the weekend to observe her, and so she could recover, if need be, before returning to kindergarten on Monday. I always noted the hour, as well as the date, of testing because I generally saw symptoms within thirty minutes. Zimmerman indicated that body temperature increased when the body is exposed to an allergen, so I also recorded body temperature. This was when I found the opposite to be true. Sarah's body temperature always went down by at least one degree. We used a brand new oral digital thermometer. Then I remembered we were mostly testing salicylates, which, as I previously described, are fever reducers. Sarah's dyslexia made it crucial to do writing tests both before and after consuming the test food.

All in all, we found very little to return to Sarah's diet. There was not a phenol that we could put back. Here is a copy of the food report I prepared for Sarah's school so the staff would be sensitive to her diet and not feed her anything that might upset her. In reality, they agreed to feed her nothing at all, and I packed all of her meals for each day. There is also a list of the foods Sarah was able to eat.

> *The elimination diet is temporary until all the metabolic systems are balanced and restored using energy medicine, then foods can be returned to the diet.*

Sarah's Total Sensitivities

Medications and Toiletries
All salicylates, including: aspirin, and aspirin derivatives.
(In reality, we refused all over-the-counter medications.)
Breath fresheners, chewing gum, or toothpaste, bath powder with cornstarch.
Fluoride and chlorine—all water must be filtered.

All artificial colorings, flavorings, and preservatives, including: ADA, BHA, BHT, casein, citric acid, disodium inosinate, disodium guanylate, FD&C blue, FD&C red, FD&C yellow, MSG, maltodextrin, modified food starch, TBHQ.

Food Allergies
Gluten products including: wheat bread, pasta, cookies, cupcakes, baked goods, corn, cornmeal, cornstarch, corn syrup, high fructose corn syrup, ALL CANDY, rye, barley, oats

Dairy products: milk, cheese, ice cream, the dairy protein casein used to emulsify soy and rice products, yogurt

Soy and all legumes, including peanuts and carob

Salicylates, including most fruits: apples (juices and cider) all citrus, apricots, cherries, all berries, pickles, grapes, raisins, peaches, plums, nectarines, tomatoes, vinegar

Herbal aromatics including: peppermint, spearmint, wintergreen, thyme, rosemary, sage, oregano, basil, plus vanilla extract, all spices, including cinnamon, nutmeg, clove, ginger, allspice

Most root vegetables including: potatoes, carrots, onions, beets, radishes (garlic is a safe food)

Nightshades including: eggplant, tomatoes, cucumber

All nuts including: cashews, Brazil, pistachios, almonds, pecans, walnuts; and seeds, including: pumpkin, and poppy seeds

Deli meats, hot dogs, processed meats, ham

Vinegar and all condiments

All processed snack foods and beverages

Most roots were also hazardous to Sarah and caused extreme mood swings. (We had her treated very early on using NAET to end the reactions so we could keep potatoes in her diet. Otherwise we would have needed to remove them too.)

Foods Sarah Did Eat

Meats: All free-range minimally processed, no added hormones, no antibiotics Meats include: Beef, poultry, lamb, veal, DHA-enriched organic eggs, fresh fish/shellfish

Grains:
Organic whole-grain brown rice - the protein structure of rice gluten is different than that of other grasses and is less offensive

Fruits: non citrus tropicals only including: bananas, papaya, mangoes

Vegetables:
Leaf: Spinach, romaine, iceberg, arugula, parsley, kale, chard
Other: asparagus, peas, broccoli, green beans, in other words, dense greens

Extras (for cooking)
100% pure maple syrup (organic)
Cod liver oil
Olive oil (first cold pressed extra virgin)
Gluten-free baking powder
Organic sunflower seed oil (Non GMO)
Sea salt
Xanthan gum

Sarah's Specific Food Responses

Food	Reaction
Casein	Clinginess, overly affectionate Short-term memory loss Severe mood swings Hiccups Leaves reality Hives
Concentrated salicylates Mints Apple cider	Severe mood swings Dark circles Vomiting Temper tantrums
Vanilla extract	Short-term memory loss Dark circles Sleeplessness
Corn syrup	Total loss of inhibitions Drunken behavior Dyslexia
Mint herb family	Headaches Hyperactivity/sleeplessness Dyslexia Skin redness and inflammation
Cinnamon (aromatic aldehyde) Oatmeal (gluten)	Dyslexia Calming Hallucinogen Fabulous Artwork
Orange Juice Fruit salicylates	Hyperactivity Performed math problems three to Four years ahead of age level Photographic memory Instant auditory memory

Sleepless Nights

This is just a note to those parents who suffer sleepless nights with hyperactive children. Sarah rarely slept through the night between the ages of eighteen months and four and a half years, when we began removal of the offending foods. She was fussy, whiny, and had nightmares. We could not convince her that she was safe and she could sleep. Once we removed the salicylates, she slept like a top.

A Summary of Sarah's Elimination Stage of Recovery

1. Observe the symptoms
2. Journal symptoms and dates
3. Eliminate recommended foods
4. Journal and date all foods eaten
5. Wait through the 3-day withdrawal period and journal foods and withdrawal symptoms
6. Begin searching for dietary substitutes

ten
Nutritional Supplements

Supplements are a real catch-22. All people should be able to absorb the nutrients they need from their food. Yet, it's not always possible. Supplements are a necessary part of the journey, but they are not the cure. In the short term, supplements only address the symptoms. In the long term, they nourish the body and aid recovery. Unfortunately, they are expensive. Every supplement used must be from an all-natural source, organic, gluten-free, dairy-free, soy-free, and free of artificial colorings and flavorings. A few safe brands we found include Country Life, Solgar, Bluebonnet, and Twin Labs. Artificial vitamins are not well absorbed by the system. We also had access to the Apothecary, now called Village Green Apothecary, in Bethesda, Maryland, for compounded supplements.

Here is the catch-22 concerning supplements. They only work if the body can see them and utilize, or "uptake," them. Most children with autism have such compromised intestines that they neither see nor utilize nutrients well. Due to their faulty digestive systems, they do not absorb supplements into their bodies correctly. I supersaturated Sarah's body with large doses of supplements, forcing her body to utilize them. I later discovered that large doses were not necessary. Her body did retain a memory of this saturation, and energy medicine corrected it. Average recommended doses would have been quite adequate. At the same time, while using supplements, I discovered how energy medicine could treat Sarah's metabolic systems and corrected for the "uptake" of vitamins. Sarah's recovery progressed faster and faster. I feel certain the speed of her recovery was due to her healthy diet and the nutritional supplements combined with her new therapy.

It was important for us to proceed with caution concerning the supplements. Some supplements, such as iron, are dangerous. However, guided by Marcia Zimmerman's book, Sarah and I headed for the whole foods store. Zimmerman does an excellent job of providing listings for age-appropriate dosages. The doses that worked for Sarah may not be exactly right for another child, so I will generalize. Sarah was four years old and weighed forty-three pounds at the time we began supplements.

DMG (Today TMG is Available)

N,N-dimethylglycine (DMG) is one of the simplest aids to autism recovery that exists. I did not find it in Zimmerman's book. I found it on the Internet at the website of the Autism Research Institute, founded by Dr. Bernard Rimland. DMG is a metabolite. It is classified as food, not as a drug or even a supplement. It comes in the form of a tiny, sugary-sweet tablet, and it can boost the immune system by as much as 300 percent. There are no known side effects. This tiny metabolite has been known to make speechless autistic children talk within forty-eight hours. Sarah took two tablets (250 mg) each morning. (After energy treatments, we reduced the dose to one tablet.) Within forty-eight hours of taking DMG, Sarah's kindergarten teacher began reporting more good days at school.

Vitamin A in Cod Liver Oil

Many children suffer from the inability to focus their vision well. Many others have what is known as the "autistic gaze." Sarah would gaze off into space for long periods as if her mind were miles away. Someone once said to me, "It looks as though she is seeing God." One optometrist finally told me that there were dark patches on the retina. One way to improve this phenomenon is with large doses of vitamin A. It comes in the form of cod liver oil. I gave Sarah an adult dose at 2,500 international units each morning.

This is where supplements begin to get interesting. Small children cannot swallow the capsules. I would place a spoon on the counter, hold the capsule and pierce it with the point of a knife, then squeeze the contents into the spoon. Sarah would take the oil from the spoon. I really wished I had had a bottle with an eyedropper.

B-Complex Vitamins

Most B vitamin supplements include the entire B-complex plus folic acid, inositol, choline, and PABA. BEWARE! MANY INCLUDE IRON. We purchased only iron-free B-complex.

B vitamins are essential cofactors for the enzymatic processes in the brain. Faulty neurotransmissions are considered the leading cause for inattention, hyperactivity, impulsivity, forgetfulness, and sleep disorders. B vitamins elevate the levels of neurotransmitters in the brain. They are calming and focusing.

Sarah took Action-B 100 by Country Life. I gave her one-half of a tablet each morning, so she was receiving 50 milligrams of everything daily, with the exception of folic acid, which was 200 micrograms and PABA, which was 15 milligrams. Once again, she was not old enough to swallow tablets. I got out the mortar and pestle and pulverized the half tablet to powder. B vitamins taste horrible. I needed to disguise them, yet Sarah was sensitive to all standard flavorings. I thought of 100 percent pure maple syrup and mixed a teaspoonful in the mortar to form a thick solution Sarah would swallow. It smelled and tasted awful, but she heroically chased it down with water each morning, repeating, "I don't want to be sick."

My journal entry from Thursday, August 24, 2000, reads:

> Is it a fluke or is she really improving? She slept through the night without waking for four consecutive nights. Yesterday she swung herself on the swings at the park, pumping her own legs. This morning she danced in a circle in the living room coordinating arm movements by slapping her thighs and clapping her hands. A week ago, she could do none of these things. I have been pulverizing B-complex and mixing it with maple syrup since Monday. Is this a fluke or a road to recovery?

Essential Oils

What are essential oils? They are the oils that give many plants and flowers their characteristic fragrance or essence. The body uses them to form connective tissues, replenish skin cells, and form neurons. Neurons are covered with a layer of fat called the *myelin sheath*, which is made of long-chain fatty acids. This sheath insulates the entire neuron and aids electrical impulses to travel at dramatic rates by preventing the loss of any of the current. Impulses travel at a rate of one hundred meters per second on myelinated nerves. Thirty percent of the brain's total fat content is comprised of one essential fatty acid known as *docosahexaenoic acid*, or DHA.

As discussed in the previous chapter, omega-3 oils are long-chain fatty acids that have carbon-carbon double bonds, making them flexible. There are two major food sources for omega-3 oils. The vegetable sources are flax seed oil (or linseed) and walnut oil. The animal source is deep-sea,

r fish. The very finest DHA supplement, however, according to nmerman, is Neuromins DHA, which is cultured from micro-
...h's were soft gelatin capsules with 100 milligrams of oil in each. As with vitamin A, she could not swallow the capsule, so I punctured them and squeezed the contents into the spoon along with the vitamin A, 400 milligrams in the morning and 400 milligrams in the evening. Neuromins is in fact the finest, as I later tested other brands and found that some contained soybean oil, rendering them ineffective.

Curiously, I discovered another source of DHA. While looking for organic eggs, free of artificial dyes, I came across a couple of suppliers that feed their chickens with DHA-enriched chicken feed. The eggs laid actually have six times more DHA than regular eggs. Just a little added boost.

The other oil crucial to Sarah's recovery was the omega-6 oil known as evening primrose oil. It is an excellent source of gamma-linolenic acid, or GLA. It has both immune-boosting and inflammation-fighting properties. Sarah both ate it and wore it. That is to say, she consumed one 500-milligram capsule (which squeezed into the same spoon as the DHA) each day. Plus, I found a lotion that was mostly evening primrose oil and put it on her skin following her bath. Within days the oozing mosquito bites and hives calmed down. All signs of redness and inflammation abated.

Minerals

Minerals were fairly easy to obtain. Most of the companies I named at the opening of the chapter supply gluten-, dairy-, yeast-, and egg-free, chelated minerals. The chelation process dramatically improves absorption.

There are a few cautions that many authors forget to mention. BEWARE OF IRON. I was very careful after purchasing one bottle of supplements with iron to examine subsequent bottles so that they would be iron-free. I READ THE LABELS.

I was careful to pick a mineral supplement that was high in calcium since Sarah's diet did not include dairy products. She needed a minimum of 500 milligrams daily (which was increased to 750 as she grew and 1,000 at puberty). Calcium-fortified juices were not a substitute for Sarah because of salicylates, aldehydes, and phenols. We discovered that calcium-fortified soy beverages were not an option either due to the fact that soy promotes estrogen production, which is not desirable in small children.

It is also important to state that in many children with autism, minerals are severely out of balance. Erythrocyte tests for Sarah indicated that both copper and selenium were at the ninety-ninth percentile. This meant that her body could no longer process those particular minerals since her blood cells were packed; they would absorb no more of any supplements. Now that she has been detoxified using energy medicine, this condition has been reversed and her blood cells now carry the correct mineral levels.

So Sarah's mineral supplement was a fairly standard total mineral without iron. One tablet a day went into the mortar and was pounded along with the B-vitamins and mixed with maple syrup. I spooned it into Sarah's mouth every morning and chased it with a little water.

Antioxidant OPCs

Antioxidants are a large group of compounds that prevent the formation of free radicals in the body. Free radicals are molecules in which one electron is not paired with anything. They circulate through the body, damaging healthy molecules with which they come into contact because the unpaired electron likes to bond with anything it can. One group of antioxidants is called *oligomeric proanthocyanidins*, or OPCs. They have an antihistamine, anti-inflammatory, immune-boosting effect on the body.

I was directed to a particular type of OPC called Masquelier's, named for the physician who originally refined it. He made it from grape seeds. I had difficulty understanding why Sarah could not have grapes, yet she should take grape seed extract. Unfortunately, at the time, the only producer of true Masquelier's OPCs in the United States bound the powder into a tablet with maltodextrin made from cornstarch. Sarah had quite an adverse reaction. Two small wounds that were not healing well grew dramatically worse, swelling and turning bright red.

Straightaway we switched to more generic grape seed extract in a capsule form that I could simply open and pour into the mortar along with the B-vitamins and minerals to mix with the maple syrup and spoon into Sarah's mouth. I gave her 50 milligrams a day. There was a noticeable change in her mental clarity. She began to sit through dinner and make more lucid conversation.

Amino Acids

Amino acids are the building blocks of all proteins. The body uses twenty of them, eight of which it cannot manufacture by itself. They must be ingested. However, a child with a compromised digestive tract (covered in chapter 12, Body Out of Balance) will not absorb these essential amino acids. I did not discover the powers of amino acids for a full year after I had initiated this food program in Sarah. They are remarkable.

One is tryptophan, which is a precursor to serotonin. Another is tyrosine, which is a precursor to norepinephrine and epinephrine. These are all neurotransmitters in the brain. They are responsible for balancing our moods as well as regulating the five senses. Because Sarah's eyes, ears, and tactile senses were always stimulated, she was continually distracted. Once she had an adequate supply of amino acids, the hyperstimulation calmed and she found peace, which was all I ever wanted for her. She was calm and tranquil.

I did not waste money purchasing amino acids in the whole foods store. Most amino acids are found in milk, which Sarah could not drink. Later in her therapy, I learned of an excellent food source available cheaply and naturally, bone marrow. I learned to make a stock from beef bones and to add all the marrow to the stock. I, in turn, used the stock as a base for all of my soups, sauces, and gravies. I even used it to moisten mashed potatoes, since we could not use milk. Sarah loved it and continued to calm down.

We used all of these supplements each day throughout the duration of Sarah's energy medicine therapy until all her metabolic systems were normalized, at which time the doses were cut back.

Every child is different and the supplements that worked for Sarah may simply be a launch point for another child. Even so, these supplements only treat the symptoms. They do not address the underlying imbalance to the body— that is to say, why my child's body could not process them normally. What follows will rebalance the entire system and resolve the problem.

Marrow Bone Stock

I asked the butcher to cut me beef shanks small enough to fit into my largest pot. I covered them with filtered water and added sea salt. Then I simmered them on a low to medium heat until the marrow naturally fell out of the bones. I either used the stock as is, or waited for it to cool and pureed it in the blender for added thickness in sauces. The natural amino acids in bone marrow helped calm all five of Sarah's heightened senses. Clothes stopped scratching. Loud noises stopped hurting her ears. Her whole body seemed to calm down naturally.

from the kitchen of Sarah Evans

Recipe for: Marrow Bone Stock

Ask the butcher to cut beef shanks small enough to fit your largest pot. Boil them in purified water with salt until the marrow falls out of bones naturally. Let cool. Push the marrow into the pot and discard the bones. Once cool, puree in the blender. Use stock as a base for gravy, sauce and soup.

Sarah's Supplements
May 2001
Compare to the revised post-therapy supplement list on page 170.

Oils	
Neuromins DHA	800 mg in 2 divided doses
Cod liver oil (vit. A)	2,500 IU in the morning
Evening primrose oil	500 mg in the evening
DMG 30 mins. before breakfast	250 mg upon waking
Antioxidant/OPC Grape seed extract	50 mg morning

Country Life Iron-Free Total Minerals	1 whole pill in the morning
Calcium	500mg + 250mg additional
Magnesium	250 mg
Potassium	50 mg
Zinc	7.5 mg
Manganese	5 mg
Sulfur	4 mg
Boron	1 mg
Copper	.5 mg
Silica	5 mg
Chromium	50 mcg
Selenium	25 mcg
Iodine	112 mcg
Molybdenum	25 mcg
Vanadium	1.5 mcg
L-glutamic acid HCl	50 mg
B-complex (Country Life)	1 half pill in the morning
B1 thiamin	50 mg
B2 riboflavin	50 mg
B3 niacin	50 mg
B6 pyridoxine	50 mg
Folic acid	200 mcg
B12 cyanocobalamin	50 mcg
D-Biotin	50 mcg
Pantothenic acid	50 mg
Choline bitartrate	50 mg
Inositol	50 mg
PABA	15 mg

Sarah's supplements were revised over time and always reduced in quantity as she healed. One important thing we learned was that calcium as a supplement (in lieu of dairy) should be given apart from vitamin D. Since calcium is a mineral and vitamin D is an oil, the two combined in a single pill cannot be absorbed by the body.

part three
The Cure

eleven

A Brief Explanation of Integrated Chinese Medicine, or Energy Medicine (as I experienced it)

In all of my years in undergraduate school, studying microbiology, and my years in graduate school at the University of Texas Southwestern Medical Center in Dallas, I studied what I believed to be all of the major pathways of the human body: the circulatory system, the respiratory system, the lymph system, the central nervous system, the endocrine system, the immune system, the digestive system, and so on. I believed I had it all covered. What I did not know, and what is not studied in American medical schools, is that there is yet another complete system in the human body. It has been extensively documented and studied for over three millennia in the Orient. It is well documented in Oriental, Russian, and some German medical literature. It goes by many names, the Qi, Chi, vital energy, élan vital, eloptic energy, and the meridian system to name a few. In eastern Europe, it is occasionally referred to as submolecular biology or bioelectricity.

So how does the energy heal, and what is energy medicine (EM)? The energy itself does not heal; it simply exists, in the same way that blood exists. It runs along pathways in the body called meridians, as blood runs through the veins. When a blood vessel is broken, it must be repaired. When a meridian is blocked, it too must be repaired or the body is out of balance and disease sets in. This is what acupuncture does. It clears blocked meridians and allows the body to heal itself. On young children acupressure is often used instead of acupuncture. In fact, for Sarah, the pressure was quite ticklish, so she dubbed her practitioner the "tickle doctor." Not just any acupuncturist can perform a complete energy medicine program. It is unique and requires a specially trained practitioner. The practitioner does not need a degree from a Western medical school, but should have a degree from a school of traditional Chinese medicine and does need to be licensed by the state. A good EM practitioner combines several techniques, and he must be sufficiently trained in all of them. The combination used on Sarah consisted of traditional Chinese medicine, including acupuncture, kinesiology (muscle response testing), and NAET, or Nambudripad's Allergy Elimination Technique. There is an additional technique, derived from scalar energy, known as Field Control Therapy (FCT®). It has it's roots in homeopathy and involves the analysis of the body using a conventional clinical algorithm to determine the level of tissue stress and degeneration for each organ individually. The FCT® algorithm was derived by Savely Yurkovsky MD and William Tiller PhD, the former chairman of the materials science department at Stanford University. FCT® greatly enhances the combination of the first three techniques by enabling increased detoxification of specific organ tissues at a deeper level.

The backbone of EM is traditional Chinese medicine (TCM). The principle behind TCM, in addition to the vital energy, is the five-phase theory in which ten major organs of the body are arranged into a system where one organ either nourishes or inhibits the functioning of another. The organs are subsequently divided into two groups, those associated with fluid properties and those associated with warming properties. In examining a patient with an immune system breakdown, the physician does not use any invasive techniques such as blood tests, scratch tests, or biopsies. Instead, he uses a general inspection of the patient's complexion, body language and tongue, plus a patient history, aural inspection of the patient's voice, detection of any body odors, and a sophisticated pulse test, which includes six pulses from each wrist. The entire system is thousands of years old.

The second major component of EM is applied kinesiology, which is a modern use of the ancient techniques. It was developed by George Goodheart, DC, of Detroit, Michigan. Dr. Goodheart discovered that when an allergen comes into contact with an allergic person it blocks the flow of vital energy and creates muscle weaknesses. From this concept he developed a method of testing patients for individual sensitivities by having them hold a suspect item and pressing against the opposite arm to measure muscular strength. If the individual is not sensitive to the item, he or she will remain strong and can withstand pressure on the arm. If the individual is sensitive to the item, there will be a disruption in the individual's energy field causing him/her to lose muscular strength and the arm will drop. With a well-trained practitioner this method is very revealing. A patient can discover sensitivities he never knew he had. Another name for the technique is muscle response testing or MRT.

The third major component of EM is NAET, which is an acronym for Nambudripad's Allergy Elimination Technique. NAET is based on a centuries-old technique of balancing the body's energy for individual substances. Devi Nambudripad MD PhD LAc DC is the doctor who has standardized this technique in the United States. A personal discovery led her into the field.

Numerous sources state that Dr. Nambudripad was a nurse in Southern California in the mid 1970s. She had suffered from severe allergies, eczema, bronchitis, and migraine headaches. An acupuncturist speaking at a chiropractic college recommended a diet of white rice and broccoli, which were the only foods she did not react to when tested. She did recover; yet, if she attempted to eat anything else, her illnesses returned. She remained strictly on this diet for three and a half years.

One day, while in the kitchen, cooking rice, she absentmindedly put a few bites of carrot into her mouth. She began to feel faint. Her husband recognized that she needed help and brought his acupuncture needles. He inserted the needles at the prerequisite acupuncture points, and she slept for forty-five minutes. Upon waking, she felt unusually refreshed and filled with energy. She noticed that pieces of carrot had remained stuck to her hand. She quickly made the connection between holding the food she was sensitive to and the energy fields and acupuncture points. She then tried eating carrots and was amazed to find that she was no longer allergic to them.

After testing other foods, she soon standardized a technique that eliminates allergies permanently and rebuilds the immune system from the inside out. She and her husband have built the NAET Research Institute, which is rapidly systematizing and designing protocols for the energy medicine industry. In 2001, there were a thousand NAET practitioners in the United States. Today, the number has reached twelve thousand worldwide, with most of them in the United States.

Today, the technique is performed by holding a small glass vial containing only energetic frequencies, also labeled electromagnetic signatures, of the offending substance in a substrate of distilled water—just enough to contain the unique energy of the substance. The patient holds the vial while the practitioner inserts needles at the acupuncture sites (or uses acupressure in children). The patient rests for an hour and is then free to go. However, for the twenty-five subsequent hours, the patient may neither eat nor touch the item being treated for. During that time, the energy passes through all of the meridians of the body. Once the patient "tests strong" for a substance using MRT, he is referred to as being "cleared" for that item. The patient may continue to "process" the substance, however, as the body rids itself of the stores in the organs, blood, and tissues. After the twenty-five-hour period has passed, the patient may once again touch and/or eat the item for which he is being treated.

The combination of kinesiology (for detecting weakness), acupuncture (for an understanding of the energy), and NAET and FCT® (for clearing specific substances from the body) is extremely powerful in restoring the body to health. With this combination a practitioner can isolate very specific tissues and rid unwanted toxins, parasites, latent viruses, and heavy metals from the body without the use of chemicals.

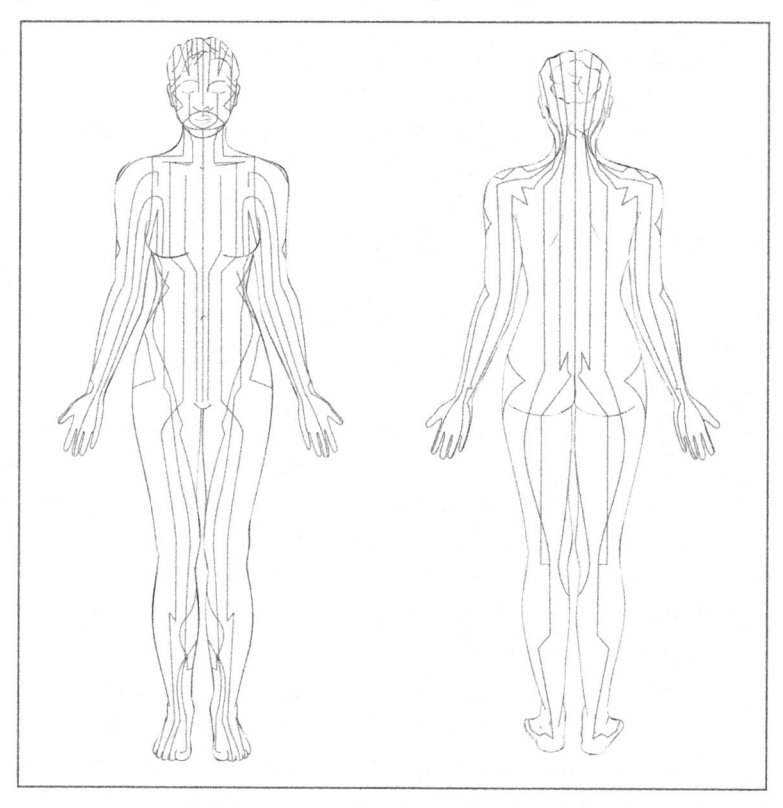

The figure above shows the pathways, or meridians, the energy follows throughout the body. There is one meridian for each major organ.

twelve
Body Out of Balance

Sarah had been on her dairy-free, gluten-free, sugar-free, salicylate-free, and artificial ingredient–free diet with supplements for nearly a year when my friend handed me the business card of the EM physician. In the meantime, I continued my search to find someone who was qualified to permanently heal Sarah. Living as we were was like walking on a tightrope. She was well as long as no irritant came along to bump her off the rope, but irritants lurked everywhere. I called holistic physicians, none of whom would take a child. I was finally referred to a nutritionist who specialized in children on the spectrum. Once again, I found we were blessed.

In April 2001, Sarah and I drove to Rockville, Maryland, where we met Dana Laake. She is a remarkably businesslike and accomplished woman. It turned out that she is part of a larger holistic medical center called Autism Source. Ms Laake is a published author, has had two governor's appointments to the State Dietetics Board and the State Dental Board, and has had her own radio talk show, "Health Talk," She is also the subject of numerous YouTube videos.

Sarah was not in her office more than ten minutes when Ms Laake had her little body summed up. She performed a reflex test on Sarah's joints, a clever hearing test, and an equally clever eye test. Immediately, she deduced that Sarah was cross-dominant. That is to say, Sarah was right-handed yet she was left-eared, left-eyed, and left-legged. In fact, this was when we discovered that her right leg was "turned off." Ms Laake examined Sarah's food plan and supplements and agreed with all I had done. She modified the supplements and had a very convenient compound mixed especially for Sarah at the Village Green Apothecary in Bethesda. The most informative actions she took concerning Sarah's health were the tests she ordered. They were completely outside the realm of the routine blood serum tests normally run by the average medical doctor. They were a far cry from the RAST tests my pediatrician had run. She ordered two urine tests and one for blood. The first test was for gluten and casein peptides or protein chains. Though Sarah had been off of dairy and grains for nearly a year, they would still be present in her system since the body carries a memory of everything that passes through it. The second, urine test, was an organics profile for forty different intestinal metabolic markers. The blood test was by far the most intriguing to me. It was one of the tests I had asked Sarah's pediatrician to perform and he refused. It was a live-cell blood erythrocyte test. It actually peeks inside the red blood cells (not just the serum) to see what the cells are carrying through the arteries. (The results of all of these tests and metabolic markers are listed in appendix B.) Conventional medical laboratories, such as Quest Diagnostics, do not perform any of the tests Ms Laake ordered. They were all performed in specialty labs out of state.*

    What we found was frightening. Yet, because I had struggled for so long all alone in the dark, I was actually relieved when the test results arrived to discover that Sarah's precious, little body was extremely toxic for heavy metals. Her mercury level was at 99 percentile, nearly double the toxic range. Her copper and selenium levels were in the ninetieth percentile as well. The numbers were significantly overinflated for an adult, to say nothing of a five-year-old child. Links between particular minerals can cause both substances to be thrown out of balance simultaneously. In Sarah's case, the mercury had linked to the selenium and was pulling it up. Her energy doctor treated both. In addition, copper was difficult to lower since it was energetically linked to vanadium. It had also displaced zinc, which required rebalancing at a later date. While the blood tests revealed a great deal, they still did not disclose what was hidden inside the tissues. Energy therapy would reveal everything over time.

    Also in Sarah's case, some elements were slightly low; yet, due to all of the supplementation, she was not terribly deficient in any one thing. Ms. Laake and I discussed where to proceed from here. I had told her that we had just begun working with a NAET practitioner. We agreed not to attempt mercury removal with any of the conventional chemical therapies for the time being and to wait for the energy to work its magic.

    The results of the gluten and dairy peptide profiles were quite remarkable because it looked as though Sarah had dairy products in her

---

* The Red Blood Cell Elements analysis was performed by Doctor's Data in St. Charles, Illinois. The casein and gluten tests were performed by the Great Plains Laboratory in Lenexa, Kansas. The Urine Organix Profile was run by MetaMetrix Clinical Laboratory in Duluth, Georgia.

diet all along, even though she had been dairy-free for nearly a year before running this test. However, she had received two energy treatments from the EM practitioner prior to the urine test. This is where I learned about the body's ability to "hold a memory" of the things passed through it. A few days before the urine test, Sarah had been treated for casein using NAET. Even though she had drunk no milk, casein peptides were leaving her body at the furious rate of fifteen times normal as if she been drinking gallons. Her body had never processed the casein in the milk she had drunk the first four years of her life, and it had simply been building up in the cells of her tissues, stagnating. Once her energy was altered, and the energy blocks removed, she was relieved of the dairy stagnation or detoxified. (These test results are in appendix B.) All offending trigger foods have this cumulative effect in the body. After the energy is balanced and the body is subsequently relieved of stagnation, trigger foods can be eaten without reaction.

The organics profile was quite revealing as well. Three of the eight intestinal dysbiosis markers proved to be extremely high, three or four times the normal rate. This is indicative of intestinal parasites, a phenomenon conventional pediatricians and psychiatrists routinely overlook. The parasites were absorbing the amino acid tyrosine, leaving none with which to balance Sarah's dopamine and epinephrine levels in the brain. No wonder she was being robbed of her peace of mind. (I will explain the source and further diagnosis of the parasites later.)

Ultimately, Ms. Laake demonstrated very clearly that Sarah was toxic with heavy metals, had stagnant levels of peptides, and was sorely lacking in essential amino acids due to parasitic action in the gut. That explains why Sarah was incapable of focusing on anything for very long. Parasites and toxicity were a real diagnosis that could be worked upon and a far cry from the "label" of autism, which was a dead end for us. I maintained contact with Ms. Laake's office through the course of treatment with our energy physician. We ran tests during and after his treatments to verify Sarah's recovery. I maintain that I have a more valid case study with Ms. Laake as a third party documenting the treatment.

This description of Sarah's body being radically out of balance also explains why there are so many different symptoms and manifestations of this disorder throughout the population. Why it appears as hyperactivity in one child and as vomiting in another, perhaps depends on the levels of toxicity and which minerals are out of balance, the locations of the parasitic colonies, and the locations of the energy blocks.

So how did Sarah get like this? Where did the mercury come from? Where did the infecting intestinal parasites come from? I had made some discoveries through my research and on the Internet, but Ms. Laake verified all of my suspicions. The infant inoculations Sarah had received contained thimerosal, or mercury, as a preservative. Children are injected at such a young age that the liver is not yet producing bile and processes neither the virus nor the substrate it is in. Sarah was inoculated at twenty hours of age with hepatitis B, a liver disease, before her liver was even functional! Furthermore, who's to say that the viruses she was inoculated with were denatured or "dead"? A virus is not a living organism to begin with. It is merely a chemical machine. A snippet of DNA or RNA injected into an infant can enter any organ and colonize it. This is referred to as an indwelling virus. What about those intestinal pathogens? Could they be the very viruses my pediatrician injected into Sarah at birth? Many pediatric gastroenterologists are agreeing that they are finding measles, mumps, and rubella colonizing the intestines of autistic children. In fact, in 1999, the recently vindicated Andrew Wakefield, MD, of the Royal Free Hospital School of Medicine in London, found that out of 151 autistic, pediatric patients he biopsied, an amazing 97 percent had rubella lining the intestine and the surrounding lymph glands. It was Dr. Wakefield who coined the new phrase autistic enterocolitis. There is historic precedence to suspect measles and rubella. In major cities, such as New York, following measles epidemics, there have been significant increases in the numbers of infants with autism. If the infant inoculations can be implicated, it is no wonder the autism rate has skyrocketed. Ms. Laake was very careful to get a copy of Sarah's inoculation record for her file.

Fortunately for Sarah, I stumbled onto the cure that would completely rebuild her metabolic pathways, intestine, and central nervous system from the inside out; would wash the existing viruses and heavy metals from her body, (which my pediatrician said was not possible); and would desensitize her to the trigger foods that made her so sick, all without harsh chemicals or invasive techniques. In short, I discovered a technique that would put her entire body back into balance.

Following is a list of ingredients in the prescription compound Ms. Laake put together for Sarah. It included a good deal more inositol and choline than my original formula. These are calming and focusing. It also included carnitor and carnitine, amino acids that aid in muscle development. Each morning and each evening, I mixed three-fourths of a teaspoon with one teaspoon of maple syrup and spooned it into Sarah's mouth.

Powder Supplement Formula
3/4 teaspoons in the morning and
3/4 teaspoons in the evening

25 mg P-5-P
.5mg folic acid
2 mg biotin
300 mg choline
250 mg inositol
30 mg B-complex
250 mg TMG
100 mg magnesium
30 mg zinc
50 mcg chromium
25 mg lipoic acid
50 mg carnitor
250 mg carnitine
750 mg glutamine

thirteen
The Tickle Doctor

Very late one evening, March 2001, the telephone rang. It was the energy physician, Ross Stark, returning my phone call. I thought it odd, in today's world of regimented medical centers, that a physician I'd never met would call my home at ten o'clock at night, but there we were. He spoke to me concerning the numbers of people he had healed of autism. He began to ask questions concerning Sarah's sensitivities, the types of questions I wished the pediatrician would have asked, but didn't. This man clearly understood the link between food and chemical sensitivity and mental behavior. Then, he inquired about how she handled chlorine. Something struck a chord in me; it seems trivial now, but at the time it was monumental. No one had ever asked that question. How did he know to ask? I never told anyone about the swimming pool incident and what the chlorine had done to Sarah's skin. Nobody knew that I double washed every load of laundry—once with soap, once with water alone to get all of the soap out, so Sarah wouldn't break out in hives. Not a soul knew the struggle I had bathing my child and shampooing her in special formulas so her scalp wouldn't turn flame red, or the extremes to which I went to keep Sarah balanced. His one question brought back all the memories of her body self-destructing. I made an appointment for the week after Easter, April 2001.

Had I known of some specialist, I would have been prepared to travel thousands of miles for his services. Yet, we were greatly blessed to have the Stark Clinic right in Annapolis. Upon entering his clinic there was an immediate sense of tranquility. Everything was dimly lit and there was soft music playing. All was quiet. It was humble; the office and waiting area were one. There were no receptionists or triage nurses milling about. Presently, a very tall man with long white hair pulled back in a Thomas Jefferson-style ponytail, Dr. Stark, showed Sarah and me to an exam room.

He spent an enormous amount of time taking Sarah's history, three hours in all. He was remarkably enthusiastic about his own craft and delighted in teaching newcomers about it. He placed Sarah on the exam table and slowly ran his hands through the air above the top of her head. I stared in wonder, not knowing what he was doing. He turned and looked me squarely in the eye and said softly, "Her mind is good." I was confused, but relieved at the same time. He also stated that there was crossing in the corpus callosum. In seconds, by waving his hands over her head, he had discovered the same cross dominance that Dana Laake had found with physical tests!

I later understood that he had extremely sensitive hands and could feel the human biofield surrounding Sarah's body. As an experienced physician, he could sense the difference between a healthy biofield and a damaged one. Since he knew all of the points of the meridian system along the head, he could determine if there were any breaks along the meridians. The locale and severity of the break in energy would indicate the type of disorder a patient might suffer. Apparently, Sarah's meridians were in fairly good shape. There were not any points along the meridians where the energy completely dropped out, or she might have been much sicker. Seeing this exercise practiced for the first time looked really mysterious to me.

Dr. Stark went on to explain the Chinese pulses, holding Sarah's wrists for a very long time. Then, he said he would demonstrate how the energy worked. He let me feel Sarah's pulse. It was steady. He opened a case filled with tiny, capped, labeled glass vials. He slowly brought one vial near to, but not touching, a point on Sarah's hand. Her pulse raced like crazy. As he pulled the vial away, her pulse calmed to normal. I was amazed and intrigued. The vial was labeled MMR for measles, mumps, and rubella.

Next, Dr. Stark showed me how the energy worked and how he could affect an individual organ within the body. I removed my shoes and lay on my back on the exam table. He lifted a couple of vials from the case. First, he said he would demonstrate the energy with a substance that very few people are ever sensitive to, human tendon. As I lay on the table, he brought my right arm up in the air and turned my thumb toward my feet to align the energy the full length of my body. He placed the vial in my left hand. While my right arm was still in the air, he pushed against it to try to knock it over. But, I could hold my arm fast.

Dr. Stark switched the vials in my left hand. I suddenly felt fatigued. I stretched out my right arm and he pressed against it. I didn't have enough strength to withstand his pressure. My arm folded. Next, he stated that he would touch an acupuncture point. He touched my left side and my arm collapsed. I had no strength to hold my own arm in the air. It fell down to my side. I was amazed. I asked him what was in the vial that he switched. He said it was sugar. Incredible! He told me that I was an undiagnosed diabetic. The point he had touched was my pancreas. He stated that Western medicine recognized two types of diabetes, insulin dependent and non-insulin dependent, while Chinese medicine recognized thirty different types.

It was very clear that Dr. Stark loved his chosen profession and was convincing about the manipulation of the energy. Yet somehow, I felt as if I were in a science fiction drama. It was all too new to me. I asked him about his credentials. He told me that he had originally been an electrical engineer, and that had assisted him in his understanding of the flow of the Qi and the meridians. He also told me that he had graduated from the Maryland Institute of Traditional Chinese Medicine and was licensed by the state of Maryland. In short, he is a Chinese medical doctor. At the time of this writing, he sat on the board of directors of the Maryland Oriental Medical Association (MOMA) and was a charter member of the NAET Research Institute. Then he confided something that caused me to sit up in awe. This man had worked with the Frontiers in Science Program at the National Institutes of Health in Bethesda, Maryland. Today it is called the National Center for Complementary and Alternative Medicine (NCCAM). He was on the cutting edge of a new science that will reshape the way medicine is taught and conducted. Sarah and I had fallen into a therapy that the world does not yet know, but may be commonplace in a hundred years because of men like Dr. Ross Stark, William Tiller PhD and Savely Yurkovsky MD.

Dr. Stark diagnosed Sarah as being "deficient in spleen Qi." I discovered that the spleen can be affected by improper functioning of the lungs and that blood problems are the result since the spleen supports the functioning of the liver and kidneys. Unusual symptoms can occur, such as bleeding without hypertension and an unsettled mind. No wonder my child had been vomiting blood and suffered frequent bloody noses. How come my conventional practitioner could not have told me these things?

toxins that induce an immune response

He also described her as having "reactive stagnation." This meant that there were blockages in her system that did not allow various nutrients to flow freely. It is an energetic response to an antigen in the system that impedes the flow of the Qi. Antigens build up in Sarah's red blood cells, adipose tissue, and organs, and stagnate there. The addition of any more of these nutrients resulted in the inability of her body to "uptake," and utilize them. That is why I had been forced to give Sarah incredibly large doses of supplements to super-saturate her body to achieve any benefit. Anytime the Qi is impeded, disease ensues.

The cure for her condition was to remove the blockages for each individual nutrient one at a time. This is precisely what energy medicine does. Dr. Stark started Sarah on her very first treatment that day. It was to remove the blockages for fundamental proteins. The vial he used was labeled "egg mix," containing components of egg white, an extremely pure protein, along with other components from poultry.

Since Sarah was such a small child and not prepared to fully cooperate with the muscle response tests, Dr. Stark performed the tests through me. The technique is called "surrogate testing." I lay on the exam table, with Sarah sitting next to me with the palm of her hand on my arm. Dr. Stark proceeded to touch various acupuncture points on my body while pressing my arm to measure the resistance. Sarah's energy passed right into me, giving my arm strength. If she let go, the change in energy was quite noticeable. After Dr. Stark discovered all of Sarah's weak points for the substance being tested, he proceeded to treat her.

Once Sarah was on the exam table, Dr. Stark handed her the vial of egg mix and instructed her to hold onto it. He rolled her onto her tummy, then asked her to take a deep breath and hold it. Using a small rubber hammer, he tapped the length of her spine with it. He repeated it as she exhaled. Next, he asked her to pant like a dog, which she found quite amusing. She giggled while he tapped the entire length of her spine a third time.

He began to apply pressure to the points of her feet, ankles, and legs. Sarah giggled, squirmed, and wiggled. She pushed him away and he begged for her to let him finish. They played a little game in which he pleaded with her to let him energize her points, and she would hold out one hand at time like a princess. The five-year-old maintained complete control at all times. This was when she first dubbed Dr. Stark "the Tickle Doctor."

Next, he produced a small electronic device called an electrostim from an instrument table. He switched it to the lowest setting and proceeded to energize all the appropriate points on the right side of her body, then on the left side of her body. And that was all there was to the treatment: no chemicals, no needles, no scalpels, no radiation, nothing invasive.

Now, Dr. Stark dimmed the lights, put on some comforting music, and instructed Sarah to relax as she continued to hold the vial of egg mix. He left us alone and went to treat other patients. We were alone in the exam room for about twenty minutes. This would be the format for each treatment session throughout Sarah's recovery.

Shortly, he returned and was amused to find that Sarah had stuck the vial between her toes so she could better play with her stuffed toys. He tested her using kinesiology to see how she was clearing. She passed muster. We paid for our first appointment, scheduled the next visit, and departed with an instruction sheet, which was to be rigorously followed. Sarah was not to eat or even touch any poultry products for the next twenty-five hours while her body processed the treatment.

fourteen
The Basic Treatments

I learned through reading and through Dr. Stark that the treatments needed to follow a specific order for two reasons. First, the body may use a particular element to help it process a second element. Second, the rotation of the electrons of one molecule may cancel out the rotation of another molecule, making it impossible to clear them simultaneously. Therefore, they must be cleared in order, causing the therapy to proceed slowly. There were moments when I felt this therapy was too long and slow; I grew impatient. Yet, Sarah's recovery was so profound it was worth the wait.

During the waiting periods, I learned something very powerful about how toxins affected Sarah's body. Even though she cleared in minutes, it took her body days to process each treatment and detoxify the substance for which she was being treated. During the processing and detoxifying time following each treatment, I saw her pass through a number of strange symptoms. Each toxin appeared to have its own set of peculiar symptoms. Processing periods always made me fearful that she would never recover. Yet, when she would finish processing in a few days, a new, healthier, more vital and focused child always emerged.

The treatments seemed to be broken into several categories. There are ten basic treatments (15 at the time of the publication of this book) for essential vitamins and minerals. Following these, the practitioner can customize the treatment for each patient depending on the symptoms and the allergens the patient reacts to. The protocol is based on what the patient's body tells the doctor. Dr. Stark proceeded to treat Sarah for her lack of amino acids. Next, he treated for the colonized viruses from her inoculations. This is the step in which he rebalanced her entire immune system. Afterwards, he moved to the heavy metals. It was like peeling away the layers of an onion. One layer gone could, and did, reveal some surprising things in the underlying layers. Sometimes it became necessary to address an issue before moving to the next phase of treatment. For example, I had wished Dr. Stark to treat Sarah for mercury when we mysteriously uncovered a parasite creating anomalies. It became an issue to treat the parasite before moving ahead with the heavy metals.

The subsequent chapters will move chronologically through Sarah's treatment process. I will make every effort to explain why she was treated in the order seen, the symptoms following each treatment, the duration of the processing time, and her behavior post processing. The last thing I need to mention is that on treatment days I did not give Sarah her supplements for twenty-five hours post treatment for fear that they may contain one of the items she was being treated for and would harm her recovery.

Treatment 1: Egg Mix (April 17, 2001)

For the twenty-five hours post treatment, Sarah could not eat or touch anything having to do with eggs, poultry, or feathers. Following is a report of what I observed at home. Sarah's food that day was good:

Breakfast	250 mg DMG, 400 mg DHA, 2,500 IU cod liver oil Organic farm-raised trout Long grain brown basmati rice Vruit*—salicylate free juice B-vitamins, minerals, antioxidants bound with 1 tsp maple syrup
Lunch	Shrimp, rice cakes, Vruit*
Snack	Tuna, pineapple
Dinner	Lamb, mashed potatoes, broccoli,
Evening Supplements	B-vitamins, 400 mg DHA, 500 mg evening primrose oil

Because Dr. Stark had said Sarah would be tired, I fully expected her to go home and nap. Instead, quite unusual behavior ensued. She appeared to be more hallucinogenic than I had seen her in a long time. If I hadn't known better, I would have thought she had gluten in her system. She entered her world of ballerinas all over again. Her speech became choppy as she was indexing her thoughts. She became obsessive and compulsive about her world, until I pulled out a large pad of paper and crayons for her to draw with. She spent four to five hours, immobile on the floor, engrossed in her artwork, compulsively drawing. The quality of the artwork was poor. She suffered a case of hiccups after eating her snack.

---

* Vruit is a children's boxed beverage of 100% fruit and vegetable juices. The tropical blend is low in salicylic acid.

For the remainder of the week there were no dramatic changes. The indexing and obsession dissipated overnight. There was a very subtle improvement in her awareness by the end of the week. She suffered a bloody nose on Saturday.

Treatment 2: Calcium Mix (April 23, 2001)

This time the small, clear vial contained calcium-carbonate, calcium-gluconate, calcium-ascorbate, cow's milk, goat's milk, milk casein, and milk-albumin. Sarah's food that day was:

	Breakfast	No supplements GF, DF, SF* pancakes with maple syrup Watermelon (we later discovered she was allergic)
	Lunch	White basmati rice cooked with distilled water
	Snack	White basmati rice cooked with distilled water
	Dinner	White basmati rice cooked with distilled water
	Evening Supplements	No supplements on treatment nights

*GF = Gluten-free, DF = Dairy-free, SF = Sugar-free

Since calcium is naturally occurring in our water supply, Sarah was not permitted to wash with or drink anything but distilled water for the twenty-five-hour follow-up period. I gave her a bath before the treatment. Of course, she was already off of dairy products, so they were not an issue.

Following this treatment, Sarah was much sleepier (as sleepy as ADD children become). She napped for half an hour in the car. When we reached home, she suffered a pretty severe, spontaneous bloody nose, which was surprising. She usually only got those from salicylates. The following day, Tuesday, April 24, there were tremendous mood swings, the likes of which I hadn't seen since she had given up dairy products the previous year. I was absolutely amazed that she was having a full dairy reaction without having ingested any dairy products. Wednesday, April 25, she seemed to be back in her disease. She was distant, in her own world, obsessive, and temperamental. I noticed some of the characteristic autistic, sideways glancing with her eyes. She was hiccuping in the evening and was up in the middle of the night. By Thursday, April 26, however, her journal reports, "She is a joy." By Saturday evening, April 28, a tiny light broke through a year of darkness. There was a small miracle. Sarah's speech became completely lucid; she showed interest in others and asked questions; she showed interest in her appearance during her bath and dressing for dinner. The experience lasted for about an hour and a half. She fell asleep one hour early.

Treatment 3: Vitamin C (April 30, 2001)

This treatment included ascorbic acid, oxalic acid, citrus mix, berry mix, fruit mix, vegetable mix, vinegar mix, chlorophyll, hesperidin, rutin, and bioflavonoids. Sarah's food that day was as follows:

Breakfast	No supplements	
	GF, DF, SF* pancakes	
	Watermelon	
Lunch	Chicken, lima beans, white rice	
Snack	Rice, lima beans	
Dinner	Chicken, lima beans, white rice	
Evening Supplements	None	

*GF = Gluten-free, DF = Dairy-free, SF = Sugar-free
We drank bottled spring water all day.

With the first two treatments there was uncertainty and curiosity. With this treatment I felt as if I had entered the Twilight Zone, I was being drawn into Sarah's science fiction melodrama. Once in the exam room, Dr. Stark handed her the vial of vitamin C and performed the acupressure treatment. Within minutes her cheeks and ears went flush red. She looked like a little matchstick, without having been exposed to any allergens. Then he said that he was going to do "brain work." On our first visit he had felt the top of her head and explained that there was crossover in the corpus callosum. (Through the energy, he had identified the cross dominance that Laake had observed.) He said that he would "make her at peace with it." He waved his hands over her head. I felt the energy across the room. Sarah fell limp like a little rag doll in his arms. Following the rest period, he applied pressure to the points on her right leg, then asked her to stand and jump on it. She rested for the remainder of the treatment until it was time to leave.

We attempted to attend afternoon kindergarten, but it was hopeless. She was physically drained, so much so that she dropped to her knees following the Pledge of Allegiance. I took her home. She began mixing up opposite ideas: love was hate, red was blue. I saw impatience, frustration, and tears. Her coordination and balance were completely affected. She remained topsy-turvy and rosy-cheeked all day long.

The following morning, May 1, Sarah's color was improved. After school she did her homework unsupervised and read, what for her, was an advanced book. By Wednesday, May 2, the miracle came again. She had completed processing the vitamin C. She was like another child. She actually played tag on the playground with her classmates before school. By evening she was hopping across the living room floor on her right leg—the one that had been "turned off" was now "turned on." I was ecstatic! What a change in just three treatments.

This was the morning I captured the urine sample ordered by Dana Laake. Sarah had gone for forty-eight hours without her supplements in preparation for the sample. I shipped the sample to Great Plains Laboratory in Lenexa, Kansas, that evening. In two weeks, they sent us the anticipated results. (See appendix B) In spite of the fact that Sarah had not had any dairy for a year, she had experienced the full-blown caseinate reaction, temper tantrums and all. The test result indicated her casomorphin level in her urine to be fifteen times higher than the normal level. This was real evidence that the energy was causing the stagnant casein to leave her body through the urine. The built-up memory of casein stored in her body's tissues was being relieved. All of this was done without enzymes, laxatives, or any other harsh chemicals.

This concept of the body's ability to store a memory of every substance that passes through it is the basis for the remainder of this book. Every substance that ever passed through my body had crossed the placenta and had come to be stored mostly in Sarah's brain. During detoxification, Dr. Stark found and removed casein, mercury, copper, selenium, other heavy metals, cadmium, solvents, herbicides, pesticides, pathogens, parasites, vaccination materials, and more. The remaining treatments will describe Sarah's recovery through the detoxification process.

Treatment 4: B-complex Vitamins (May 4, 2001)

B-complex vitamins include B1, B2, B3, B4, B5, B6, B12, B13, B15, B17, PABA, inositol, choline, biotin, and folic acid. Her food was as follows.

Breakfast	250 mg DMG, 400 mg DHA, 2,500 IU cod liver oil Carrot juice, banana, turkey meat B-vitamins, minerals, antioxidants with 1 tsp maple syrup
Lunch	Tuna fish, cauliflower, distilled water
Dinner	Swordfish, homemade french fries in canola oil (discovered a potato allergy)
Evening Supplements	None post treatment

We drank distilled water all day.

Back in the exam room of the Stark Clinic, Sarah was showing a good deal of improvement before the appointment. She was very responsive in the morning, even before her supplements; she actually went bicycle riding in the morning. She had also been very responsive with her speech and was playing little word games.

During the B treatment, Dr. Stark performed more brain work on Sarah. This was when he started to address the issue of her over-stimulated senses, her hypersensitive hearing, touch, smell, and vision. I watched as he waved his hand over her head, putting energy in her brain. Again, she fell limp like a little rag doll in his arm. He spoke to her about beautiful sounds she could listen to and words she could read and flowers she could pick. In reality, he was balancing specific meridian points on her head to calm her over-stimulated senses. The remainder of the treatment was as normal.

The following day, Sarah was an amazing child. She was extremely observant of her surroundings. She made an effort to read signs and billboards. The most amazing thing she did, however, was to join me in the yard for a ride on the lawn mower. She rode with me as I mowed nearly an acre of ground. The reason this is so astonishing is that many autistic children are extremely fearful of loud noises, such as lawn mowers. Sarah would never have gone near the lawn mower before treatment; in fact, she had often barricaded herself in the house and cried herself to sleep on mowing day.

All in all, the B vitamins were extremely difficult. She took a very long time to process them; in fact, she was still processing when we went for her next appointment with Dr. Stark six days later. I anticipated this to be the case since she had been on such high doses of B vitamins. Her journal reports nearly six days of obsessive-compulsive behaviors, fussiness and frustration, and she was sometimes retreating into her own world. Her obsessive-compulsive behaviors were always at their worst when she was angry, and her journal reports a lot of anger during the B processing. There was even some paranoia of her classmates on the ninth of May.

Treatment 5: Sugar Mix (May 10, 2001)

The sugar mix included cane sugar, beet sugar, brown sugar, corn sugar, rice sugar, maple sugar, molasses, honey, fruit sugar, sucrose, glucose, dextrose, maltose, lactose, date sugar, and grape sugar. Her food for the day was:

Breakfast	250 mg DMG, 400 mg DHA, 2,500 IU cod liver oil Vruit Ezekiel bread and cream of rice with maple syrup B vitamins, minerals, antioxidants with 1 tsp maple syrup
Lunch	Sardines
Dinner	Hamburger (no carbohydrates)
Evening Supplements	None

The morning of Thursday, May 10, I was delighted when Sarah remarked on a little bird out the kitchen window, the details of a video, and the stripes on the road on the way to the Stark Clinic. I knew she was beginning to emerge from the vitamin B processing just in time for her next treatment.

In the clinic exam room, the sugar treatment went as normal. Sarah was a little bit woozy following the treatment; Dr. Stark suggested I give him a call in a day or two, perhaps on Saturday afternoon, to let him know how she was. He had never required this before; it felt a bit unusual. Why would he want a report? Did he know something I didn't?

My feelings were not unfounded. Sarah awoke the next morning, Friday the eleventh, screaming with a tightness in her chest and scarcely able to breath. I called the Stark Clinic immediately. My husband and I took her into his office. She vomited in the car several times on the way. Obviously, the treatment had gone straight to her gut, Sarah's weakest point. Once we reached the office, she vomited again. Dr. Stark used the energy to locate the source of the irritation in her small intestine. He surmised that she had voided some diseased portion of her intestine that she needed to be rid of. He treated her both energetically and homeopathically with some topical drops.

Sarah slept in the car on the way home. Once there, we put her to bed. She slept the day away and missed kindergarten. At one o'clock, exactly twenty-five hours after the treatment, I heard "Mom, my throat is dry!" I went to check on her and she was up, chattering and feeling better. She was still a little pale, with the shiners beneath her eyes, but she was cheerful.

I was carpool mom that afternoon (the other mother was not available), and I was forced to bundle Sarah up and stick her in the car for school. We picked up her girlfriend, and I was amazed to hear a conversation in the backseat that I had never heard before. Sarah was able to follow everything her little friend said. She was more focused than I had ever heard in her life. She was like a new child. She must have completely processed the B vitamins and sugars simultaneously, and her brain was functioning normally. But a few other symptoms of sugar processing arose.

On Monday, May 14, we were forced to make a third trip to the Stark Clinic for symptoms of the sugar treatment. Sarah had come down with a bladder infection. It was obviously related to the treatment since she had not had such an infection since the special diet. Dr. Stark merely touched some points on her forehead. He said they related to the bladder. She was relieved of a mild headache, and the infection cleared up in no time. The following day her journal reports a mild skin reaction, perhaps hives, but it isn't carried over several pages, so it must not have been severe.

Vomiting, a bladder infection, mild headache, and skin reactions were all the symptoms seen with the sugar treatment, and Sarah was a new child in a few days when she finished processing. She was better focused, aware of her environment and could maintain a conversation all without antibiotics, psychostimulants or harsh chemicals of any kind.

Treatment 6: Vitamin A (May 16, 2001)

Next, Sarah and I went for her vitamin A treatment at the Stark Clinic, which included beta-carotene and fish. Sarah's foods on May 16 were:

Breakfast	250 mg DMG, 400 mg DHA, 2,500 IU cod liver oil Vruit Cream of rice w/maple syrup B vitamins, minerals, antioxidants with 1 tsp maple syrup
Lunch	Vruit, radishes, carrots, Ezekiel bread, and watermelon
Dinner	Chicken and rice
Evening Supplements	None

I had preconceived notions about vitamin A. I was sure it would affect her vision and the sideways glancing. It did to some extent, but there were other symptoms that were greatly affected as well. The treatment at the Stark Clinic proceeded as normal.

Afterward, Sarah suffered some minor, short-term memory loss. Sarah's teacher reported a lot of obsessive-compulsive behavior at school. Her ballet teacher said that she could not hold her attention. On Friday, Sarah said to me, "Things keep going out of my mind, and I want them to stay in." I was so relieved to hear this. While Sarah knew that certain foods made her sick and would not touch them, she never indicated any understanding of her mental and behavioral problems. This was the first indication to me that she was aware that she was not always in control of the things passing through her mind. By Saturday, she had completed processing and became a healthy child. Sarah, who had never worked a puzzle in her five years of life, built a three-dimensional model of a triceratops dinosaur and proceeded to build a house from Legos with a heliport on top. It seemed that the vitamin A treatment cured her problem with spatial relations. On Tuesday, May 22, Sarah completed two big, floor puzzles in ten minutes and cut out paper dolls without any help or supervision.

Treatment 7: Mineral Mix (May 24, 2001)

Sarah's food on this day was as follows:

Breakfast	250mg DMG, 400mg DHA, 2500IU cod liver oil Vruit (a salicylate-free juice) Cream of rice w/maple syrup
Lunch	One hard-boiled egg
Dinner	Lamb, rice pasta
Evening Supplements	None

An unusual coincidence surrounding this treatment reminded me to remain keenly aware of God's hand in the process of Sarah's recovery. My husband arrived home from a doctor's appointment with a report that he was deficient in zinc. This was no coincidence. Immediately, I checked Sarah's zinc supplements. She was taking a full adult dose of 45 milligrams per day. Therefore, it was obvious to me that her body was not "up-taking" zinc. On arriving at Dr. Stark's Clinic, he decided to treat Sarah for mineral mix, which includes forty-five trace minerals, including zinc. The treatment went as usual. post treatment, she was not permitted to touch metals or minerals of any sort. Sarah became very restless, full of life, and creative. She gravitated toward metals. I had to hide her Erector® set and her magnet set. We used all plastic utensils for cooking and eating.

By evening, a new level of awareness emerged from within her. She began recognizing sounds she had never noticed before. She ran to the front door two or three times to listen to the spring peepers in the yard. She reacted to distant sirens as if she had never known the sound before. She had a new awareness of thunder during a storm in the night. She maintained her focus for a longer period of time than she ever had before. She watched an entire three-hour video and followed the plot.

The following day was our second visit with Dana Laake, the nutritionist. A second coincidence occurred when she began to explain the minerals to me and how specific ones were linked to the heavy metals, such as mercury. At this point she had a staff optometrist look at the retina of Sarah's eyes. He discovered dark shadowy patches which, I was told, are indicative of mercury poisoning. Coincidentally, the very next day, Sarah came down with a pronounced case of dyslexia the likes of which I had not seen for eight months. For the first time in the entire school year, her teacher caught a few hints of her dyslexia on a test. (Before this, Sarah had shown no signs of dyslexia in the classroom.) Dr. Stark found the suggestion of dark patches interesting and recommended that we photograph her retinas. A simple trip to the vision center in the local shopping mall was all it took. Her episode of dyslexia only lasted about a day and a half. I have always wondered if the mercury in her system was linked to one or more of the minerals being treated and as the minerals were processed through her system, the mercury, in turn, was being moved around. (The treatment had selenium in it, which is linked to mercury.) By Saturday afternoon, she finished processing the minerals and the dyslexia was gone. Following are two photographs, one taken while Sarah was playing in the kitchen on her chalkboard during the processing period. Note the top "I love you" is written in mirror image. Her father walked into the kitchen and caught her writing backwards and corrected her. The second photo was a test I gave her the following day to make sure the dyslexia was gone. She recognized and correctly circled all of the backwards numbers and letters (as I asked), demonstrating that her symptoms had cleared for that processing period.

Treatment 8: Iron (June 1, 2001)

Her food on treatment day included:

Breakfast	250 mg DMG, 400 mg DHA, 2,500 IU cod liver oil Vruit Ezekiel bread with raw honey B vitamins, minerals, antioxidants with 1 tsp maple syrup
Lunch	Chicken leg
Dinner	Chicken leg, raw cauliflower, potato, and distilled water
Evening Supplements	None

For Sarah, iron was a very rough treatment. It took her a long time to process, nearly ten days. During the twenty-five-hour follow-up period, she was a little sulky, but she rallied toward the end. For the subsequent days, there was a good deal of obsessive-compulsive behavior. Yet, when she finished her processing, I saw one more new level of awareness and fluidity of speech. There was also an increased level of independence in her household activities.

Treatment 9: Salts and Chlorides (June 11, 2001)

Sarah's foods on the treatment day included:

Breakfast	250 mg DMG, 400 mg DHA, 2,500 IU cod liver oil Vruit Ezekiel bread with pasteurized organic honey (I later discovered she was allergic to both.) 1 hard-boiled DHA-enriched egg Banana B vitamins, minerals, antioxidants with 1 tsp. maple syrup
Lunch	White rice, distilled water and cauliflower
Dinner	Chicken leg, raw cauliflower, white rice and distilled water (no salt on any of the food)
Evening Supplements	None

Salts and chlorides were an enormously amusing treatment. Sarah became very clumsy for the day following the treatment. Nothing serious happened, so we could all laugh when she walked into walls, fell off her dinner chair, and got the hiccups, as if she were drunk. Yet, the next day, when the twenty-five hours was up, her journal reports "cheerful, compliant, picked up all her toys." By the thirteenth, the few blemishes she had were healed. She was able to withstand extreme outdoor, summer temperatures during a trip to the park. Her childlike, distended tummy slimmed right down. Something struck me and gave me the impulse to measure her. Sarah had not grown in two years and was still in her four-year-old clothes at age five and a half. She was next to the smallest in her class. Upon measuring, I found she had grown an inch and a half.

As a courtesy to us, Dr. Stark performed one additional treatment at this time. Sarah was ready for swimming lessons, but was allergic to the chlorine in the swimming pool. I took a sample of pool water with me to the clinic and Dr. Stark treated her for the pool water at the same time as the salts and chlorides.

Dr. Stark performed two more basic treatments for Sarah before moving to the next phase of recovery. The two combined had quite a profound effect. They were the essential and nonessential amino acids.

Treatment 10: Amino Acids I (June 14, 2001)

Sarah was treated for lysine, methionine, leucine, threonine, valine, tryptophan, isoleucine, and phenylalanine. Her foods on treatment day included:

Breakfast	250 mg DMG, 400 mg DHA, 2,500 IU cod liver oil Vruit GF, DF, SF* pancakes with 100% pure maple syrup
Lunch	Rice pasta
Dinner	White rice and romaine lettuce
Evening Supplements	None

*GF = Gluten-free, DF = Dairy-free, SF = Sugar-free

Occasionally, with many of the treatments and during the ensuing processing period, I would see the symptoms that a particular treatment was meant to cure. This was such a case. For the twenty-five-hour, follow-up period, Sarah was very tired. The next day, I saw hyperactivity, attention deficit, and smell, sound, and light sensitivities. It was as if she had reverted back to her illness. I had to reassure myself that these were, in fact, the symptoms that this treatment was going to cure. After three days of processing, it cleared, and once again I had a child who was completely at peace. On the seventeenth, her journal reports: "Sarah was at peace while coloring and working with play dough. She was so quiet I had to check on her." She was also extremely mentally alert.

The foods Sarah ate during this treatment were extremely strict. She ate white rice, romaine lettuce, and distilled water with no supplements.

Treatment 11: Amino Acids II (June 18, 2001)

This treatment included alanine, arginine, aspartic acid, carnitine, citrulline, cysteine, glutathione, glutamic acid, glycine, histidine, ornithine, proline, serine, taurine, and tyrosine. Sarah's food for that day was:

Breakfast	250 mg DMG, 400 mg DHA, 2,500 IU cod liver oil	
	Honeydew (we later discovered an allergy to all melons)	
	Turkey	
	Vruit	
	B vitamins, minerals, antioxidants with 1 tsp maple syrup	
Lunch	Ezekiel bread with raw honey (allergy discovered)	
Dinner	White rice and Romaine lettuce	
Evening Supplements	None	

This was about the time that Dr. Stark taught us how to use bone marrow, an ancient Chinese remedy. Since Sarah did not drink milk, her amino acid supply was sparse. By boiling down the beef marrow bones, I could make a stock filled with amino acids and stem cells. I used filtered water and added salt. Then I used the stock for sauces and gravies, meat pies, and for moistening mashed potatoes and boiling pasta. Sarah ate it with pleasure and continued to calm down and focus.

Sarah was tired during the twenty-five-hour period following her treatment. But my journal reports that Sarah was "sharp as a tack" the next day.

This ended the basic treatments. Sarah was so dramatically improved, it is nearly impossible to put my gratitude into words, and certainly worth every penny we paid. There were no more repetitive speech patterns, no more awkward gait, no more hives, and no more hallucinations. Sarah was in our world.

Fifteen
The Vaccine Link

Many thoughts passed through my mind during this entire healing process. I read countless books and articles, listened to talk shows, and searched online. Most practitioners spoke of managed care through diet and drugs. No one addressed the cause of the disorder. At long last, I came upon the website of Andrew Wakefield, MD, mentioned earlier. While Wakefield performed biopsies on the intestines of autistic individuals and discovered colonized viruses, Dr. Stark performed energy tests on Sarah and discovered something much more profound. Sarah had been colonized not in the intestine alone, but in several organs, including the brain, with a variety of viruses all stemming from her inoculations. At times, I wonder why she was so affected by the inoculations; but when I review her record, I find it is no surprise. When I was a child in the 1960s, I was inoculated perhaps eight to ten times. Sarah was inoculated for ten different viruses over five different occasions, for a total of thirty viral injections, at which point I refused to let the pediatrician give her any more. Is it so far-fetched to believe that a few live, active, virulent strains would set up housekeeping in a child's body?

The next five treatments that Dr. Stark performed boosted Sarah's immunity toward MMR, diphtheria, tetanus, hepatitis B, and the substrates they were in, including the preservative thimerosal. Her body, in turn, created immunity to the colonized viruses and eliminated them from her system. Her entire immune system functioned more efficiently following these treatments. In fact, before them, Sarah rarely suffered from a cold or the flu or any other form of infection. Her immune system simply didn't work properly. It couldn't recognize a cold virus. After the treatments her immune system began to work.

At this stage, because we were no longer treating for vitamins, minerals, or food-related sensitivities, the twenty-five-hour follow up period was less restrictive. Sarah maintained her normal gluten-free, dairy-free, salicylate-free diet plus supplements. I continued recording her food, potty habits, and treatment reactions.

Treatment 12: Measles, Mumps, Rubella (June 23, 2001)

By June, Dr. Stark determined that we were ready to get down to the more causative factors of Sarah's disorder, the colonized viruses. Through me, he began testing Sarah using a small glass vial containing MMR, measles, mumps, and rubella.

The search procedure in Oriental medicine is what makes it so valuable. This integrated version of Oriental medicine is extremely sophisticated in locating pockets of disease and weakness within human tissues, without biopsies or MRIs. Acupuncture is even more sensitive than the use of a magnetic resonance imaging machine. There are several ways for an alternative practitioner to find an area of disease within a body. A patient can hold a vial containing a suspect virus, bacteria, tumor, or parasite, and the physician will press specific acupressure points around the body, which in turn affect meridians that pass through specific organs. Then the physician can do one of several things: he can feel the patient's pulse for a reaction; feel the resonance of the energy at a given point along the meridians; or use muscle response testing, which is useful because the patient participates. After testing many acupressure points and watching for muscle weakness or pulse changes, the physician can determine which organ the microbe has colonized and can treat for it.

As I held the MMR vial and Sarah touched my arm, Dr. Stark began testing the acupressure points for all the major organs in the body. He tested her blood and her bone marrow for viral colonies. There were none. He found MMR lodged in her brain and her small intestine. The intestine came as no surprise to me, but learning that a virus was colonizing my child's brain was very hard to take. How was he going to remove these colonies without chemicals? He used the same procedure as before. Sarah held the vial. He tapped all the points along her spine; then he massaged the points for her brain and intestine and used the electrostim. She continued to hold the vial for thirty or forty minutes post treatment. Afterward, Dr. Stark tested her to see if she had cleared; that is to say, if she had grown strong for the MMR. Then we were ready to go home.

Sarah had a very strong reaction to this treatment, which is not surprising for something lodged in the brain. I saw obsessive-compulsive behaviors, attention deficit, and groggy, drunken behavior. Her drawing ability disintegrated, and she mixed up the verses of songs. There was a lot of forgetfulness and a new twist to the dyslexia I had not seen before.

Instead of turning letters backwards or upside down, she transposed whole syllables into adjacent words.

MMR processing took quite a long time, and she was still processing when we went for her next treatment five days later.

Another one of Sarah's more unusual symptoms was a small hematoma, about the size of the head of a pin, on her right cheek. It was like a raised blood blister. It had vascularized, and spider veins were spreading across her cheek. I had taken her to a pediatric dermatologist at John's Hopkins when she was four. He said he could laser it, but that she was too young and it might return. He said we should wait until she was six. At the time, I did not know how fortuitous that was. Once we reached this stage of integrated Chinese medicine, I began to notice a change in the hematoma. After Sarah had been treated for the measles, mumps, and rubella vaccine, it was no longer raised. It was flush with the surface of her cheek and the redness was greatly reduced. It eventually disappeared.

Treatment 13: Diphtheria (June 26, 2001)

Sarah was continuing to process MMR when we arrived for the next treatment, which Dr. Stark determined to be diphtheria. Using the method described previously, he tested to find the location of the colonies. He found it growing in her heart, somehow that struck a nerve with me, and I was enraged. I felt that the seat of her precious little soul had been attacked. Until this time, I had accepted the damage done to my child in the name of a good cause. I had channeled all my energy into finding a cure for her. But learning that diphtheria had colonized her heart made me angry enough to take action. This was the moment at which I decided to pen this book. Other mothers needed to know that their children were not being properly diagnosed and that a real cure existed for children with ADD, PDD, Asperger's, dyslexia, and autism.

The diphtheria treatment proceeded as all the others had. Apparently, the energy used for the diphtheria treatment pushed the MMR processing to completion. That afternoon, my journal reports that she was, once again, sharp as a tack. Her reading improved quite noticeably. She was energetic and very independent the following morning. While processing the diphtheria, I saw a whole new focus to Sarah. There was motivation and purposefulness to her behaviors that she had never displayed before. This relieved a huge worry for me. Sarah had been learning and memorizing things without a sense of purpose or usefulness to the learning. I was concerned that she would never find purpose in her life. Now I could see differently. What a burden to have lifted for any parent of a sick child. She was really approaching normalcy.

The afternoon of July 29, Sarah had her first summer ballet lesson with a group of other girls. It was exactly one year from the day when the teacher had asked me to enter the class to observe Sarah's erratic and dyslexic behavior. What a transformation! Sarah told the teacher that she was going to set an example for the rest of the class. The teacher invited her up front and center. She performed every dance perfectly. She was no longer distracted by the other students. She led the class in the open floor work. To think, the preceding summer she had been turning upside down, dancing backwards and had a right leg that didn't work properly.

To date we had only spent seven hundred dollars using EM to heal Sarah, and it was the best seven hundred dollars we ever spent!

Treatment 14: Tetanus (July 3, 2001)

We returned for Sarah's next treatment with the good news of the week. Dr. Stark tested her to see if she had completed the diphtheria treatment. She had, and so he wanted us to move on to tetanus. He placed the tetanus vial in her hand and began a search to locate the colonies. It was lodged in her brain, small intestine, and eyes. Dr. Stark performed the acupressure treatment while Sarah held the vial. Everything proceeded as usual.

Later in the evening, the symptoms of the treatment hit. Sarah had sudden fatigue. Her handwriting was worse than I had seen it a long time. Her pupils reduced when she tried to focus on something specific. The morning of the Fourth of July, I was sure she wasn't going to enjoy the holiday. She had no energy and was completely exhausted. Around twenty-two hours post treatment, she began to rally. By the time the evening picnic, parade, and fireworks rolled around, Sarah was ready.

The family spent the following day at Rehoboth Beach, Delaware, under the hot sun and on the hot sand. I was sure we would see a reaction from the heat. I waited for the temper tantrums, the tears, the screaming, and the complete fatigue. They never came. Sarah withstood the heat. She acted mature the entire day, as well as in the car for the two-hour drive home.

Treatment 15: Hepatitis B (July 10, 2001)

During this treatment, Dr. Stark explained more to me about the actual contents of the vials for the viral inoculations. In addition to the individual virus, there was some of the substrate that the inoculation would normally contain. There was a stabilizer, poultry tissue protein that the virus is grown in, grain alcohol, and the infamous preservative thimerosal, complete with the mercury that had been injected into my child. The MMR, diphtheria, and tetanus vials had all contained these ingredients. That meant that with each treatment, Sarah's body was growing more and more resistant to the mercury that was in her and was hopefully passing it out the stool. Dr. Stark did conduct a search for the mercury and found it settled in the Broca's region of her brain, or the speech center. No wonder she would search for words and not find them. It also explained why echolalia was part of her normal speech pattern. The hepatitis B vial that Sarah held for this treatment contained all the same ingredients. It held the virus, the tissue protein, grain alcohol, and thimerosal. My hopes were that, perhaps, much of the mercury was being removed without even addressing the mercury issue.

I knew that Sarah had the hepatitis B vaccine when she was only about twenty hours old, because I left the hospital twenty-three hours after she was born. We were forced to return to the hospital twice for bilirubin tests due to jaundice that I feel certain was brought on by the hepatitis B inoculation. I was quite sure this treatment would bring out something rudimentary in Sarah's disorder. I was not at all prepared for what we discovered.

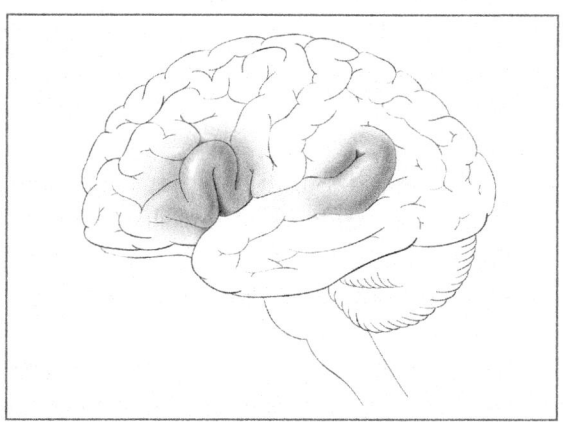

Situated in the left hemisphere of the brain at the posterior end of the third convolution, the Broca's region is responsible for the motor aspects of speech.

Sarah displayed many of the routine symptoms with this treatment including poor attention span, squirminess, and skin reactions to soaps. But, something new cropped up. She began to play with light switches as if she couldn't see and the rooms were too dim for her. She had nightmares of things crawling. After we woke her, and turned on the lights, she continued to see things squirming and wiggling. After five days, she told me that she was quite aware that the things she was seeing were not real. She was making an effort to distinguish between hallucinating and defining what she was truly seeing. She was eventually able to describe the sight as numerous wiggling, squirming lines, some red, some blue. They overlaid everything she looked at. If she looked at a picture on the wall, she could describe the picture accurately; however, she would go on to say that it was overlaid by these squirming lines. Sometimes they were fat; sometimes they were thin. They were everywhere. This did not sound to me like a hallucination. I made the assumption that it was some chemical or heavy metal clearing out of her brain. Little did I know that it was the herald of the next phase of Sarah's recovery.

Treatment 16: Hepatitis B—Power Treatment (July 17, 2001)

Since Sarah was still processing hepatitis B when we arrived for our next treatment, Dr. Stark determined that it would be necessary to do a "power treatment" for hepatitis B. Using some science of his own devising, he had determined that her problem was not so much the virus as the suspension it was in. He said that the energy from the poultry tissue proteins and grain alcohol were so strong that her body was not differentiating the virus from the suspension. So this time, Sarah held two vials: one containing pure hepatitis B, and the other containing the suspension. He separated them so energy from the hepatitis would be stronger. Then he treated Sarah.

The amplification worked. Sarah completed processing hepatitis B in four days. She passed through a period of slow mental processes and searched for words. Within a couple of days, however, a healthier, brighter, mentally sharper girl emerged. Her skin problems cleared up and she was bright, happy, funny, and speaking normally.

Following the treatments for the inoculations, Sarah's father and I thought it best to repeat her initial blood tests to see how her body was healing. We received quite a surprise. On August 31, 2001, we returned to Dana Laake's office in Rockville and the blood was drawn. As before, the test for packed red blood cell elements was performed by Doctor's Data, Incorporated in St. Charles, Illinois. Mass spectroscopy was used to analyze the elements of the packed blood cells. (The results are printed in appendix B, "Medical Test Results.") Without any chemical chelation, no DMSA, without even so much as one mercury treatment, Sarah's mercury level had dropped from 0.019 to 0.004, merely by realigning her energy for MMR, diphtheria, tetanus, and hepatitis B. Her level dropped to approximately 20 percent of what it had been! Her red blood cells had been 80 percent detoxified of the mercury merely by treating for the inoculations! What a miracle!

sixteen
Customizing the Program

At this stage of the recovery program, Dr. Stark began to customize the treatments to meet Sarah's special needs. He addressed her sensitivities to salicylic acid and gluten. Then, he began his move toward the heavy metals, with copper first, since her blood test revealed a high level.

Treatment 17: Salicylic Acid (July 24, 2001)
Sarah's food that day was as follows:

Breakfast	250 mg DMG, 400 mg DHA, 2,500 IU cod liver oil 1 hard-boiled DHA-enriched egg Chicken leg No morning vitamin or fruits	
Lunch	Chicken and organic potato chips	
Dinner	White rice, ground beef, lima beans	
Evening Supplements	None	

Upon returning to the Stark Clinic, Sarah was tested and cleared for hepatitis B. In fact, she was quite strong for it. I had wanted Dr. Stark to clear Sarah for grape seed extract. Her body really needed it to develop blood vessels and to carry nutrients into the brain. He tested her and she was weak for it. Dr. Stark, however, was ready to treat Sarah's sensitivity to salicylic acid. Next, he demonstrated something to us which I found nearly unbelievable.

First, he tested Sarah using kinesiology (muscle response testing) for the grape seed extract. Her muscles were weak for it and, therefore, she could be treated. Next, he tested her with a vial of salicylic acid. Likewise, she was weak for that and could, therefore, be treated. We decided to see whether or not she could be treated for both at the same time. Sarah held both vials and he tested her, but she remained strong. What had happened? She had been weak for both; yet, when she held the two vials together, she became strong. Therefore, he would not be able to treat the two together in one session. Dr. Stark explained that occasionally the electron spin of one compound cancels out the electron spin of another compound, making it impossible to treat for two at once. I was amazed at how the very compounds themselves indicated their own hierarchy of behavior in the body. He tested her again and found her to be weaker for the salicylates than for the grape seed extract. So he finished the session by treating her for salicylic acid.

    He scanned her body to find the weak areas. None of her organs were weak. It was entirely neurological. Only her brain was affected. He performed the treatment. The ensuing twenty-four hours were not an issue in terms of what she could not eat or touch, because Sarah's diet was completely salicylate free.

    Back at home following the treatment, Sarah's processing period was uncanny, yet predictable. Without ingesting the first salicylate, she had a complete salicylate reaction. At the end of the twenty-four-hour period, she began to transform. She became inattentive, demonstrated confusion, and hearing was painful. She became obsessive and fixated on things. At the dinner table, I watched before my very eyes as the color slowly drained from her face and the allergic shiners emerged below her eyes. Following dinner, nausea set in. She went to bed with her familiar "big silver bowl" by her side.

    The morning brought with it the other side of salicylate reactions. She woke up hungry, singing, and free of nausea. However, her spontaneous word usage was years ahead of her age. She chattered incessantly, and the dyslexia had grown worse. The next day brought withdrawals. She was extremely moody, crying, and was up in the night. Her long-term memory had also been slightly affected. She could not remember one of her favorite videos. By July 30, however, I noted in my journal that she was great in the car, on a two-day road trip to her grandmother's house. The subsequent pages report on a normal, bright, cheerful little girl. The processing was complete. Sarah's tremendous program of recovery continued.

Treatment 18: Calcium Salicylate (August 14, 2001)

Sarah's food for the day was as follows:

Breakfast	250 mg DMG, 400 mg DHA, 2,500 IU cod liver oil
	GF, DF, SF* waffles with maple syrup and honeydew
	B-vitamins, minerals, antioxidants with 1 tsp. maple syrup
Lunch	Hamburger, raw broccoli, cauliflower, carrots,
	Ezekiel bread with raw honey
Dinner	Baked potato, lima beans, flank steak
Evening Supplements	None

*GF = Gluten-free, DF = Dairy-free, SF = Sugar-free

I was not at all aware that salicylic acid takes a completely different form in liquids than in solids. Dr. Stark would need to give Sarah a second treatment of the acid in this additional form. It would desensitize her for beverages that carry the acid and prepare the way for future treatments that would, once again, allow her to drink such beverages as grape juice, orange juice, tomato juice, and apple juice.

Her processing symptoms were similar to the preceding treatment, but not as severe. She experienced dark circles under her eyes, loss of appetite, and exceptional word usage. When the processing was complete, Sarah was very clear-minded. My journal reports, "bright-eyed and bushy-tailed." She was reading absolutely perfectly without transposing a single syllable, word, or letter.

Yet, a dark shadow was hanging over this spectacular recovery. Sarah continued to report that she was seeing the squirmy, writhing lines on a regular basis. They overlaid everything she saw.

Treatment 19: Copper (August 17, 2001)

Dr. Stark continued customizing Sarah's program by focusing on her heavy metal load. I was more concerned about the mercury, but he was moving ahead according to her body's needs. Sarah was under no additional exposure to mercury, having no fillings in her teeth and no future inoculations. Some mercury was contained in the vials used to treat her inoculations; therefore, she had already begun to release mercury from her body. Yet, mercury must be meticulously monitored because it can potentially build up in delicate organs, such as the kidneys and liver.

Yet, we lived in a home with copper pipes (as do most people), so Sarah was continually exposed to copper. Her blood test showed that her body was not processing it. Therefore, Dr. Stark tested Sarah's body using kinesiology and discovered copper locked up largely in her adipose tissue and some in the frontal lobes of her brain. He then did something I had never seen him do, or at least he had never verbalized it before. He pressed on the testing arm in three different locations and determined the number of days that it would take for Sarah to clear. He reported that in two and a half days she would begin to feel better following the treatment. She held the copper vial and he performed the acupressure treatment to her points. She had an immediate reaction.

Within fifteen minutes, Sarah showed signs of color-blindness, a headache, dizziness, and general malaise. By the time we arrived home, she couldn't unzip her backpack or pick up a juice box. Within a half hour, at four o'clock, she suffered a severe, spontaneous bloody nose and lay on the kitchen floor crying, "Mommy, all the copper's coming out my nostrils!" She had a tummy ache, backache, and headache. She was extremely fickle and changed her mind every few seconds. It was so obvious how this heavy metal had destroyed her ability to reason. I was delighted to see her being treated for it. At seven o'clock in the evening, she was back on the kitchen floor with a second bloody nose, worse than the first. Within an hour she began spontaneously spouting nursery rhymes and knock-knock jokes. She was zany and confused right up to bedtime.

The following morning, Saturday the eighteenth, she suffered a third bloody nose, had dark circles under her eyes, and continued spouting nursery rhymes. The next day brought relief from the bloody noses. It was just as Dr. Stark had predicted, in two and a half days, she began to feel better. However, she became mentally very dull; the dark circles remained for several days, as did forgetfulness, inattention, and the inability to find things. At one point, she didn't recognize one of her own girlfriends. At another moment, she was too fearful to turn the bathroom light on. At yet another moment, she said to me, "Mom, I have so much going on in my brain that I can't tell you."

A few weeks later, we returned for a follow-up visit with the nutritionist, who took another blood test. Sarah's copper level had fallen from .94 µq/g in April to .78 µq/g in September. I felt this was an amazing achievement with just one copper treatment. Dr. Stark used no chemicals to remove heavy metals from Sarah. It could only get better from here.

Treatment 20: Albumin (August 21, 2001)

When we arrived at the Stark Clinic, Sarah was still processing copper. I wasn't quite sure what would happen when I knew she was processing a heavy metal and we were preparing for another treatment. Dr. Stark used kinesiology to determine that Sarah would continue to process copper for five more days on top of the four days she had already spent. He wanted to treat her for something that would not present a risk to her body while processing the heavy metal. He attempted benzoate, which is the benzene ring discussed in chapter 9, Food Elimination. It is the base of all phenolics and potentially one of the substances that was making Sarah the most ill. Of course she was weak for it and, therefore, needed to be treated. However, using the arm resistance technique, Dr. Stark determined that there would be a risk to some of Sarah's organs if he attempted to treat in combination with the copper processing. He chose another vial of something a bit less caustic, albumin. Sarah was weak for it and it posed no risk to her body. So he had her hold onto the vial while he performed the acupressure treatment.

The course of the following week was very confusing, frustrating, and painful for me. It was one of those periods when I was asking myself if this therapy was really working at all. I was beginning to second-guess why I was coming and spending the money. Sarah appeared to show no improvement over the week. She remained inattentive, fearful, tripping over words and unable even to make eye contact. One unusual symptom did occur on the ninth day of copper processing, however. Until now I've refrained from discussing bowel habits, but I did recommend recording them in the journal, and this is one of the reasons why. Sarah had a bowel movement that smelled so rank I had to air the room. There was a distinct chemical odor to her stool. It made me wonder if, indeed, she was passing the heavy metal from her body.

At long last, on the eleventh day of processing, the longest of any treatment up to this time, the miracle came again. Sarah's speech cleared up, the attention deficit was gone, she was problem solving, her strength was good, she was loaded with energy, and she had good coordination. I had my fabulous little girl back. The only thing that did not seem to part was the mass of wiggling lines before her eyes.

Treatment 21: Gluten (August 28, 2001)

Gluten is the protein found in the seed coat of all grasses. In Sarah, it had accumulated and stagnated in the cells of her organs, adipose tissue, and red blood cells. If Dr. Stark identified a specific location, I failed to record it. Since gluten is a hallucinogen, we wanted to remove any stored in the body before the start of the school year. Sarah had been gluten-free for one year and two months before the treatment. That is to say, she had not eaten any grains for over a year. Sarah's food on treatment day was as follows:

Breakfast	Watermelon, Steak
Lunch	Vruit, Steak, potato chips
Dinner	Chips, eggs, Vruit
Evening Supplements	None

Sarah fell asleep immediately upon leaving the Stark Clinic at five o'clock in the evening and slept until seven the following morning. Fourteen straight hours of sleep following a gluten treatment did not surprise me in the slightest, as the over eating of grains always made me groggy and sleepy. The next morning, Sarah was very clear-headed and well-spoken. Unfortunately, some of her obsessive-compulsive behaviors were back in full swing. There was some occasional daydreaming, and she was tired and depressed. There was a gradual improvement as days went on. On Labor Day, her journal reports one word:"sharp." The following day would be the first day of first grade. I really felt that Sarah was ready.

There is much more to "customizing the program." This was just a brief introduction. Customization will become more evident as the story progresses. I will explain how Dr. Stark resonated each tissue and addressed each weakness Sarah had. I believe any child's weaknesses can be individually tailored in the same way.

seventeen
Unwelcome Guests

Treatment 22: Toxoplasma gondii (September 4, 2001)
    I wanted to remain in a state of denial about the squirming, writhing lines that Sarah viewed overlaying every image she saw. I wanted to believe they were some phenomenon of the detoxification, perhaps something disturbing her nervous system. But with each treatment slowly eliminating her symptoms one by one, and with that symptom remaining, I was forced to come to grips with it. Dr. Stark knew what it was all along and probably anticipated this day. He pulled out a vial to test Sarah and confirm his suspicion. She had a colony of parasitic protozoa, some small coccidia, growing in her retinas, as well as along the optic nerve and in the visual cortex of her brain. It was called *Toxoplasma gondii* (*T. gondii*) and is carried and transmitted by cats. Dr. Stark tested me and found that I was a carrier. I confessed to having been raised with numerous cats. I must have been carrying it for decades. Half of me was repulsed at this discovery. The other half was grateful that Sarah was actually able to see the protozoa or they might have gone undiagnosed for years. In addition, he tested her with a second vial, containing twenty-nine different parasites and oocytes. She was weak for some of those as well. While he was testing her, my mind harked back to her former pediatrician's office and his words to forget the search. "It will only make you crazy. Besides, even if you do find something, there will be no way to remove it." Well, I had found something. I, at long last, had a true diagnosis (not just a label of autism), and I had a way of removing the causative agent—a gentle, nonsurgical, non chemical way of healing my child.

The Optic Nerve and Visual Cortex:

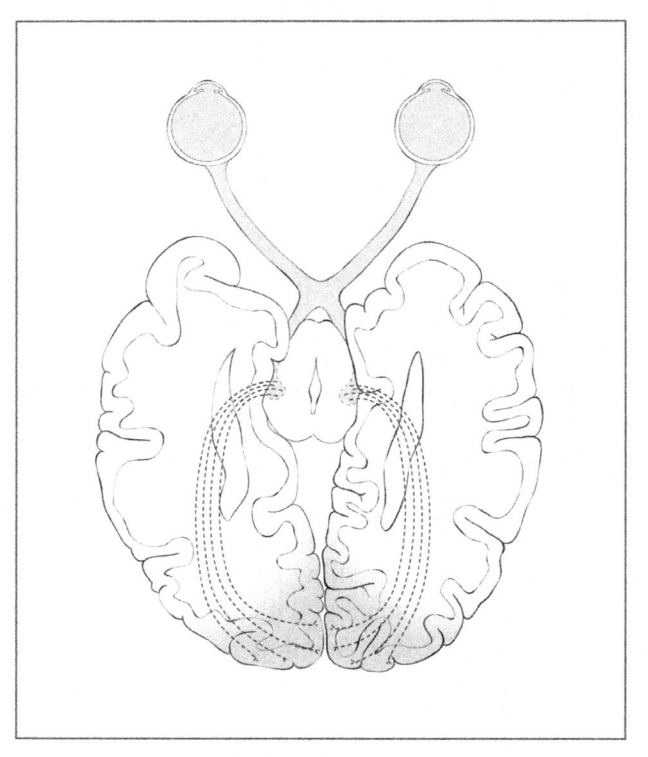

The eye is considered part of the brain, along with the optic nerve, and the visual cortex which is located at the center rear of the brain.

To document this portion of Sarah's recovery, we photographed the retinas of both of Sarah's eyes, before, during, and after treatment. In the pretreatment, diseased photo that follows, there are milky white strands of infection encircling the arteries in her retina, plus a triangle of milky white parasitic-like strands in the lower right quadrant of the photograph. The subsequent photos, in Sarah's file, show gradual diminishing of the white infected area in the tissue.

> *I wanted to remain in a state of denial about the squirming, writhing lines that Sarah viewed overlaying every image she saw.*

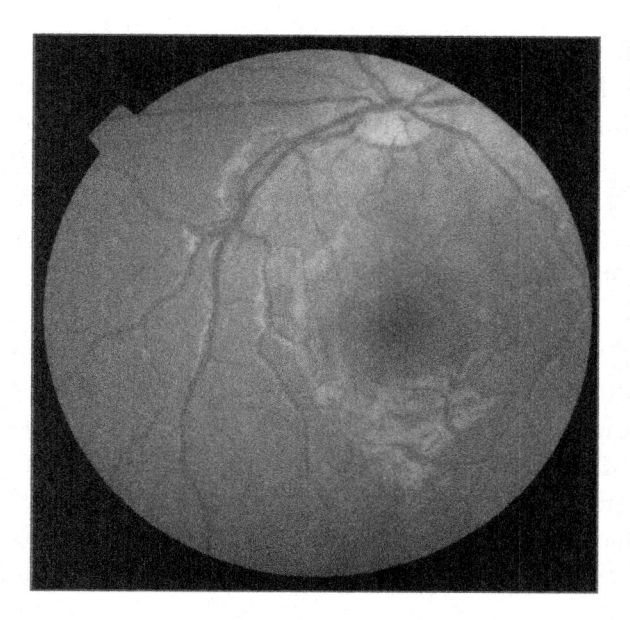

Sarah's right retina, August 2001. Note the large white triangle in the lower right region; this is a colony of *Toxoplasma gondii*.

Conventional medicine uses sulfonamides and pyrimethamine for the treatment of parasites. They work synergistically to block a metabolic pathway. Even Dr. Stark explained that parasites can be extremely tenacious and that it may be necessary to resort to a few time-tested, ancient Chinese herbs to remove them. Sarah held the vial as Dr. Stark performed the acupressure treatment and realigned her body's energy for *T. gondii*.

It was a bit difficult to follow Sarah's reaction at first. It was the first day of school, and she was away from me, so I really could not judge her behavior. A conversation with the schoolteacher two days later was revealing. She stated that she really saw no difference between Sarah and the other children. I breathed a sigh of relief and gratitude that the summer of Chinese medicine had brought so much healing to my child. She continued to say, however, that Sarah had difficulty staying on task and liked to speak out in class. I was not sure how to interpret this. Was it ongoing attention deficit, the reaction to a treatment, or merely Sarah's own personality emerging?

At the end of her first week of school, seventy-two hours post treatment, Sarah came home in a state of total attention deficit. It was very clear that she was incapable of being still and at peace. She was so squirmy, in fact, that by early evening she actually hurt herself and we spent the remainder of the evening at Nighttime Pediatrics. Other symptoms included the refusal to accept change, inflexibility, clumsiness, and moodiness. None of these symptoms was really quite what I anticipated for the removal of the parasite from her eyes. I asked her if her vision had changed at all, and there had been no change.

Treatment 23: T. gondii Power (September 11, 2001)

We returned to the Stark Clinic with little to show in terms of recovery for the preceding treatment. I felt disappointed. Perhaps my expectations of the energy had been too high. I knew that parasites were extremely tenacious; perhaps the energy was not enough to kill them.

Dr. Stark, however, was prepared, even anticipated this lack of response. He explained that there was a special method of amplifying the body's response to a given substance. Each parasite gives off its own particular level of energetic resonance, and Dr. Stark described a method of absorbing the resonance electronically and suspending it in solution with a stabilizer. I later learned that this was the basis for a therapy known as Field Control Therapy® developed by Dr. Yurkovsky MD, (described in Chapter 11). Performing an acupressure treatment while holding the amplification vial for *T. gondii* (which Dr. Stark referred to as a power treatment) would magnify the innate frequency of the substance being treated. If the frequency were not supposed to be there, the body would eliminate it. For this treatment, Sarah held two vials, *T. gondii* and the amplification vial for *T. gondii*. Dr. Stark massaged her acupressure points. She continued to hold the vials for approximately forty-five more minutes. It was a routine treatment in that respect.

The following day, exactly at the twenty-four-hour mark, Sarah came to me and said that she had a headache and that the lines were changing continually before her eyes, and she stated, "Mommy, I have to lie down." This is an unusual statement for any five-year-old. She fell asleep at 6:30 p.m. At 8:00 p.m. she awoke with her face, ears, and scalp flame red. I felt her face, and she was burning up with fever. I took her temperature, and it was 101.4° and climbing. Of course, Sarah was completely sensitive to fever reducers, and I knew better than to give her any. I called the Stark Clinic in the evening for advice. Dr. Stark explained that Epsom salts baths would draw out the parasite. Her father bought some, and we bathed her and put her to bed.

The following morning, her fever was 102°. She had a headache, achy joints, visual problems, and nausea. A second Epsom salts bath reduced the fever to 99.6°. She could eat a little bit and went back to sleep. She awoke in the afternoon and the fever had returned to 102°. She described the lines in her eyes as changing all the time, "Now they're skinny . . . Now they're fat . . . Now I can't see them."

At long last, Sarah's immune system had woken up, and it was taking charge of her body in way it never had before! This was the miracle I had hoped for throughout the entire five months of treatment! Her immune system, having been ravaged by vaccines, mercury, and toxins, was now functional. It was building a fever that was burning the parasite out of her body. The energy had done it!

Sarah passed through three more days of high temperatures, achy joints, hoarse throat, and sinus drainage. I was delighted when the drainage came, because I knew the unwelcome guests were leaving her body. Additional Epsom salts baths aided in the removal of the parasites.

Monday morning, September 17, 2001, on the thirteenth day of processing *T. gondii*, Sarah told me that the wiggling lines seemed to be coming together into a shape. My heart leapt. Could this be the healing plaque into which her own antibodies and killer cells were forcing the parasites? Thursday morning, September 20, Sarah reported that she saw something like a ball, and the wiggling lines were inside that ball. She said that there were a few outside, but not many. Sunday morning, September 23, Sarah reported that the ball of lines was breaking up and spreading to the corners. I felt blessed that my child could see all of this happening before her eyes and could report on her own condition. Saturday, September 29, I asked Sarah about the lines. She stated, "They are still grouped," and continued to say that the "big ones" were on top of the "little ones." I interpreted this to mean that her own body's immune system and killer cells were destroying the parasite. By mid-October, Sarah reported that she could still see the round ball, but that it had moved far away from the center of her field of vision, was smaller, and tended to move around. On the first day of November, Sarah said that the ball of lines was completely gone! We later found that the ball of lines was simply shrinking to the point where it moved outside of her field of vision. It would take another two years to remove the parasite completely.

I had been so impatient throughout the course of this treatment. No other treatment had taken over a month to process, yet it was very clear that Sarah's body was doing a better job than many of the antibiotics and stimulants my friends and relatives used on their children to fight parasites and attention deficit. But there was more. On the twenty-fifth day of processing, Dr. Stark tested Sarah once again for the vial marked "Parasite II" containing twenty-nine different parasites and oocytes. She was strong and cleared for all twenty-nine at once. She was being healed of parasites without chemicals. The fever had destroyed every living unwelcome guest in her precious little body.

However, as I said earlier, parasites are tenacious little creatures, so we closely monitored Sarah's retinas for many months. During those months, her treatments continued for her other needs, such as neurotransmitters and heavy metals. (Therefore, in this chapter we jump from treatment 23 to treatment 33. The treatments in-between will be covered in the next chapter.) On November 10, about two months following the treatment, we returned to the vision center in our local mall and had the retinas of Sarah's eyes photographed a second time. The white, diseased areas were significantly reduced; however, some white patches remained. Dr. Stark surmised that parasitic spores, or oocytes, had hatched out and commenced recolonizing. It was time for another *T. gondii* treatment.

Treatment 34: T. gondii Power (November 29, 2001)

This treatment differed from the preceding *T. gondii* power treatment in that no amplification vial was used. Sarah only held one vial containing energy from the parasite *T. gondii*. Apparently, the amplification vial was not necessary since the only areas of recurrence in her body were the eyes and the vision center of her brain. Dr. Stark directed Sarah's energy to those areas during treatment. (He did test her for the twenty-nine other parasites before treating to be certain nothing else had hatched out. Nothing had.)

By late November, Sarah's recovery was so successful that her treatment reactions were dramatically reduced. At forty-eight hours, I took her temperature, but there was no fever. She was a little bit fidgety and couldn't sit still. Otherwise, she was completely well.

It took a week for the changes to begin. Finally, on December 11, I asked Sarah where "the lines" were. We were standing in the kitchen. She told me that there was a "big cloud" in the dining room. After some additional questioning, I understood that the parasite was moved far into the peripheral vision (the dining room), and the coccidia were coming together into a "cloud."

By December 16, the lines were gathered together into a ball in the left of Sarah's area of vision. I surmised that this was a repeat of the healing plaque Sarah described during the first treatment, this time condensing the newly hatched oocytes.

Treatment 37: T. gondii Power no. 3 (December 20, 2001)

Nearly a month had passed since Dr. Stark had checked Sarah's strength for the parasite. (During this time he had been treating other issues.) Sarah was weak for it. The tenacious little bug was not going down without a battle. Her weakest point continued to be her eyes. So Dr. Stark performed a third treatment to rid Sarah's body of the nasty bug. The reaction came within twenty-four hours. Sarah came to me saying, "The big colors keep getting in the way of what I want to see." The macrophages were back on the attack of the parasite. By Christmas Eve the lines had moved far out into the peripheral vision and remained in a ball throughout the holiday.

Treatment 38: T. gondii no. 4 (January 3, 2002)

Dr. Stark wanted to stay on top of the parasite and was unrelenting. He tested Sarah's strength and found that she was weakest in the left eye. He searched the rest of her body because he was certain that another area of disease was feeding the eye condition. Nothing had revealed itself as of yet. So he performed a fourth acupressure treatment for *T. gondii* on Sarah. Twenty-eight hours after the treatment, Sarah reported in her own words seeing "large gray shapes behind the lines." This gray, shadow-like shape seemed to persist for several days. The appearance and shape of the ball of parasites seemed to change on a daily basis. Some days Sarah would report a ball, some days a distorted ball. Some days she would report it in her peripheral vision; a couple of times she reported not being able to see it at all. Apparently, the ball of parasites was migrating around her retina and moving into areas where she could no longer keep track of it. Possibly, the parasites were hiding in regions where antibodies and macrophages would find it difficult to follow.

Dr. Stark continued to treat Sarah for *T. gondii* periodically, throughout the duration of her time with him. There were approximately two dozen *T. gondii* treatments in all.

eighteen
Returning to the Custom Program

In the midst of processing her first *T. Gondii* treatment, Sarah had an appointment for her next treatment. It turned out to be another power treatment. Two power treatments at one time proved to be more than Sarah's little body could stand.

Treatment 24: Salicylate Power (September 20, 2001)
Sarah had already been treated once for salicylic acid and once for calcium salicylate, the dissolved form. However, during testing, when the two were found in combination, her muscle resistance was quite weak. Therefore, it was necessary to treat for the two together. Sarah's food for September 21 was:

Breakfast	No morning supplements Rice
Lunch	Ezekiel bread with raw honey, rice, chicken
Dinner	Lamb and rice
Evening Supplements	None

Within twenty-four hours Sarah displayed signs of confusion, lack of awareness of her surroundings, obsessive-compulsive behaviors, fickleness, and a headache. It was the third week of first grade. I attended her class at school all day on the twenty-fourth and witnessed a child who was completely attention deficient. She was incapable of sitting still in her chair. She had no idea where the rest of the class was in their studies. She was unable to complete exercises. It was painfully obvious that, for Sarah, salicylates, among other things, were the cause of the attention deficit disorder.

These symptoms lasted the entire week. It was one of those dark times when I was beginning to wonder whether or not she was really getting well, or if I was just deceiving myself with this therapy. I could barely communicate with her, and it was breaking my heart. The teacher was beginning to say things to me like maybe the first grade was not such a good idea and perhaps returning Sarah to kindergarten would be better for her. Due to the long months of recovery I had already seen Sarah pass through, I was not about to admit defeat. I also knew that there was more recovery to come.

Treatment 25: Copper, Vanadium (September 27, 2001)

I did not enjoy returning to the Stark Clinic with the news of Sarah's attention-deficit week at school. Dr. Stark was very quick to remind me that he had performed a power treatment during the previous visit. Naturally, her body was disturbed by it. Then, he tested her and said she would finish processing the calcium salicylate in three days and the *T. gondii* in one more week. In truth, Sarah began to show improvement the next day. In fact, the teacher sent home a letter describing how good she was.

At this stage in the therapy, we received the results of Sarah's second blood test. (See appendix B.) While Sarah's copper levels had dropped from 0.94 μg/g to 0.78 μg/g, well within normal ranges, her selenium levels remained high. Dr. Stark assumed that the selenium was bound up together with the copper. He began testing individual blood minerals in combination with one another. He determined that vanadium was an intermediary element that was linking both copper and selenium. One element would not leave the body's tissues without the other. Therefore, he decided to treat Sarah for the combination of copper and vanadium first, with the thought of a following treatment to balance the selenium levels. To me, the balancing of these linked elements is one of the great values of FCT®.

There were no severe restrictions for the twenty-five hour follow-up period. I did, however, refrain from giving Sarah her evening bath due to our copper pipes and the potential copper load in our water.

Sarah's reaction to this treatment was more like autism than attention deficit. She grew very quiet and distant. She also grew so forgetful it had me concerned. I looked up her reaction to the past copper treatment and found that forgetfulness had been a key symptom. She also suffered a severe loss of independence and loss of her ability to problem solve.

Six days into the copper and vanadium treatment, Sarah completed processing the salicylate power treatment. There was quite a change in her personality. Homework became easy; she was eager to play, self-motivated, and independent. Once again, I saw the child God had promised me. It was time to return for the next treatment to balance selenium.

Treatment 26: Selenium (October 4, 2001)

This treatment did not require special dietary restrictions for the subsequent twenty-five hours; however, we did forgo Sarah's vitamin and mineral supplements so as not to give her a large dose of selenium. Sarah began to react the very first day. Her memory began to grow poor. Around the twenty-seventh or twenty-eighth hour, she complained of bug bites on her knees and wanted ointment for them. I looked down and saw hives popping out in huge wheals all around her knees. She developed dark circles under her eyes, hiccups, and tactile sensitivity. I put her in a warm Epsom salts bath for the hives and followed up with a lotion of evening primrose oil. These symptoms were reduced, but persisted for several days.

In addition to these physical symptoms, Sarah suffered mental ones. By October 10, she came home with an extensive note from the teacher. It stated that she was doing no work and was staring into space for long periods. When the teacher called her back to attention, she behaved as if she were just waking up from a deep sleep. What a perfect picture of autism she described. How well she put it. She wrote in a tone that indicated she was distressed to give me such news. I, on the contrary, was overjoyed. I now knew how the treatments were working and realized that this note meant the selenium treatment had been very effective. I knew it was just a matter of time before she would complete the processing.

It took her twelve days in all to process selenium. Other symptoms included an inability to comprehend very simple requests, fussiness, and fatigue. She was like a baby and could do very little for herself.

On the twelfth day, the magic came again, and the beautiful, new child, I was coming to know, emerged in the middle of her ballet class. She impressed her ballet teacher so much that the teacher asked me personally to come and observe her in class. "I want you to see this," she said. I came and sat in the corner of the dance studio and watched. Tears of joy came to my eyes as I beheld her following each step perfectly.

Treatment 27: Zinc (October 18, 2001)

At long last we completed treating the minerals that were out of balance for Sarah. Zinc was the last mineral displayed on the packed red blood cell test, which still required treatment (see "Red Blood Cell Elements" in appendix B). Her level was too low. During the twenty-five-hour follow-up period, we avoided root vegetables and her vitamin and mineral supplements. I did, however, supplement her DMG and essential oils.

While low zinc levels were probably not doing as much damage as many of the other minerals and metals that were too high on her test results, it was certainly something her body needed.

Once again, Dr. Stark performed the surrogate test with me on the examination table, and with Sarah at my side, holding my shoulder to provide the energy. I held the vial of zinc in my left hand and extended my right into the air. Dr. Stark asked me to close together the thumb and ring finger of the extended hand as he applied pressure. My arm held fast. Next he brought together the thumb and middle finger and applied pressure. My arm gave way as it lost all its strength. Next, he had me bring together the thumb and forefinger of the extended hand while he applied pressure, and my arm held fast. He explained that Sarah could utilize zinc but that there was a problem with her ability to uptake it. So he performed the usual acupressure treatment.

The following morning found Sarah in tears after a restless night. She complained of nausea, yet I knew she was hungry. She did not have a fever, or the allergic shiners, or the pale complexion of a child preparing to vomit, although she complained that she was going to throw up. Then it hit me. Sarah had always had confusion over her sense of hunger, since she was an infant. I had heard that people with eating disorders suffered from low zinc levels. Could it be that her body was now regulating its ability to deduce hunger? She maintained that she was nauseated until noon, at which time she ate an enormous lunch and all of her complaints disappeared.

The zinc also had an effect on her mind. Her motivation and creativity were heightened. She was alert, and her speech was good. Unfortunately, the improvement did not affect her classroom performance enough to suit the teacher. While Sarah had never been hyperactive in class, she simply refused to complete assignments and would disrupt the class by growing fussy. While she had made huge leaps in her physical recovery, in her social skills, in her ballet class, and in physical education class, she still needed fine-tuning to be able to concentrate for long periods sitting at a desk in a classroom. With the minerals finished, it was time for the next phase of recovery.

nineteen

Rebuilding the Central Nervous System

Treatment 28: Acetylcholine and Neurotransmitters (October 25, 2001)

I was amazed by this next phase of recovery. The idea that individual neurotransmitters could be addressed by integrated Chinese medicine, or energy medicine (EM), was just phenomenal. There are around one hundred neurotransmitters in the body relaying messages from one nerve to another through the synapses. Contemporary Western medicine has no way of addressing individual neurotransmitters, but Chinese medicine does. Dr. Stark began with acetylcholine, which is found at neuromuscular junctions, in the brain, as well as junctions in the internal organs, notably the intestines.

For the treatment, Sarah held two vials. The first was labeled "neurotransmitters," and although it was clear to the naked eye, it contained the energetics of human neurotransmitters. The second contained the energetics of acetylcholine. Dr. Stark performed the customary acupressure treatment by rapping her spine and massaging her points. Sarah's posttreatment, follow-up period had no restrictions. She was simply told to drink lots of water.

The subsequent days were confusing. There were no real symptoms, as with previous treatments. I had hoped that the neurotransmitter work would improve her class work instantly, but that was not the case. She remained behind the rest of the children.

Completely coincidentally, however, she came down with an unrelated symptom, which had me elated. Sarah caught her first cold at age six! To an unknowing individual this would not be remotely interesting; however, I was jumping for joy. She had never been sick or caught colds. She had food reactions, but never a common cold. Initially, I believed she had been too healthy to catch a cold. I did not realize that her immune system was completely tied up wrestling with its own breakdown. <u>She was incapable of recognizing a cold virus and fighting it</u>. This cold meant that her immune system was now doing what it was designed to do, ward off invading germs. I shared my delight with no one, because I knew that no one could understand why I was overjoyed by my child's first cold. I was having my own private, little party in my head.

Treatment 29: Brain Balance Plus (November 1, 2001)

This treatment was beyond anything that modern Western medicine addresses; it touches the heart of mental illness. Modern medicine only addresses one or two neurotransmitters. Selective serotonin re-uptake inhibitors are the state of the art in Western medicine to "manage" mental illness. Yet they cannot hold a candle to the treatment that Dr. Stark performed on Sarah in one hour.

Until this time, Sarah had been treated one vial at a time. However, there are close to one hundred neurotransmitters, not to mention the enzymes that break them down, in the neural synapses. How could Dr. Stark test for dozens of vials at one time? How could he possibly know which ones to balance? Would he simply go straight to serotonin, like the general practitioners? In his intuitive way, he allowed Sarah's body to show him the order of her recovery. He entered the exam room carrying a small device and several cases of vials. I hopped on the exam table for surrogate testing. Sarah laid her palm on my shoulder to pass her energy to me. He placed in my left hand a small, copper rod connected by a wire to a metal probe. The wire was to conduct Sarah's energy through me up to the cases of vials. Dr. Stark opened the cases and placed the metal probe across an entire row of a dozen vials. I raised my right arm in the air, and he pressed against it. My arm held fast. He moved the probe to the next row of a dozen vials and pressed against my right arm. The arm held fast. How come Sarah, who was so obviously ill, remained strong for so many neurotransmitters? Usually she fell weak for anything for which she had not yet been treated. Dr. Stark placed the probe on the next row of vials. My right arm was raised, and he pressed against it. It was ever so slightly weak but did not collapse. He said that was the row. He lifted the probe and touched each vial individually while testing my arm's resistance for each. When he arrived at nitric oxide synthase, my arm collapsed. Then he went back to the beginning of the case of vials and started all over again.

He held the probe against each row he previously tested, and my arm went weak in several places. It was as if the nitric oxide synthase was a key that unlocked the order of Sarah's neurotransmitter recovery. Upon retesting all of the vials, my arm went weak for norepinephrine, phenylethylamine, and serotonin.

In addition to these four vials, Dr. Stark handed Sarah a vial labeled "brain balance," which he explained held some energy from each lobe of the brain. This would not only make the treatment more specific, but would support her during processing.

All together Sarah held five vials for this treatment: brain balance, norepinephrine, phenylethylamine, serotonin, and nitric oxide synthase. Dr. Stark performed the usual work on her spine plus the acupressure massage of her points. We waited the customary amount of time holding the vials. There were no restrictions for the next twenty-five hours.

The next day, the miracle came faster than it ever had before. The schoolteacher reported on a new child, one who was focused, who finished her work on time, and who kept up with the class. The other children even cheered for her as she completed her assignments on time. She received her first happy face on her math paper. It was a miracle, indeed. To think that modern Western medicine has no viable means of testing individual neurotransmitters and thousands of people live in managed care situations, but in one hour my child had her entire central nervous system rebalanced, is mind-boggling to me, yet all true! Nothing in Western medicine can compare to this form of healthcare.

At seventy-two hours following the treatment, the neurotransmitter receptor sites in her small intestine must have rebalanced. Sarah suffered one small bout of vomiting. It did not last long, and she was fine immediately after. There had been nothing out of the ordinary in her diet and all of her food was fresh, and there had been no changes to her supplements.

Treatment 30: Serotonin and Methionine (November 8, 2001)

This was to be the last phase in rebuilding Sarah's central nervous system. When we returned to the Stark Clinic, Sarah was retested for the stability of her neurotransmitters against other compounds in her system. Dr. Stark discovered that Sarah was weak when serotonin encountered the amino acid methionine. Methionine is very important because it carries sulfur into the body, which is crucial to the molecular construction of proteins, especially enzymes. It was no wonder that Sarah had trouble with many of her digestive enzymes.

For the treatment, Sarah held three vials: serotonin, methionine, and brain balance. Dr. Stark performed the acupressure treatment and we waited through the subsequent hour-long processing time. Sarah had no treatment restrictions for the following twenty-five hours. She had suffered one processing symptom at thirty-six hours when there was a small bout of vomiting. She recovered immediately. There were no foods or supplements out of the ordinary in her diet, and everything was fresh.

Addressing Neural Inflammation

There is one more aspect to rebuilding the central nervous system that needs to be addressed. When there are indwelling pathogens in any tissue of the body, the body's own immune system will send out an inflammatory response to protect against the pathogen. When that inflammation is in the brain and neural tissues, it obstructs the individual's ability to function normally. Dr. Stark was able to address the inflammatory response by treating with vials that included inflammatory agents such as soluble fibrin monomer, cytokines, eicosanoids, vasoactive amines and more. Energetic balancing treatments using these vials together with vials of the energetics of brain tissue gently reduced the amount of inflammation in Sarah's brain, restoring normal function to daily tasks. Her visual scan rate improved, hence her reading picked up. Her fine motor skills improved making her handwriting more comfortable and legible.

twenty

Food, Supplements, and Concentration

When I least expected it, by complete accident, or by divine providence, an incident occurred that ushered in the next phase of Sarah's recovery. While Sarah had made tremendous strides physically, behaviorally, emotionally, and neurologically, we could not call her a well child if she could not eat normal, everyday foods and was still taking hundreds of dollars' worth of nutritional supplements every month. In fact, there were three hurdles she needed to overcome to be deemed healthy: one hurdle was to reduce her supplements to more common dosage levels; the second was to focus her attention; the third hurdle was to have her eating more common foods again.

In the midst of working on the neurotransmitters, we began to run low on Sarah's prescription supplements. Village Green Apothecary was very close, and in the past they had always refilled the order in two days. I had intended to telephone the Apothecary the minute I realized the bottle was low, but was too busy to get to it. Then a weekend came. First thing Monday morning, I placed the order. Quite out of the ordinary for them, but fortuitous for Sarah, it took ten days to fill the order instead of the customary two. During this time, Sarah's bottle ran dry. There was little I could do on my own to make up for what she would be lacking during the dry spell before the new order would arrive. I believe God was counting on that.

While Sarah had been demonstrating a slow, steady improvement in the classroom all fall long, there was nothing to compare to the improvement she had in that one week. It was as if her mind had been set free. She received more happy face stickers and "great job" compliments on her work in that one week than she had all year. I was stunned and began to scratch my head in wonder.

Monday of the following week, the prescription refill arrived. Doing what I believed was the right thing, I immediately put her back on it as the nutritionist had prescribed. In one day she began to decline. The remainder of the week at school was poor. She could neither focus nor complete her tasks. At this point, it dawned on me that the supplements were just too much for her. I was over-supplementing.

On the thirty-first visit to the Stark Clinic, November 15, 2001, I lugged a small bag with a pharmacy's worth of bottles (including all of Sarah's essential oils, the DMG, all of the minerals, B-complex, the grape seed extract, and the prescription mix) into Dr. Stark's office. Once ushered into an exam room, he began to practice energy medicine in a way we had not yet seen. We reviewed every supplement, starting with the essential oils. Sarah sat on the exam table and touched my arm to pass the energy from herself to me. I held out my left hand while he placed ten of the DHA capsules in it. Then he performed the muscle resistance test on my right arm. He removed two capsules and pressed my arm again. He removed two more and pressed my arm again. He removed two more capsules from my left hand, reducing the number to four, and pressed again, then he put one back and pressed again. He said that 500 milligrams of DHA was the correct dosage for her. He performed this procedure with all of the supplements:

Revised Supplement List

	Original Dose	Revised Dose
DHA	800 mg	500 mg
Evening Primrose Oil	500 mg	500 mg
Cod Liver Oil	2,500 IU	2,500 IU
DMG	250 mg	125 mg
Grape seed extract	50 mg	50 mg
Prescription mix	1.5 tsp/day	none
Calcium	500 mg	750 mg
Zinc	0 mg	30 mg
B-complex	50 mg	25 mg

This was the first major change in Sarah's routine in seven months. It meant that her recovery had reached the point where she could uptake her own nutrients from her food! While she had needed all of the supplements in the beginning, they had become overwhelming to her system now that she was growing healthier. These revised doses were far more in keeping with the average recommended doses. All I needed to do was institute the new program of supplements and wait to see the results. Within a week, Sarah was happier, more independent, more assertive in her needs, and cooperative with others. As an added bonus, our monthly budget for supplements dropped by three-fourths. Sarah had overcome the first hurdle toward normalcy!

Treatment 31: Acetic Acid (November 15, 2001)

Acetic acid is one of the world's oldest flavoring agents and is naturally occurring in cheeses, coffee, grapes, peaches, berries, and more. It is the major component in vinegar and extra-dry wines. It can also be synthetically produced and is used in large quantities in pickling, ketchup production, and other condiments.

Derivatives of acetic acid, such as vinyl acetate and solvent esters, are used in the manufacture of water-based paints and adhesives. Other derivatives are used in packaging and household products. Many children with autism are sensitive to acetic acid in any form.

Following the review of the vitamins, Sarah held just one vial labeled "acetic acid," and Dr. Stark performed the treatment. During the first twenty-four hours of her processing period, I witnessed only mild symptoms, such as allergic shiners under her eyes. Her schoolteacher, however, reported a great deal of distraction and inability to remain on task. The second day was more severe, with ringing in the ears and nausea in the evening. By the fourth day, she was completely helter-skelter, doing four or five things at a time. She remained energetic and unfocused until the next treatment. The subsequent treatment appeared to push through any blocks Sarah had for acetic acid. Following the thirty-first treatment, Sarah was alert, focused, and well-spoken. It is hard to believe how one chemical can have such a profound effect!

Treatment 32: Heavy Metals (November 20, 2001)

While Sarah had completed treatments for most of her inoculations and her mercury level had dropped 80 percent, she still had not been treated for individual heavy metals. I guessed that Dr. Stark would treat individually for mercury and lead, but I was wrong. He simply handed Sarah a vial labeled "heavy metals." It contained energies from every metal that the body deemed problematic, including lead, mercury, and aluminum, which are frequently implicated in many mental illnesses.

Sarah held her little vial and underwent the energy treatment with Dr. Stark tapping the points down her back and massaging the points of her hands and feet. She held the vial for the next forty-five minutes, and we were through.

Her post-treatment symptoms were quite subtle. There was no more of the vomiting, temper tantrums, or hyperactivity. She was alert and well-spoken. Yet, there was a short-term memory loss that made learning difficult. We practiced reading. She would sound out a new word, move to the next page, see the word, and forget that she had just sounded it out. Then she would have to sound it out all over again. At forty-eight hours she did complain of mild nausea and painful hearing. After five days, she was cooperative, easygoing, helpful, and her short-term memory was restored.

Treatment 33: Chemicals (November 26, 2001)

Upon returning to the clinic, Sarah tested strong for both lead and mercury. I was very pleased with this. Dr. Stark said it was time to move on to something new. He handed her a vial simply labeled "chemicals." This time I asked for a list of what was in the vial. He photocopied a two-page printout for me with a list of eighty different chemicals on it. I could scarcely believe the energies of so many chemicals were in one small vial. I was delighted to see arsenic among them. It covered most inhalants, ingestants, contactants, and injectants. There were twenty-two acids, nine ammonia derivatives, and several sulfates.

Sarah appeared to display no specific symptoms at all to this treatment. I was pleased because this meant that her body was calming down. I could be more confident that she was really on the mend. Even though Sarah was showing tremendous improvement, was asserting her needs more, and was working more quickly, her schoolteacher still was not satisfied with the quality of her classroom work. She still had a problem remaining fully focused and completing her assignments.

Treatment 35: Mercury and Hypothalamus (December 6, 2001)

Hypothalamus

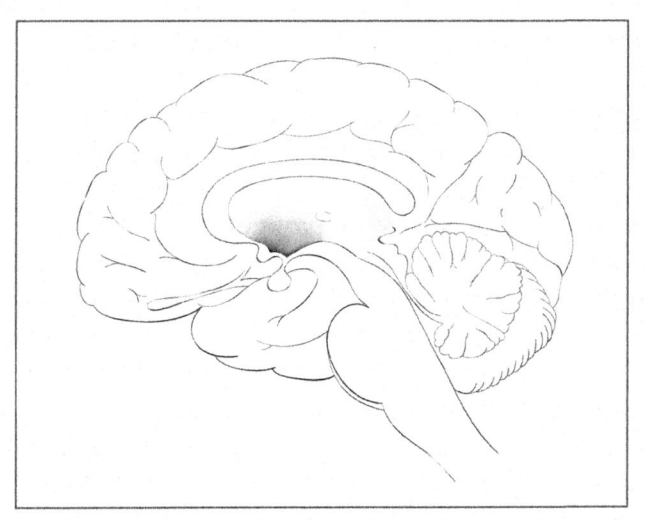

The hypothalamus, seen in the shaded area, is responsible for coordinating both the autonomic nervous system and the activity of the pituitary, controlling body temperature, thirst, hunger, and other homeostatic systems, and is involved in sleep and emotional activity.

For two days Sarah behaved like a whirling dervish. Hyperactivity was definitely the primary symptom of this treatment. Unfortunately, I was unable to observe any more after those two days. Saturday evening, December 8, we went out to dinner. Try as I might to control Sarah's food, she was exposed to a dish that had monosodium glutamate in it. This completely disrupted any symptoms of the mercury withdrawal. She grew fussy, inconsolable, and had temper tantrums for three days. Her classroom behavior deteriorated rapidly; I felt we had lost much of the ground we had gained in the fall. We certainly lost ground in our relationship with her teacher. I received several notes from her indicating that Sarah was unable to follow directions, answer questions, or keep up with the class. She had even been crying in the classroom.

Treatment 36: Monosodium Glutamate (December 13, 2001)

During the next appointment, I explained the situation to Dr. Stark, especially about eating in a restaurant. He apologized immediately for not having treated her for monosodium glutamate earlier in her therapy. He said it was normally his routine, but Sarah had so many needs that he treated her for other things at the time he normally would have performed an MSG treatment.

The treatment was very ordinary. She only held the MSG vial. Since it affected both her brain and small intestine, he directed energy to those two sites. (Dr. Stark always sent energy throughout the entire body, but at times he would concentrate on particular areas when needed.)

Sarah exhibited dark circles under her eyes for a couple of days and was completely contrary, teary, and unreasonable. The week was a complete loss as far as schooling went. No education took place. Since it was the middle of the grading period, the interim reports were due to be sent out. Pressure was mounting for her to demonstrate some recovery at school. The principal had issued a warning to my husband and me. We had had many closed-door meetings. As many frustrated parents have experienced, emotions were high on my part and the teacher's part. I knew we were up against Sarah's second hurdle.

twenty-one
Chinese Emotions

One of the major sets of symptoms shared by many autistic children is severe emotional outbursts. Any number of things can cause these outbursts, from altering a normal pattern of events, or changing their environment, to introducing something new they haven't come in contact with before. Changes in the environment create severe anxiety that the child cannot cope with. The type of outburst varies from cowering fearfully, to tearful, to screaming and raging.

One afternoon in January 2002, while in the Stark Clinic, waiting for a treatment, Sarah suffered one of these screaming, raging temper outbursts. As I write this I can't remember what triggered it. We were in one of the exam rooms, not in the lobby, thank goodness. Sarah was seated on the far end of the exam table with her back to the door, facing the wall, screaming hysterically. Dr. Stark walked into the exam room prepared to treat the parasite. When he witnessed Sarah's behavior, he looked at me calmly and said, "She needs Chinese emotions." Then he disappeared out the of the exam room.

Shortly, he returned carrying a small box of vials. Sarah never noticed his first arrival, departure, or reentrance. She was continuing her little tantrum against the wall. Dr. Stark lifted the lid on the box and I noticed that these vials were different from the ones he usually used. Instead of being filled with a liquid substrate, they contained tiny white tablets, about the size of commercial saccharine pills. I asked what they were. He replied that this was a very ancient technique. These pills were standardized extracts from herbs and other plants. Each plant extract is energetically tuned to an individual emotion and can cause a disturbance or can strengthen a person against a weakness in his or her emotional pattern. Again, here was another completely customized protocol to deal with emotional disturbances.

Sarah continued with her tearful fit of temper in the corner, six feet away from Dr. Stark. He held the box with one hand and ran his other hand over the vials. He felt one and said, "This is it." He removed the vial from the box and held it in the air, facing Sarah. From six feet away, he waved the air next to the vial in her direction. She immediately calmed down and was pacified. The tears and screaming stopped. He left the room again and returned shortly with an eyedropper bottle and told me to place a few drops under her tongue and on her belly button each morning and at night before bed. The drops were made from distilled water and the tablet of the plant extract in the vial he had used. The drops have stabilized Sarah's mood ever since. We get refills every couple of months.

In future visits, I learned more about Chinese emotions—how they are diagnosed and how they are treated. For individuals with extreme anxiety, they can be a true asset. Dr. Stark had several boxes containing about twenty vials each. The plant extracts are specific to individual emotions. If a patient suffers from a phobia or anxiety, Dr. Stark could determine the exact specificity by placing individual vials inside the patient's energy field and determining those he is weak for using muscle response testing. Then, by placing other emotion vials inside the energy field, the doctor can determine the one, or more, that will make the patient strong (in other words, calming the phobia or anxiety). Then, the doctor can prepare a drop solution for the patient to use daily, from the tablet extracts. This specified approach is far more customized to the patient than the shotgun approach offered by many of the herbal companies. This approach is an energetic one and relies on the frequencies of both the patient and the plant extract. It is not a chemical approach. It is specifically tailored to the patient.

twenty-two
The Coil

Sarah's interim report was due from school. Her teacher, out of an act of charity, sent home a personal letter without submitting an official report to be placed in her permanent file. The teacher knew our struggle to bring Sarah to wellness. Parts of that letter are attached, and the teacher's concern over the correct educational environment for Sarah is very apparent. The arrival of the letter and our decision toward action took place about one week before Christmas 2001.

Here is an excerpt from the teacher's letter dated December 14, 2001:

> I know that Sarah is able to learn. However I am becoming more and more concerned that this learning environment is not helpful to Sarah. She is sending strong signals in her actions in class and in her comments to [the principal] and me that the work is too difficult for her. Her crying is a signal the she is under too much stress. Her distractibility is affecting the amount of material she is learning.
>
> I am concerned about the class dynamics and how that involves Sarah. Her crying really disrupts the classroom and makes everyone feel ill at ease. It is difficult for the class to work with one classmate so obviously upset. It is also difficult for me to teach when one of my students needs so much extra attention. I know I cannot keep stopping to help Sarah each time, yet I see she needs that help.

I took the letter to Dr. Stark on December 14. He reviewed it and we discussed the matter. It was clear that Sarah had made huge strides at home. She was focused and well behaved during church and Sunday school. She participated well at parties. She had been promoted in ballet class. Yet at school, there remained a problem. Dr. Stark surmised that there was something in the classroom itself that was disturbing Sarah. He referred to it as "pernicious energy." He said that many people are extremely sensitive to the ambient energies produced by lights, radios, televisions, and computers, as well as by large groups of people in auditoriums, theaters, and classrooms. This was an entirely new concept to me, that large groups of people could generate pernicious energy—enough to disrupt a sensitive individual's thought patterns. Yet I've known many people who deliberately avoided crowds because they grew uncomfortable in them. What made me even more amazed was that Dr. Stark had a remedy for pernicious energy.

Before attending the Chinese medical school, Dr. Stark had studied and practiced electrical engineering. He had an excellent understanding of the flow of electricity and the physics behind energy medicine. The idea that he could somehow control incoming energy that had no obviously generated source and no conductive wiring was beyond anything I had ever been exposed to. I asked if there is solid physics behind his remedies. He replied that there is and that the Russians and Chinese were at the forefront of the studies on energy medicine. Their medical databases contained numerous research studies supporting the validity of energy medicine. I asked, "If this pernicious energy were floating around a room, what wavelength would it have on the electromagnetic spectrum?" He replied that the energy would be close to the microwave range, not a microwave itself, but close. Then he proceeded to write out some equations that I did not understand.

Even though I had a limited understanding of what Dr. Stark had explained to me, the teacher had already corroborated his theory while recounting an event from the classroom one day. Apparently, Sarah had been reduced to a fit of tears during the week of the monosodium glutamate. The children sitting at the desks adjacent to hers simply could not do their work with her sulking. The teacher described how she took Sarah's desk and moved it a few feet back, out of the row and away from the other children. Once seated, within minutes Sarah calmed down, and the crying stopped. She was able to return to work. So altering seating arrangements and moving her out of the energy patterns of others had made a difference to Sarah. In fact, the teacher went on to recount that normal children sulk when separated from the group, yet Sarah always improved when she was sent to the back of the room to complete an assignment. This sounded to me like another corroboration that pernicious energy, generated by people in one's surroundings, disturbs those who are sensitive to it. How was Dr. Stark going to remedy this situation?

On Thursday, December 6, a routine appointment became not quite so routine. As always, I climbed on the exam table and Dr. Stark tested Sarah's sensitivities through me. Sarah stood at my side, with her hand on my shoulder. I raised my right arm for muscle response testing. In my left hand, Dr. Stark placed a copper tube with a wire attached to a frequency generator. He began to generate frequencies and send them into Sarah's body through me. As he reached the first one, he pressed on my arm, with Sarah touching me, and my arm held fast. He continued generating frequencies, the numbers were climbing on the digital display, and he pressed my arm all the while. He hit the frequency 104 and my arm collapsed. He quickly jotted it down in her file. He continued generating frequencies as I raised my arm again. Sarah continued touching my shoulder. The numbers on the digital display climbed. Dr. Stark continued testing the resistance on my arm. When he reached 209, my arm lost its strength and collapsed again. He recorded the number in her file. Again, I raised my right arm and we continued the procedure. He found a few weaknesses at higher frequencies that he referred to as harmonics of the first two frequencies. So the same remedy would work for them as well. That completed Dr. Stark's data collection.

Next, he explained what he would do with this information. He would bend a thin copper wire into a sort of spring with a specific diameter and spacing between each coil. It would run interference for the frequencies to which Sarah was sensitive. It would squelch electrical noise and shield Sarah against pernicious energy. He would test the coil against the frequencies using his generator. I asked if he had done this before and he said yes, and that people felt a great clarity when they wore their coils in crowded public settings. Sarah's, it turned out, was special because she was sensitive to two frequencies instead of one. I asked if he had ever made a coil before for a child in a classroom setting. He had not. Sarah would become the first child in the world with such a device to balance and improve her classroom behavior. The goal was to have her focus and concentrate without the use of Ritalin, Adderall, or Dexedrine.

I grew incredibly excited and impatient waiting for the coil to be made. I made a pest of myself nagging Dr. Stark to complete it. Christmas was upon us, and I wanted a few days in the classroom to test it before the break. My wish did not come true. Time constraints did not allow Dr. Stark to complete the coil before the school's Christmas break.

When he did present it, I was delighted. The coil was packed in resin to hold its shape and wrapped in black electrical tape. It was quite small, an imperfect cube, approximately one half inch by one half inch (one and a half centimeters by one and a half centimeters). I placed it in a small jewelry bag, ready to safety pin to Sarah's clothing when school reopened in January.

My husband and I never told the teacher about this aspect of the remedy for her classroom behavior. We felt we did not have enough knowledge to explain it intelligently. Dr. Stark felt that we would get more unbiased feedback from the teacher if she was unaware of Sarah's coil.

As it turned out, the coil was remarkably helpful in crowds, such as malls, movie theaters, and chaotic environments, such as children's birthday parties. In fact, Sarah was invited to a swim party at our local county pool not long after she received the coil. I witnessed the dramatic results of its effectiveness. While in the pool, Sarah was only wearing her swimsuit, without the coil. She remained by herself, fearful of the water, never leaving the shallow end, refusing to participate with any of her friends. All of the other girls were in the deep water, diving and playing games. After swimming, all of the girls returned to the locker room to change. Sarah put on her play clothes with the coil attached to her shirt collar. When the girls finished changing, they played a variety of games. Sarah joined in all of them, and her reaction time, playing speed, and concentration were as good as any other child's. It was as though she had transformed before my very eyes. She was instantly a normal child. Unfortunately, it was too little too late for the classroom. There was much improvement in Sarah's concentration, yet in her case, not enough for her classroom needs.

Immediately before Christmas break, Norm and I sat down in a meeting with Sarah's teacher and the principal. It was a huge disappointment. They wanted to remove Sarah from the first grade classroom and return her to kindergarten, which would have been the death knell for her intellect. We refused and the principal said that she was just taking our money and that Sarah was not learning. In truth, she was learning an extraordinary amount but was simply not demonstrating it to them. As the toxins were retracing their pathways out of her body, she was exhibiting symptoms too overwhelming for the teacher to deal with. We asked if the processing and detoxification from the treatments were too much to handle, and the teacher's answer was a resounding "Yes." We agreed to cease the treatments for a period so Sarah would not suffer processing reactions. (We did, however, say that we would continue controlling the parasite.) Both the teacher and the principal agreed to give this a try and resolved to leave her in first grade.

This turned out to be the worst decision we made in the entire course of Sarah's recovery. For an entire month, through January 2002, we performed no detoxifying or curative treatments. We only took Sarah to the Stark Clinic for *Toxoplasma gondii* treatments. Treatments 37 through 40 are all one week apart and are all for *T. gondii*. Sarah desperately needed additional energy for her immune system to remain in control of the other viruses, bacteria, and toxins. Over the subsequent weeks, she slowly began to fade back into her trancelike world in the classroom.

To make matters worse, she contracted a midwinter virus that many of the children were passing around. It weakened her even further. At this point the teacher ceased to make comments and references about Sarah's work. At the end of January she simply requested another conference. Norman and I both knew this was bad news.

twenty-three
Unlocking Sarah's Organs

February 2002, Norman and I attended an early morning conference with Sarah's principal and teacher. They insisted the class work was too difficult for her and that she really must be returned to kindergarten. Fortunately, an idea had come to mind the night before the meeting. It had always been very clear to me that Sarah's recovery took precedence over everything, including her education. I discussed the idea with my husband and he agreed that she really needed more treatments. At the conference, I presented the idea that we would remove Sarah from school on a medical leave of absence, during which time I would home-school her and simultaneously double up on her energy treatments to push through the therapy. Everyone was delighted with this plan. We all agreed to return her to the classroom at the end of the year to test her progress. The principal also requested that we have Sarah's learning abilities evaluated. We agreed to it. Little did we know how fortuitous that request was would be.

I contacted the Stark Clinic and scheduled Sarah for two visits the following week. Sarah and I returned to the clinic Monday, February 11. I told Dr. Stark our agreement with the school and he agreed this was the best thing for Sarah's recovery. He immediately began a new protocol to unlock her organs. He referred to it as a "stressed level system". The official name is Field Control Therapy (FCT®). He defined "stress" as any event that affects the workings of a major system; immune, circulatory, neurological, digestive, or hormonal. He explained that it worked like Chinese boxes. The problem may be inside a box that is inside another box that is inside yet another box. It may be necessary to remove mercury, lead, and parasites from one organ before we could work on another organ. The stress levels tell us which organs the body wants to treat. Each individual is different, so FCT® can be completely customized for each patient. As the energy passes through the stressed organ, tapping into it's energy diagnostically and then therapeutically, it unlocks each cell and drains it of toxins and pathogens.

Each zone of the body can become unlocked, one treatment at a time, until the entire body is drained of morbid causes of disease. The order of unlocking Sarah's stress levels was as follows:
1. Whole body
2. Connective tissues
3. Red blood cells
4. Hematopoietic zone
5. Seven brain levels
   a. Cerebrum
   b. Cerebellum
   c. Pituitary
   d. Brain Stem
   e. Hypothalamus
   f. Amygdala
   g. Corpus callosum
6. Lymph

FCT® uses a clinical algorithm to determine the level, or severity, of stress for each organ. First stress is very severe, and fifth stress is minor.

Treatment 42: First Stressed Hematopoietic Zone (February 11, 2002)

Dr. Stark entered the exam room carrying a small metal platform, with holes bored into it and wires running from it, with two handles, one copper, and one aluminum. Sarah held the copper handle in one hand and touched me with the other. I raised my right arm for testing, as a surrogate for the patient. Dr. Stark placed a vial labeled "first stress" in the metal platform. Using the aluminum handle he began testing dozens of vials of organs and whole body systems. He explained that frequently a person would test strong in a given organ (a sort of false positive) until another organ is unlocked and releases toxins. Then, the organ that was previously strong will reveal its true toxicity, go weak, and can then be treated. This is the Chinese box theory, or FCT® algorithm of corresponding grades in stress levels of the organs. He continued testing my arm for resistance and hit upon two weak zones, red blood cells, and the hematopoietic zone, which is the body's system for producing blood. The hematopoietic zone includes the liver, bone marrow, and red blood cells. He placed the vial in the metal platform along with the first stressed vial. Then he switched the vial cases and said he would search for things that were causing the stress to that zone. I raised my arm; Sarah continued holding the copper tube and touching me. Dr. Stark used the aluminum handle to touch dozens of vials of toxins and stressors in order to determine the causes of malfunction or stress to the hematopoietic zone and red bloods cells. My arm fell weak for several vials labeled "heavy metals," "lead," "supplements," and "mercury." The two main sources of mercury in a child usually are mercury in dental amalgam fillings of the mother, due to it's ability to cross the placenta and being secreted into the breast milk, and childhood vaccines. He placed those vials in the metal platform along with the first stressed and hematopoietic zone vials. Lastly, he added a vial labeled "lymph" to direct her body's energy to help drain the mercury, lead, heavy metals, and extraneous supplements from her body. Sarah continued to hold the copper tube connected to the platform while Dr. Stark performed the acupressure treatment. With the use of the platform, Sarah could be treated with seven different vials at one time. (The clinic had platforms allowing for up to fifteen to twenty vials, meaning hundreds of compounds could be drained at one time.)

 I was a little confused by the extraneous supplements he found. I had always believed that taking vitamins was healthy. Apparently, Sarah's body had overdosed on them, which according to Dr. Yurkovsky common. She had an abundance of supplements accumulated in the tissues of her hematopoietic zone. The vial contained the energies from literally dozens of vitamins, minerals, and amino acids. In addition to draining extraneous supplements, this treatment would also improve her body's ability to utilize supplements.

 The next day, following the treatment, Sarah was deeply disturbed by the "unlocking" or toxic release process. All of the toxins coming out of her retraced a pathway through her body that caused a number of symptoms to erupt. There were tears, dyslexia, delayed speech, memory loss, fidgetiness, and some limited hyperactivity. I was so glad I was home-schooling her at this point. She never could have functioned in a classroom following this treatment, yet as time has proven, it was so necessary.

Treatment 43: First stressed Hypothalamus (February 14, 2002)

On Valentine's Day we returned to the clinic. We used the same metal platform with wires and handles as before. Dr. Stark placed the first-stressed vial in the platform. Sarah held the copper handle and touched me. I raised my arm. Dr. Stark used the aluminum handle to go through his vial case. This was the day he explained that there was an order he followed to determine which organs and systems were stressed and how he would unlock them. He begins with a whole body vial. If the muscle resistance test is strong, he moves on to connective tissues. If those are strong, he then tests the hematopoietic zone, and so on, as well as the five regions of the brain. Sarah first fell weak for hypothalamus. He placed the hypothalamus vial in the metal platform. Then, he reached for the next box of vials to find what was stressing the hypothalamus. He tested dozens of vials, and my arm grew tired of all the pressure. He found heavy metals, mercury, herbicides, pharmacological materials, lead, vaccine material, and cadmium, which took us both by surprise. We did not know where it could have come from. He placed all nine vials in the metal platform along with a lymph vial for drainage. His search was complete for that treatment. I found it astounding that the human body could be so toxic and still go on functioning. He replied that many people could not. It amazes me that conventional medicine still looks for one cause and effect to illness.

Dr. Stark performed the acupressure treatment on Sarah as she held the copper handle connected to the tray of vials. She waited forty-five minutes, holding the copper handle, and her treatment was complete.

The processing symptoms were quite remarkable. Sarah experienced nausea, total exhaustion, dizziness, headaches, and joint aches. At one point, her right leg strengthened even more than before, improving her dancing. There was occasional use of her left hand for writing. "The lines," as she referred to the alleged protozoa in her eyes, had peculiar shapes behind them. These symptoms lasted right up to the next treatment.

In the meantime, I was very curious as to the source of the cadmium. How could she possibly have acquired it and gotten it lodged in her brain? I read about cadmium and quickly discovered that it was a by-product of zinc refinement. After talking to friends who were using holistic healing methods, I discovered cadmium was a common problem. I thought about reducing her zinc, but she really needed it. I was very relieved that cadmium could be found and detoxified from her brain without incident using FCT®.

Treatment 44: Second Stressed Hypothalamus (February 18, 2002)

It was Monday afternoon when we returned to the Stark Clinic. Each day was very strictly structured, with her class work in the morning and either treatments or ballet in the afternoon. I was so happy that we were doubling up on the treatments and cleansing Sarah's body. Given her blood tests, I was not at all surprised to see mercury and heavy metals coming up continually in her brain tissues. I was also delighted that the hypothalamus was being cleansed. The hypothalamus is the relay center of the brain. It transfers neural messages from one area of the brain to another. Apparently, the electric impulses between neurons can be short-circuited by the presence of unwanted metals. Neurotransmitter receptor sites can also be clogged by unwanted heavy metals. It should come as no surprise that children with autism cannot locate words or organize thoughts; they read backwards and have motor delays. Of course, these were all of the symptoms I saw with this treatment. In fact, Sarah carried these struggles with her through the next three treatments.

Treatment 45: Amygdala, Dura Mater (February 21, 2002)

Sarah was found to be at the first stress level when Dr. Stark tested her during this treatment. Her brain remained her weakest area. He placed a vial in the aluminum platform to resonate the tissues of her total brain. At the same time, he resonated the amygdala and dura mater. He then added vials for solvents, herbicides, aluminum, cadmium, paint, and heavy metals to release them from the tissues. Finally, he added a lymph vial for drainage.

The activation of the lymph system turned out to be very important. Without it, I don't think each tissue would have drained properly, and Sarah would have merely shifted symptoms from one region of her body to another. I could see the drainage in action. For a couple of days, she suffered headaches, a sore neck, swollen glands behind her ears, plus hearing and smelling sensitivity.

Treatment 46: Brain (February 25, 2002)

This treatment was very reassuring in that Sarah's total brain region dropped to the third stress level. It could rise again as toxins shift through the body, but this was a sign that recovery was progressing well. Dr. Stark treated her brain for excessive pharmaceuticals, mercury, cadmium, heavy metals, and vaccines, specifically measles, mumps and rubella. Sensitivities, joint aches, and fatigue continued to grow.

Over the course of the next few days, Sarah developed a bladder infection, and while she had frequent urination with pain, it was noticeable that her urine stunk. It had a distinct, chemical-like odor. Even her breath and the very pores of her skin stunk. She was so stagnated that she had not had a bowel movement in four days (which Dr. Stark treated her for). While there was no dyslexia, she was quite wild and hyperactive. It was growing apparent that the issue of detoxifying her brain was reaching a peak. The chemicals were shifting out of her brain and into other organs and it was clearly bothering her. She was growing stagnant in that she couldn't release enough toxins quickly enough. It was as though the very chemicals we were trying to release were clogging up the drains of her body. Her tongue was turning purple from stagnation, and she developed another bloody nose.

At this point Dr. Stark told us about a new protocol that would help to flush toxins and diminish the reactions. We started giving Sarah long, hot baths in Epsom salts. What a simple gift, yet so powerful! I drew the bath water as warm as her little body could tolerate (without burning her) and I dissolved two cups of Epsom salts in it. I had her soak for half an hour. We did this every other day for as long as we were detoxifying her body. If it were not for these baths, this phase of her recovery would have been horrible. I could smell the toxins draining from her body. In addition to the baths, she was drinking glasses of filtered water to wash her system clean. We purchased a home water filter for the kitchen sink and drank water ceaselessly.

Treatment 47: Red Blood Cells (February 28, 2002)

With her body so stagnated, it felt like an eternity waiting for the next treatment. Due to the serious nature of the stagnation and the bloody nose, Dr. Stark treated Sarah for toxins in the red blood cells at the second stress level. The toxins included mercury, heavy metals, and cadmium, among others. He used a unique new tool. It was a red laser light. He pointed it at her acupressure points and warmed them to increase the flow of the chi. Sarah loved it and kept asking that he warm her tongue with it because she tasted flavors. We went home after the treatment. She fell asleep in the afternoon and slept the night through until nine the next morning. Upon waking, she suffered one last bloody nose. But the results were astounding; it was as though the dam broke. Sarah passed, probably, the first normally formed stool that she ever passed in her life. Her dyslexia was gone and she was calmed to the activity level of a normal child. She was moving at a normal pace through her schoolwork at home. It was an overnight miracle.

twenty-four
Home-schooling and Epsom Salts

It was always clear to us that healing our child was top priority. School and everything else was secondary. It was obvious that the reactions to the treatments caused a spiraling effect, downward as she detoxified and upward again as her immune system was boosted. I knew teachers would never understand the concept of treatment reactions. I also knew the reactions could be distracting to a class.

We made the decision to pull Sarah out of school and to home-school her. It proved to be another blessing. At home, in a homogeneous atmosphere, I could see that Sarah's brain was growing better and better each day. Without dyslexia she was zipping through her work. In fact, not only was she making up for lost time, but she was beginning to surpass her former classmates in many areas as tests always implied she would. While home-schooling, I could observe her progress more closely. In addition, we enjoyed the freedom of visiting the doctor during the day, not during after-school hours or on weekends. It allowed for a comfortable routine that was conducive to recovery. We were free of the emotional upheaval caused by treatment reactions in the classroom. We wanted to continue treatments so there would be no relapse. In short, home-schooling was giving us the freedom we needed for total

Sarah's Psychological Evaluation WISC III
Age: 7 years 4 months
Reported Feb. 13, 2003

Verbal	Percentile
Information	91
Similarities	98
Arithmetic	37
Vocabulary	>99
Comprehension	37
Digit Span	75
Performance	
Pic Completion	5
Coding	75
Picture Arrangement	25
Block Design	91
Object Assembly	75
Symbol Search	63

recovery. Therefore, Norm and I made the decision to remove Sarah permanently from a classroom-style school.

We then paid to have several cognitive-linguistic and psychological evaluations run on Sarah in the spring of 2002 as well as 2003. These tests included a Peabody Picture Vocabulary Test, the Test of Word Finding, the Test of Language Competence, the Lindamood Auditory Conceptualization Test, the developmental test of Visual-Motor Integration; The Test of Nonverbal Intelligence, three Woodcock-Johnson Tests of Achievement, and the Decoding Skills Test, among others. (See appendix C for complete before and after Wechsler Intelligence Scale evaluations.) These allowed us to have a better picture of her learning patterns.

We joined a statewide home-school umbrella group. I studied curricula and chose one appropriate for Sarah's learning style, heavy on auditory learning and recitation. Sarah flourished under this protocol. It was as though she understood that she had been set free.

At the time of her WISC evaluation, we also had her observed at length by a PhD psychologist with credentials from the Kennedy Krieger Institute in Baltimore. At this point, Dr. Stark had treated Sarah for about a year and a half. The psychologist reported that she could find no symptoms of autism or even pervasive development disorder, PDD. She said that Sarah's participation level in activities was good and that she was popular with other children. However, she did observe difficulty with executive function and transitioning between tasks. She said that Sarah's activity level was on par with other children and that she was not hyperactive or overly impulsive.

I walked away from that meeting basking in the words "no symptoms of autism." I thought to myself, she never saw Sarah when she was three years old. She never saw the symptom list I recorded for the pediatrician the summer of 2000. All she saw was the child in recovery two and a half years later approaching a symptom-free state.

At this time, I was so grateful that Dr. Stark had introduced the Epsom salts protocol for us to administer at home. It was easy and even helped speed up Sarah's recovery. Every other night Sarah was to have a bath in Epsom salts. Now the whole family does it. Since we were home-schooling we could design a household routine that conveniently included both her treatment therapy and Epsom salts baths. Sarah soaked for thirty minutes in a tub with two cups of Epsom salts (four cups for adults). She enjoyed it immensely, as the salts created a buoyant effect, and her limbs floated on the water. We learned that after thirty minutes the pores of the skin open up and toxins are released directly into the bath water. It helped to reduce any toxin buildup in her brain and helped her immune system wash out pathogens. Anything unwanted went right down the drain.

I always noticed a slight or subtle improvement in her concentration and schoolwork the morning after a salts bath. Within months of beginning this new therapy, her concentration, awareness, and motivation took another dramatic jump. Her executive function began to improve, while multitasking remained a challenge.

Sarah's Psychological Evaluation WISC IV Age: 10 years 8 months Reported June 20, 2006	
Verbal	**Percentile**
Information	>99
Similarities	>99
Arithmetic	75
Vocabulary	>99
Comprehension	99
Digit Span	63
Performance	
Pic Completion	95
Coding	37
Picture Arrangement	63
Block Design	84
Object Assembly	84
Symbol Search	63

A brief overview of Sarah's Wechsler's Intelligence Scale Index is located in the sidebar. She was tested twice, once at age seven years and four months and again at ten years and eight months. Unfortunately, there were no psychological tests taken prior to seven years. Significant results are evident in two areas. The first area is called picture completion. This test determines how well and how quickly a patient can spot something that is out of place, inaccurate, or incomplete in a picture. Sarah's original percentile ranking was horribly low! She was in the bottom fifth percentile! Today, I firmly believe that was due to the *Toxoplasma gondii* obscuring her vision. Once she was rid of it, her ranking jumped to the ninety-fifth percentile, an amazing and statistically significant leap! The new percentile is also more in keeping with Sarah's other test rankings. Her verbal comprehension, arithmetic skills, and picture arrangement scores also took significant jumps.

twenty-five
More Unwanted Visitors

Treatment 49: Inoculations (March 7, 2002)

Dr. Stark performed another treatment to boost Sarah's immune system toward the offending viruses injected into her in infancy. He treated hepatitis, diphtheria, pertussis, and tetanus.

Sarah was beginning to go downhill again. Within the week she became very disorganized. She couldn't find things. She was losing the awareness of her environment. I was still keeping copious records of her symptoms to report to Dr. Stark with each visit. He would not be surprised at her recent downturn.

Treatment 50: Third Stress Chest, Thymus (March 11, 2002)

Dr. Stark realized that if she was backsliding in her recovery, there might be something feeding the parasite in her brain, some other pathogen living in a symbiotic relationship with the *Toxoplasmosis*. He performed an energetic, whole-body, stress-level, diagnostic search. Using the muscle resistance test, he tested her whole body; she held strong. Then, he worked his way down from the top, testing head, including brain, and neck, including thyroid, each individually. They all held strong. Then he tested her chest. She went weak. He tested each stress level individually and found that she was at the third stress level. Next, he tested each organ of the chest individually. It was not the heart or lungs. It was the thymus that was under duress. Next, he tested for the usual toxins: heavy metals, cadmium, excess supplements, lead, copper, and some bacteria. Then he tested for individual pathogens and discovered yet another parasite! It was almost unbelievable to me how one child's body could be so weakened that two major parasites could set up housekeeping. It was equally unfathomable to me how conventional medical doctors could miss the indicators! This newly discovered pathogen was allegedly living in the thymus—the heart of the body's computer for decoding immune response. It was no wonder Sarah suffered bizarre immune system responses to foreign agents. The new pathogen was a helminth—a family of flatworms, roundworms, and pinworms that are attracted to large concentrations of supplements, hence they are frequently found in the intestines. She probably picked it up in some under-cooked meat or by eating raw vegetables. He tested me as well to see if I had passed it on to her, and I did not have it.

Her reaction to the treatment was immediate and severe. It affected her entire body and lasted a long time. In fact, a new downward spiral erupted. I was so glad I was home-schooling at this time. Sarah developed joint aches and grew lethargic, disoriented, and extremely sound sensitive. She was unable to work independently, exhibited attention deficit, talked incessantly, cried spontaneously, and lost her memory. It was all I could do to retain my sanity watching my child go through this. She reported that the lines in her eyes were changing. They were no longer in a group. They were spreading!

Treatment 51: T. gondii and Helminths (March 14, 2002)

I reported this strong reaction to Dr. Stark and he agreed that the helminth treatment had caused a flare-up in the *T. gondii*. He gave Sarah a treatment for both of them together.

There was no improvement in her behavior or the state of her vision the entire week. In fact, her deteriorated state had me quite worried. Her hyperactivity and sensory sensitivity were out of control.

Treatments 52 through 59 (April 2002)

Dr. Stark performed seven more treatments for *T. gondii* to no avail. There was no improvement. I was growing scared. I worried that maybe energy medicine was not the panacea I thought it was. I was concerned that Sarah's immune system might never be able to fight off this infection. I had a long talk with my husband. I was nearly ready to give up and return to conventional medicine and to try antibiotics. We both agreed that was a shotgun approach, that it could cause the parasite to mutate and grow worse, and that it could damage her existing normal flora. The conversation temporarily pacified me.

Treatment 60: Biovial (April 25, 2002)

I confided my feelings to Dr. Stark at this appointment. I told him about the conversation with my husband. I told him that we had considered antibiotics. He agreed that there was definitely something feeding the parasite and that there must be a pathway linking the helminth and the *T. gondii*. He went searching for it, with FCT®, and discovered that it was the entire lymph system. These two parasites were riding it like a subway. He left the exam room and returned a little while later with a new, vial of his own creation. I thought he purchased all of his vials from laboratories in Europe and China, but apparently he had the ability to make his own. I later learned that a device called a potentizer is used by many homeopaths to imprint an energetic signature into a substrate. He said it was Sarah's own special energy frequency from her thymus, lymph, and brain energies and that it contained the energy from the pathway the parasites were using! That was the vial he used to treat her.

    Thank goodness! It did the trick. It snapped her out of her downward spiral. She said the lines in her eyes were gathering into a ball once again and the ball was shrinking. Hyperactivity, disorientation, sound sensitivity, and joint aches all disappeared. My child was back on the road to recovery. Energy medicine and FCT® were working!

twenty-six
Improving Concentration and Memory

By spring of 2002, when Sarah was six and a half, things were improving. Her emotional swings were steadying. Her concentration was still wavering, but wasn't as bad. Since we were home-schooling, the pressure to contend with the distractions of the classroom was lifted. I was spending my time planning course work each day. I had less time to journal Sarah's recovery. Since she was growing more and more balanced, there was less to record. We maintained her gluten-free, dairy-free, salicylate-free, organic diet. The treatments also began to take on a pattern. Rather than write out the next ninety treatments, I will document the pattern. First there were five or six brain detoxification treatments, and these were followed by one or two parasite treatments. The region of the brain Dr. Stark chose to treat depended on the symptoms I reported seeing in the last few days. For example, if I reported that Sarah had difficulty finding words, he treated the Broca's region. If I said she had difficulty with coordination or reaction time, he treated the corpus callosum. If she had difficulty spelling words because she couldn't recall what they looked like, he would treat the visual cortex and short-term memory. Very commonly, I reported delayed reaction time, and he would treat the hypothalamus. A typical treatment went something like this:

Sarah would sit on the exam table and Dr. Stark would bring in boxes of vials. Sarah would hold a metal wand attached by a wire to the metal tray. I would hold onto Sarah with my left hand and raise my right hand for muscle response testing. First, Dr. Stark would determine the region of the brain with the greatest weakness by placing vials in the aluminum tray and pressing my arm. The vial that caused me to weaken would be the one he would treat. Then, he would determine the energy level using vials and pressing my arm. Next, he would start with a new box containing dozens of vials with the energies of routine, environmental antigens. Sarah repeatedly went weak for the same antigens: dissolved mercury, solid mercury, cadmium, solvents, pesticides, herbicides, aluminum, lead, xenobiotics, heavy metals, fluoride, and paint. Once he determined all of the toxins disturbing her, he would place a vial labeled "lymph" in the aluminum tray. This was to activate the lymph system to drain all the toxins from the region being treated. Once he completed the tray, he would give Sarah the acupressure treatment on her back, hands, and feet. She would lie and nap or read for about forty-five minutes and the treatment would be over.

Following five or six of these brain treatments, I always noticed a downward spiral. Sarah would grow fidgety and inattentive. Her urine usually smelled like a chemical factory. I would always complain to Dr. Stark about her inattentiveness. He would invariably perform a treatment for *Toxoplasmosis* and Sarah would dramatically and immediately improve. This was the pattern we followed from spring 2002 until spring 2003 with few deviations.

Here is an example of a treatment from January 9, 2003. The vials included energetics from DNA, mercury vivus, dissolved mercury, cadmium, paint, aluminum, heavy metals, and herbicides. Following the acupressure treatment, Dr. Stark felt Sarah's head and put additional energy into the left cerebral cortex.

That night Sarah was doing her math homework (double-digit subtraction) and suddenly blurted out, "Hey, Mom I know the answers, and I don't have to do anything!" By "anything" she meant counting on her fingers or using manipulatives. I replied, "Yes dear. That's the way it is when the left side of your brain works." The next day she developed a fever of $100.5°$. I let it burn. Then she told me she had a severe headache. The fever calmed to normal the next day. The headache took two days to clear. Then she had a symptom resembling sinus drainage. I was certain toxins were clearing out of her head. Once the head problems cleared, her thought processes improved as well.

By winter of 2003, Sarah's behavior was more normal than not. Occasionally during this time period, however, we had reasons to perform other types of treatments. One such occasion was in February 2003, when Sarah took a serious downturn that lasted for two weeks. Dr. Stark could only surmise that the toxins leaving her brain were accumulating in her bloodstream during the detox process. So we tested her red blood cells energetically, and sure enough, Sarah was very weak for her entire hematopoietic zone. In addition to placing the hematopoietic zone vial into the aluminum tray, Dr. Stark tested for the stress level; which was first stress; then he tested for individual antigens: heavy metals, xenobiotics, cadmium, aluminum, fluoride, pesticides, herbicides, solvents, and large intestine toxins. At last he added the lymph drainage vial. In one day, Sarah displayed a remarkable rebound from her downward spiral. She was reading with expression. Her left and right scan rate improved, her mental recall and word retrieval both improved. She was happy and well adjusted.

Another treatment that did not follow the pattern of five brain treatments and one parasite treatment occurred in fall of 2002. Sarah was often very uncomfortable with the music in church. The organ was painful to her ears and pounded in her chest. She had never liked loud music, even from radio or CDs. During Sarah's ninety-third treatment, Dr. Stark brought a new box into the exam room. It was a large, wide, flat box. He opened it to reveal a beautiful, delicate set of tuning forks. Each one was a different color. Dr. Stark explained that each fork issued a sound that was compatible with a particular meridian of the body. So I touched Sarah and held up my right arm for muscle response testing and he removed a fork, tapped it, and held it close to Sarah's ear and then pressed on my arm. He repeated this with three or four forks until my arm went weak. The fork was in the key of B and was compatible with the lung meridian. So Dr. Stark treated Sarah for the key of B and all of the harmonics. From that point on we heard fewer and fewer complaints about noise, until the complaints eventually died out all together.

One last unusual treatment that Sarah received from spring 2002 to spring 2003 that had phenomenal effects was for her small intestine. During the years of her illness, Sarah had established a pattern on weekends of playing wildly for a few hours, until she was exhausted to the point of being overwhelmed, at which point she would have an irrational temper outburst and cry inconsolably for twenty or thirty minutes and then fall sound asleep. Since she had been in the care of the Stark Clinic I had not seen this pattern. It had been two years since I had seen it. I had completely forgotten it. In late February 2003, Dr. Stark performed Sarah's 134th treatment to clean her small intestine. He detoxified it for aluminum, xenobiotics, mercury, heavy metals, paint, measles, mumps, rubella, diphtheria, pertussis, and tetanus. It was amazing. After two years, I witnessed the recurrence of mood swings, depression, fatigue, and stomachaches. Then she fell fast asleep. When she awoke, the treatment reaction was ended and the results were phenomenal. Her left-to-right scanning ability was improved. There was increased attention to detail, better short-term memory, improved handwriting, heightened motivation, and improved recall. It was as if every evil thing had come out of her body.

Sarah continued to have ups and downs throughout the brain detoxification and immune system boosting to fight the parasite. But they were growing less and less severe with each treatment. In fact, they were becoming quite mild. Outbursts and stomachaches were becoming the exception, no longer the norm. The tissues in her brain were growing healthier. Her description of the "lines," as we referred to the parasite, was becoming less and less grandiose. The lines were no longer a problem for her vision. By summer of 2003 a photograph of the retina of her eye revealed a nearly completely healed child.

The white, milky strands of disease were nearly vanished, and all without antibiotics or harsh chemicals of any kind. I knew that if the eyes were healing, then the visual cortex of Sarah's brain was healing as well. Dr. Stark had removed an entire colony of parasitic protozoa from beyond the blood-brain barrier to heal my mentally ill child! At long last, we felt it was time to move on to the final phase of Sarah's recovery.

> *The treatments began to take on a pattern. There were five or six brain detoxification treatments followed by one or two parasite treatments.*

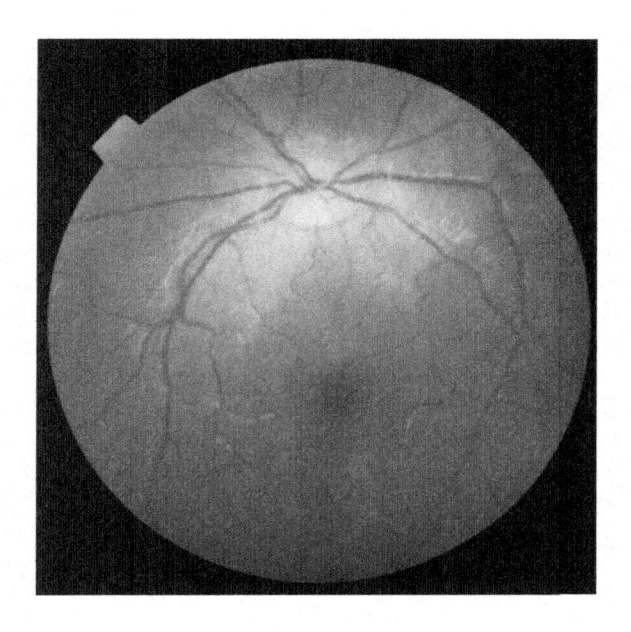

The retina of Sarah's eye taken August 2003. The large white patches of disease are gone, as well as the symptoms of autism. Dr. Stark had healed my child of an entire colony of parasitic protozoa beyond the blood-brain barrier! Compare to the 2001 retinal photo on page 153.

twenty-seven
Putting the Foods Back

Even though Sarah's mood and social activity told family and friends that she was recovered, everyone complained because she still could not eat normally. No one in the family could take care of her or have her visit for an extended stay because they couldn't feed her. I could not claim to have healed my child if she could not eat dairy, gluten, sugar, and most fruits, among other things. It was time to talk to Dr. Stark about lifting the allergies.

I was extremely cautious and apprehensive about throwing Sarah headlong into the world of processed foods. I had worked too long and hard on her recovery to have her relapse. I was aware that gluten, dairy, and sugar all promoted the growth of the parasite in her brain, so we had worked out a plan for reintroduction of foods. I would ask Dr. Stark to treat a specific food. Then, at the following appointment, I would take in an organic sample of the food, treated in the previous appointment, and ask him to test Sarah for it. Only after she passed the test would I let Sarah eat the sample. Then we would wait seventy-two hours for the aftershock, if one were coming. I would make a note of her reactions, if any. Usually there were none. I feel it is important to say at this time that I did not let Sarah simply begin eating anything just because she could. She remains on her strict diet with supplements. Sugar, gluten, dairy, and fruits are for holidays and vacations only. Until we feel certain that the parasite will never again hatch out and destroy her brain, Sarah will remain on her healthy, organic diet. When she chooses to eat off of her diet for example, on vacation, she simply treats herself for the rich foods and detoxes them.

On May 13, 2003, I took Sarah in for her first food treatment: berry mix. Since Dr. Stark had already treated Sarah for salicylic acid and calcium salicylate it was easy to go straight to the vial with the energetic frequencies of raspberries, blueberries, strawberries, boysenberries, and blackberries. He performed the usual treatment. Sarah was excited to try to eat something new. Of course, she needed to wait the obligatory twenty-five hours following treatment before testing anything. Obviously, after years of vomiting and illness, I was apprehensive, so I did not simply permit Sarah to scarf down mouthfuls of berries. I went to the organic foods store and purchased strawberries and raspberries. We grew our own blueberries. I washed and took in individual samples for Dr. Stark to test. Sarah passed on the blueberries and raspberries, but failed on the strawberries. Dr. Stark had to give her a second, independent treatment just for them. Following the test, I allowed Sarah a handful of blueberries. Then I told her that she needed to wait seventy-two hours so we could determine if she was all right. Everything else in her diet and daily routine had to remain constant.

I watched her intently for the next thirty minutes. I had known the salicylates to work that quickly. I waited for the hyperactivity, attention deficit, and dementia, and the red ears and cheeks. There was no change in her temperament. She was just as compliant as she could be. I watched her for seventy-two hours. On the third day I waited to see if the color would drain from her skin. I watched for the dark, allergic shiners to present themselves below her eyes—the telltale sign that vomiting was not far off. Nothing happened! Nothing. How exciting to have nothing happen! Sarah responded normally! I was ecstatic!

Using the same procedure, we returned wheat, corn, dairy, tomatoes, peppers, nuts, apples, vanilla extract, and much more to Sarah's diet. I asked Dr. Stark to test individually for butter, cream, milk, and cheeses. Each cheese would need to be treated separately due to the individual enzymes that age the cheeses. Other foods were like that as well; for example, each citrus fruit needed to be treated individually, as well as all of the herbs and spices.

Dr. Stark automatically and voluntarily treated her for food additives, such as ethane gas used to ripen commercial fruits brought to market, and the waxes that are sprayed on them, as well as monosodium glutamate and preservatives, to name a few. Now Sarah can travel and eat in restaurants without throwing up or departing from reality. As I stated, she only receives these foods on holidays and vacations. Following trips, we still ask Dr. Stark to perform exploratory tests to see if anything she has been exposed to is bothering any organs. (The most common thing he finds is fluoride from city drinking water, which in Sarah causes attention deficit and memory loss.) He then detoxifies for these things.

At this stage of Sarah's recovery, we had completed between 175 and 200 treatments and could really claim we had healed our autistic child.

Part Four
The Follow-up

twenty-eight
The Follow-Up

After years of treatments, and years of home-schooling, Sarah was prepared to face the world. She lacks a few of the memories neurotypical children may have, but she is in no way different. She is equally as motivated and curious about new activities as any girl ought to be. She understands the behaviors of other children very well. She is mainstream in her schoolwork. In 2005, she was on grade level with her writing and spelling and two to three years above grade level in every other subject. She passed her fourth-year ballet examination with the Academy Ballet School of Annapolis, an affiliate of the Royal Academy of Dance from London, England. (The Royal Academy sends an examiner from London to the Washington D.C. area each year to test the young ballerinas.) Sarah passed with merit in the spring of 2005 and proceeded to go en pointe the following fall. She could not have successfully achieved this without coordination and concentration. She passed the SCAT examination and was admitted to Johns Hopkins University Center for Gifted and Talented Children. In the summer of 2005, she entered a normal classroom setting with gifted children, followed class activities, took notes without assistance, remembered her own homework, and was motivated to participate normally. The teacher never knew her to be different from any other child. She also became an official craft tester for American Girl magazine. At age fourteen, she passed the College Board Accuplacer Examination and entered the local community college. In the spring of 2012, she competed in the Junior Olympics in Colorado Springs, Colorado. She was accepted into the honors program at the university of her choice for the fall of 2013. No one at any time ever commented that she was in any way different.

During the summer of 2012, Sarah was awarded an internship at Kennedy Krieger Institute. Before she could work there, she was asked to update her chicken pox vaccine. She was sixteen at the time and had not received the vaccine since infancy. Naturally, we were frightened to vaccinate her. Instead, we were permitted to offer proof of immunity. Therefore, Dr. Stark performed a NAET treatment for varicella-zoster virus. Twenty-four hours later we performed a blood test, which proved positive for chicken pox immunity, making it unnecessary to revaccinate. The NAET treatment had really boosted her immune system.

In the state of Maryland there is a program for mentally ill children. It is called the Maryland State Autism Waiver. For eligible families (at the time of this writing) it paid up to thirty thousand dollars per year from the time of diagnosis, age two or three until the child reaches the age of eighteen or twenty-one. That comes to approximately a half million dollars per child per lifetime. After that age, many of them enter institutions, also at the taxpayer's expense. We healed Sarah for approximately twenty thousand dollars, about two-thirds of one year on the waiver. Sarah will never be a taxpayer burden. She is independent.

I hope that I have made it clear how NAET, FCT® and integrated Chinese medicine can rid the body of poisons, unwanted pathogens, and allergies. It can rebalance hormones, neurotransmitters, and the immune system. I trust everyone can see how effective it is. For parents with children on the spectrum, who feel discouraged with their current choice of therapy, now there is hope. (To learn more, turn to appendix E: "How to Find a NAET or an FCT® Practitioner.") More and more families everyday are bringing their children with autism to complete wellness. As the practice of energy medicine grows, I believe it will become as standard as any other mainstream medical practice. In fact, it will be used for a variety of other disorders, not only autism. In many clinics, NAET, FCT® and ICM are used to treat cancer, ALS, Lyme disease, and more. One thing is for sure: it worked for our daughter. And this is why my husband and I wanted to share this therapy with the world.

Appendix A
Total Recovery Protocol

Sarah's Total Recovery Protocol

1. Dietary restrictions and supplements specific to her needs. We removed all artificial ingredients and as many carbohydrates as possible to inhibit the growth of pathogens.

2. Acupressure with vials specific to her weakened organs for detoxification of environmental chemical and heavy metal toxins. We found a qualified doctor of traditional Chinese medicine who understood NAET.

3. Continuous Epsom salts baths to further detoxify her body. She bathed in two cups of Epsom salts every other day for the entire duration of her detoxification protocol. This pulled the toxins directly out of her body through the pores of her skin.

4. Continued acupressure with vials to boost her immune system to fight any invading pathogen.

5. In a couple of years, we had a healthy, normal child who had never been on psychostimulant drugs or antibiotics, nor had ever used a behavior modification program.

6. Once normalcy was attained, the practitioner treated her for all of her food allergies and the foods were slowly restored to her diet.

Appendix B
Medical Test Results

THE GREAT PLAINS LABORATORY

11813 W. 77th Street
Lenexa, KS 66214

Phone 913 341-8949
Fax 913 341-6207

CLIA ID#17D0919496
William Shaw Ph.D., Laboratory Director

Patient ID #	24970	Date reported	05/14/01
Patient Name	Sarah Evans	Date of collection	05/02/01
Patient age	5	Time of collection	AM
Physician name		Patient Sex	Female

Urinary Peptides

Peptides	Value		Normal Range Children
Casomorphin (Milk)	31.3	H	< 2.5 ng/ml
Gliadorphin (Wheat)	19.0		< 20 ng/ml

Children on gluten and/or casein free diets may have normal values of the peptides in urine. Children with high values may benefit from gluten/casein free diets and/or peptidase supplementation. Children with normal peptide values may still have wheat and/or milk allergies that can be detected by allergy tests.

This test was developed and its performance characteristics determined by The Great Plains Laboratory. It has not been cleared or approved by the U.S. Food and Drug Administration.

The FDA has determined that such clearance or approval is not necessary. This laboratory is certified under the Clinical Laboratory Improvement Amendments of 1988 ("CLIA") as qualified to perform high-complexity clinical testing.

People on a diet containing soy proteins or are consuming soy "milk" may also have high peptides in their urine. Soy proteins are used as emulsifiers, extenders, binders and stabilizers in meat, poultry, snack foods, sausage, frozen spaghetti, and whipped toppings. Textured vegetable protein (TVP) is soy based and many meat substitutes are soy-based. We have found that individuals on soy may have high values for gliadorphin and /or casomorphin presumably because of peptides from soy that are similar or identical to those in gluten or casein (Zhang XZ, Wang HY, Fu XQ, Wu XX, Xu GL. Bioactive small peptides from soybean protein. Ann N Y Acad Sci 1998 Dec 13; 864: 640 - 5).

Individuals on peptidases such as Serenade or Enzymade may have high peptide values in the urine. This does not mean that these products are harmful in any way. We cannot rule out the possibility that one of the components of these products could be interfering in the tests for gliadorphin and/or casomorphin.

Form revision 2/7/01

This test was conducted following the NAET treatment for casein. Sarah had been dairy-free for one year before this test. There should have been no casein in her system. Yet, the energy unlocked her cells to release stored, stagnated casein and removed it through her urine at fifteen times the normal level.

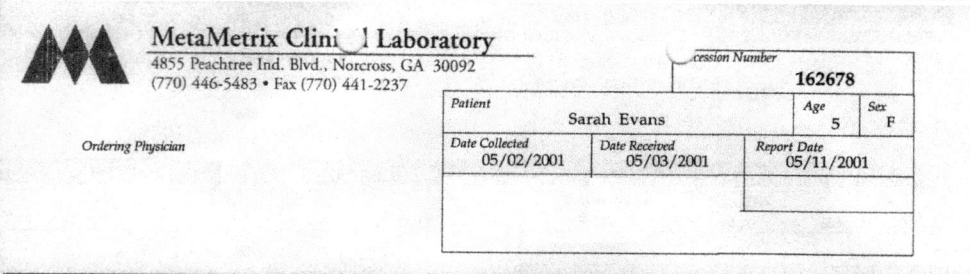

MetaMetrix Clinical Laboratory
4855 Peachtree Ind. Blvd., Norcross, GA 30092
(770) 446-5483 • Fax (770) 441-2237

Ordering Physician

Accession Number: 162678
Patient: Sarah Evans
Age: 5 Sex: F
Date Collected: 05/02/2001
Date Received: 05/03/2001
Report Date: 05/11/2001

T91 Urine Organix Profile
Methodology: GC/Mass Spectroscopy ^^COBAS FARA II

Category	#	Analyte	Results	Units	Reference Limit
Fatty Acid Metabolism	1	Adipate	2.3	µg/mg creatinine	≤ 3
	2	Suberate	2.8		≤ 4
	3	Ethylmalonate	1.8		≤ 4
Carbohydrate Metabolism	4	Pyruvate	0.74 H		≤ 0.7
	5	Lactate	10		4 - 30
	6	a-Hydroxybutyrate	39.5		≤ 50
	7	ß-Hydroxybutyrate	8		≤ 40
Energy Production (Citric Acid Cycle)	8	Citrate	306 L		500 - 2300
	9	Cis-Aconitate	167		5 - 250
	10	Isocitrate	212		50 - 800
	11	a-Ketoglutarate	5.9		3 - 25
	12	Succinate	11.6		5 - 35
	13	Fumarate	0.29		0.2 - 1.2
	14	Malate	3		≤ 6
	15	Hydroxymethylglutarate	0.32		0.2 - 1
B-Complex Vitamin Markers	16	a-Ketoisovalerate	0.36		≤ 1.5
	17	a-Ketoisocaproate	2.32 H		≤ 2
	18	a-Keto-ß-Methylvalerate	1.09		≤ 1.2
	19	Methylmalonate	5.6 H		≤ 3
	20	ß-Hydroxyisovalerate	10.1		≤ 20
Neurotransmitter Metabolism Markers	21	Vanilmandelate	0.36		0.2 - 2
	22	Homovanillate	2.3		1 - 5
	23	5-Hydroxyindoleacetate	1.4		0.8 - 5
Detoxication Indicators	24	p-Hydroxyphenyllactate	0.07		≤ 0.5
	25	2-Methylhippurate	0.7		≤ 1
	26	Orotate	59.7		≤ 180
	27	Pyroglutamate	15.8		≤ 80
	28	Sulfate/Creatinine Ratio	370		≥ 180
Intestinal Dysbiosis Markers — Bacterial	29	Benzoate	1.6		≤ 5
	30	Hippurate	320		≤ 800
	31	Phenylacetate	1.3 H		≤ 1.2
	32	Phenylpropionate	4.2 H		≤ 1.2
	33	p-Cresol	340 H		≤ 150
	34	p-Hydroxybenzoate	1.9		≤ 5
	35	p-Hydroxyphenylacetate	20		≤ 50
	36	Tricarballylate	1		≤ 1.8
Clostridial	37	Dihydroxyphenylpropionate	0.3		≤ 0.9
Yeast/Fungal	38	Tartarate	50		≤ 80
	39	Citramalate	3.7		≤ 10
	40	ß-Ketoglutarate	0.4		≤ 1

Urinary Creatinine = 50 mg/dl

Handwritten annotation: "Bacteria are absorbing leaving Tyrosine, none for Sarah Tyrosine uptake"

Georgia Lab Lic. Code #067-007
CLIA ID# 11D0255349
New York Clinical Lab Permit Code #811767AO
Florida Clinical Lab Lic. #800008124
Laboratory Directors: J. Alexander Bralley, PhD & Robert M. David, PhD

This test was conducted at the very beginning of Sarah's recovery program. Intestinal dysbiosis markers clearly indicate that something was disturbing Sarah's intestine and not allowing for nutrition absorption. We did not retest once it became obvious that Sarah was absorbing nutrients from her diet throughout her recovery.

RED BLOOD CELL ELEMENTS

10/00

LAB#: 99841-0226
PATIENT: Sarah Evans
SEX: Female
AGE: 5

CLIENT#: 18915
DOCTOR:

NUTRIENT ELEMENTS

ELEMENTS	RESULT µg/g	REFERENCE RANGE
Calcium	20.0	8– 31.0
Magnesium	52.0	36– 64.0
Potassium	85.0	65– 95.0
Phosphorus	628	480– 745
Copper	0.94	0.52– 0.89
Zinc	9.8	8– 14.5
Iron	938	745– 1050
Manganese	0.018	0.007– 0.03
Chromium	0.033	0.012– 0.07
Selenium	0.55	0.19– 0.38
Boron	0.075	0.005– 0.11
Vanadium	0.0009	.0001–0.002
Molybdenum	0.0007	.0005–0.002

POTENTIALLY TOXIC ELEMENTS

TOXIC ELEMENTS	RESULT µg/g	REFERENCE RANGE
Antimony	< 0.0002	< 0.005
Arsenic	0.006	< 0.01
Cadmium	< 0.0008	< 0.005
Lead	0.025	< 0.09
Mercury	0.019	< 0.01

SPECIMEN DATA

Comments: results checked
Date Collected: 4/18/2001
Date Received: 4/20/2001
Date Completed: 4/23/2001
Methodology: ICP-MS
µg/g = ppm

©2000 DOCTOR'S DATA, INC. • ADDRESS: 3755 Illinois Avenue, St. Charles, IL 60174-2420 • LABORATORY DIRECTOR: James T. Hicks, MD, Ph.D., FCAP
TOLL FREE: 800.323.2784 • TEL: 630.377.8139 • FAX: 630.587.7860 • EMAIL: inquiries@doctorsdata.com • WEBSITE: www.doctorsdata.com
CLIA ID NO: 14D0646470 • MEDICARE PROVIDER NO: 148453 • TAX ID NO. (FEIN): 93-0941625

This blood test was conducted at the beginning of Sarah's NAET treatments and clearly demonstrates that at age five her mercury levels were nearly double that of the normal adult reference range.

RED BLOOD CELL ELEMENTS

LAB#: 99980-0296
PATIENT: Sarah Evans
SEX: Female
AGE: 5

CLIENT#: 18915
DOCTOR:

NUTRIENT ELEMENTS

ELEMENTS	RESULT µg/g	REFERENCE RANGE
Calcium	20.0	8- 31.0
Magnesium	51.0	36- 64.0
Potassium	75.0	65- 95.0
Phosphorus	613	480- 745
Copper	0.78	0.52- 0.89
Zinc	8.8	8- 14.5
Iron	879	745- 1050
Manganese	0.018	0.007- 0.03
Chromium	0.037	0.012- 0.07
Selenium	0.41	0.19- 0.38
Boron	0.055	0.005- 0.11
Vanadium	0.001	.0001-0.002
Molybdenum	0.0011	.0005-0.002

POTENTIALLY TOXIC ELEMENTS

TOXIC ELEMENTS	RESULT µg/g	REFERENCE RANGE
Antimony	0.0002	< 0.005
Arsenic	< 0.0006	< 0.01
Cadmium	< 0.0008	< 0.005
Lead	0.029	< 0.09
Mercury	0.004	< 0.01

SPECIMEN DATA

Comments: selenium checked
Date Collected: 8/31/2001
Date Received: 9/6/2001
Date Completed: 9/11/2001
Methodology: ICP-MS
µg/g = ppm

©2000 DOCTOR'S DATA, INC. • ADDRESS: 3755 Illinois Avenue, St. Charles, IL 60174-2420 • LABORATORY DIRECTOR: James T. Hicks, MD, Ph.D., FCAP
TOLL FREE: 800.323.2784 • TEL: 630.377.8139 • FAX: 630.587.7860 • EMAIL: inquiries@doctorsdata.com • WEBSITE: www.doctorsdata.com
CLIA ID NO: 14D0646470 • MEDICARE PROVIDER NO: 148453 • TAX ID NO. (FEIN): 93-0941625

This second blood cell elements test was conducted following several NAET treatments for vaccine solutions. No mercury treatments had yet been conducted. The mercury levels dropped to one-fifth of their previous level by performing energy treatments for vaccines alone.

Appendix C
Psychological Tests Before and After

REPORT OF WISC-III TESTING
The Psychological Corporation

NAME: Sarah EVANS

REPORT DATE: 02/13/03
BIRTH DATE: 10/12/95
TEST DATE: 02/13/03
EXAMINER:
TITLE:

AGE: 7 years, 4 months
GENDER: female

TEST RESULTS

SCALE	IQ	PR	95 PERCENT CONFIDENCE INTERVAL IQ	95 PERCENT CONFIDENCE INTERVAL PR	CLASSIFICATION OF INTELLECTUAL FUNCTIONING
Verbal	121	92	114-126	82- 96	
Performance	102	55	94-110	34- 75	
Full Scale	112	79	106-117	66- 87	high average

Difference Between VIQ and PIQ = 19 ($p < .05$, Freq 14.5%)

FACTOR SUMMARY

	SS	INDEX	PR	95 PERCENT CONFIDENCE INTERVAL INDEX	95 PERCENT CONFIDENCE INTERVAL PR
Verbal Comprehension	58	125	95	117-130	87- 98
Perceptual Organization	39	99	47	91-107	27- 68
Freedom from Distractibility	21	104	61	94-113	34- 81
Processing Speed	23	109	73	98-117	45- 87

VERBAL

	RAW SCORE	SCALED SCORE	PR
Information (IN)	13	14	91
Similarities (SM)	16	16	98
Arithmetic (AR)	12	9	37
Vocabulary (VO)	32	19	99
Comprehension (CO)	11	9	37
(Digit Span DS)	12	12	75

PERFORMANCE

	RAW SCORE	SCALED SCORE	PR
Picture Completion (PC)	8	5	5
Coding (CD)	51	12	75
Picture Arrangement (PA)	12	8	25
Block Design (BD)	33	14	91
Object Assembly (OA)	24	12	75
(Symbol Search SS)	25	11	63

Sarah EVANS

GRAPH OF SUBTEST SCALED SCORES

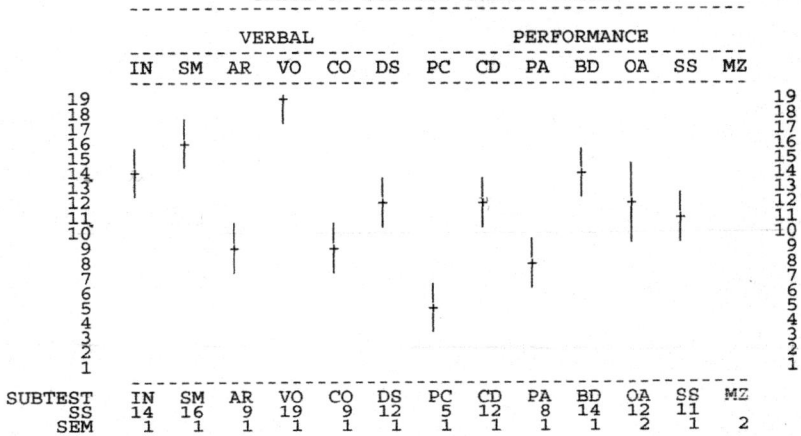

```
                VERBAL                    PERFORMANCE
        IN   SM   AR   VO   CO   DS   PC   CD   PA   BD   OA   SS   MZ
```

SUBTEST	IN	SM	AR	VO	CO	DS	PC	CD	PA	BD	OA	SS	MZ
SS	14	16	9	19	9	12	5	12	8	14	12	11	
SEM	1	1	1	1	1	1	1	1	1	1	2	1	2

TABLE OF AREA MEANS AND SIGNIFICANT DIFFERENCES

SUBTEST	SCALED SCORE	DIFFERENCE FROM THE MEAN	SIGNIFICANCE OF DIFFERENCE	FREQUENCY
VERBAL				
Information (IN)	14	0.83	ns	>25%
Similarities (SM)	16	2.83	.15	25%
Arithmetic (AR)	9	-4.17	.05	5%
Vocabulary (VO)	19	5.83	.05	<1%
Comprehension (CO)	9	-4.17	.05	10%
(Digit Span DS)	12	-1.17	ns	>25%
Mean Verbal Score = 13.17				
PERFORMANCE				
Picture Completion (PC)	5	-5.33	.05	5%
Coding (CD)	12	1.67	ns	>25%
Picture Arrangement (PA)	8	-2.33	ns	>25%
Block Design (BD)	14	3.67	.05	25%
Object Assembly (OA)	12	1.67	ns	>25%
(Symbol Search SS)	11	0.67	ns	>25%
Mean Performance Score = 10.33				

Sarah EVANS

ANALYSIS OF COMPOSITES

	AVERAGE SCALED SCORE	INDEX	PR
Bannatyne			
Verbal Conceptualization	14.7	125	95
Spatial	10.3	102	55
Acquired Knowledge	14.0	122	93
Sequential	11.0	106	66
Guilford			
Memory	11.7	110	75
Cognition	12.5	115	84
Evaluation	10.0	100	50
Convergent Production	10.0	100	50
Figural Content	10.3	102	55
Semantic Content	12.5	115	84
Symbolic Content	11.0	106	66
Horn			
Fluid Intelligence	11.2	107	68
Crystallized Intelligence	14.5	125	95
Retention Ability	11.7	110	75
Dean			
General Ability	12.3	113	81
Abstract Thought	15.0	126	96
Remote Memory	9.5	97	42
Auditory Memory	10.5	104	61
*Visual Memory	8.5	90	25
Social Comprehension	8.5	91	27
Kaufman			
WISC-R Freedom from Distract.	11.0	106	66
Simultaneous Processing	10.3	102	55
Reasoning	10.8	105	63
Verbal Reasoning	12.5	113	81
Nonverbal Reasoning	10.0	100	50
Verbal Concept Formation	17.5	139	>99
Fund of Information	16.5	133	99
Home Cultural Opportunities	12.5	114	82
Extent of Outside Reading	16.3	134	99
Long-Term Memory	14.0	122	93
Time Pressure I	10.0	100	50
Reproduction of a Model	13.0	116	86
*Visual Organiz. w/o Motor Activity	6.5	80	9
Visual Motor Coordination	12.7	116	86
*Vis. Percept. Meaningful Stimuli	8.3	90	25
Visual Closure	8.5	92	30
Visual Motor Speed	12.0	111	77
Essential vs. Nonessential Detail	9.7	98	45
Learning Ability	15.5	132	98
*Concentration	7.0	82	12
Trial and Error Learning	13.0	115	84
Ability to Respond when Uncertain	8.5	92	30
Flexibility	13.3	121	92
WISC-III			
ACID Profile	11.8	111	77
ACIDS Profile	11.6	110	75
Attention-Concentration	9.8	98	45

REPORT OF WISC-III TESTING
The Psychological Corporation

NAME: Sarah Evans

REPORT DATE: 06/20/06
BIRTH DATE: 10/12/95
TEST DATE: 06/20/06
EXAMINER:
TITLE:

AGE: 10 years, 8 months
GENDER: female

TEST RESULTS

SCALE	IQ	PR	95 PERCENT CONFIDENCE INTERVAL IQ	95 PERCENT CONFIDENCE INTERVAL PR	CLASSIFICATION OF INTELLECTUAL FUNCTIONING
Verbal	139	>99	131-143	98->99	
Performance	115	84	106-122	66- 93	
Full Scale	130	98	123-134	94- 99	very superior

Difference Between VIQ and PIQ = 24 (p < .05, Freq 6.2%)

FACTOR SUMMARY

	SS	INDEX	PR	95 PERCENT CONFIDENCE INTERVAL INDEX	95 PERCENT CONFIDENCE INTERVAL PR
Verbal Comprehension	71	144	>99	135-148	99->99
Perceptual Organization	52	119	90	109-125	73- 95
Freedom from Distractibility	23	109	73	99-117	47- 87
Processing Speed	20	101	53	91-111	27- 77

VERBAL

	RAW SCORE	SCALED SCORE	PR
Information (IN)	26	19	>99
Similarities (SM)	28	18	>99
Arithmetic (AR)	19	12	75
Vocabulary (VO)	44	17	99
Comprehension (CO)	29	17	99
(Digit Span DS)	14	11	63

PERFORMANCE

	RAW SCORE	SCALED SCORE	PR
Picture Completion (PC)	25	15	95
Coding (CD)	41	9	37
Picture Arrangement (PA)	32	11	63
Block Design (BD)	46	13	84
Object Assembly (OA)	34	13	84
(Symbol Search SS)	24	11	63

Sarah Evans

GRAPH OF SUBTEST SCALED SCORES

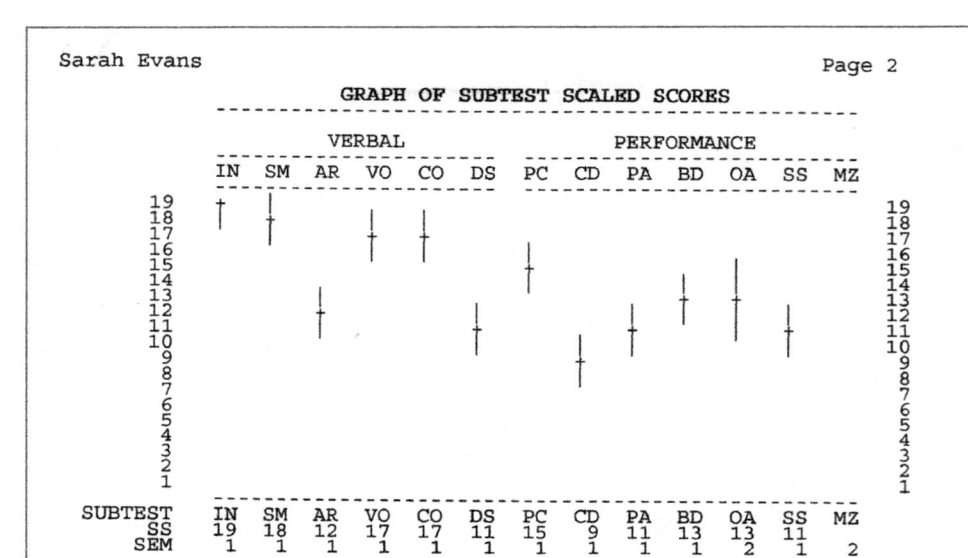

	VERBAL						PERFORMANCE					
SUBTEST	IN	SM	AR	VO	CO	DS	PC	CD	PA	BD	OA	SS	MZ
SS	19	18	12	17	17	11	15	9	11	13	13	11	
SEM	1	1	1	1	1	1	1	1	1	1	2	1	2

TABLE OF AREA MEANS AND SIGNIFICANT DIFFERENCES

SUBTEST	SCALED SCORE	DIFFERENCE FROM THE MEAN	SIGNIFICANCE OF DIFFERENCE	FREQUENCY
VERBAL				
Information (IN)	19	3.33	.05	10%
Similarities (SM)	18	2.33	ns	25%
Arithmetic (AR)	12	3.67	.05	10%
Vocabulary (VO)	17	1.33	ns	>25%
Comprehension (CO)	17	1.33	ns	>25%
(Digit Span DS)	11	4.67	.05	10%
Mean Verbal Score = 15.67				
PERFORMANCE				
Picture Completion (PC)	15	3.00	.15	25%
Coding (CD)	9	3.00	.15	>25%
Picture Arrangement (PA)	11	1.00	ns	>25%
Block Design (BD)	13	1.00	ns	>25%
Object Assembly (OA)	13	1.00	ns	>25%
(Symbol Search SS)	11	1.00	ns	>25%
Mean Performance Score = 12.00				

Sarah Evans

ANALYSIS OF COMPOSITES

	AVERAGE SCALED SCORE	INDEX	PR
Bannatyne			
Verbal Conceptualization	17.3	139	>99
Spatial	13.7	120	91
Acquired Knowledge	16.0	133	99
Sequential	10.7	104	61
Guilford			
Memory	14.0	124	95
Cognition	14.7	129	97
Evaluation	13.0	120	91
Convergent Production	10.0	100	50
Figural Content	13.7	120	91
Semantic Content	15.7	135	99
Symbolic Content	10.7	104	61
Horn			
Fluid Intelligence	13.5	123	94
Crystallized Intelligence	17.8	144	>99
Retention Ability	14.0	124	95
Dean			
General Ability	15.9	135	99
Abstract Thought	15.5	129	97
Remote Memory	17.0	138	99
Auditory Memory	11.5	109	73
Visual Memory	12.0	112	79
Social Comprehension	14.0	122	93
Kaufman			
WISC-R Freedom from Distract.	10.7	104	61
Simultaneous Processing	13.7	120	91
Reasoning	14.2	126	96
Verbal Reasoning	17.5	139	>99
Nonverbal Reasoning	12.0	111	77
Verbal Concept Formation	17.5	139	>99
Fund of Information	18.0	141	>99
Home Cultural Opportunities	16.0	135	99
Extent of Outside Reading	18.0	143	>99
Long-Term Memory	16.0	133	99
Time Pressure I	12.2	114	82
Reproduction of a Model	11.0	105	63
Visual Organiz. w/o Motor Activity	13.0	117	87
Visual Motor Coordination	11.7	110	75
Vis. Percept. Meaningful Stimuli	13.0	118	88
Visual Closure	14.0	121	92
Visual Motor Speed	11.0	106	66
Essential vs. Nonessential Detail	14.7	128	97
Learning Ability	13.0	117	87
Concentration	13.5	120	91
Trial and Error Learning	13.0	115	84
Ability to Respond when Uncertain	14.0	121	92
Flexibility	14.0	125	95
WISC-III			
ACID Profile	12.8	118	88
ACIDS Profile	12.4	116	86
Attention-Concentration	11.6	110	75

Appendix D
Sarah's Treatment List

Sarah's Treatment List

No	Date	Treatment
1	4-17-2001	Egg mix
2	4-23-2001	Calcium, casein
3	4-30-2001	Vitamin C, ascorbic acid, citrus mix
4	5-04-2001	Vitamin B-complex
5	5-10-2001	Sugar mix
6	5-16-2001	Vitamin A
7	5-24-2001	Mineral mix
8	6-01-2001	Iron mix
9	6-11-2001	Salts and chlorides
10	6-14-2001	Amino acids I
11	6-18-2001	Amino acids II
12	6-23-2001	Measles, mumps, and rubella vaccine
13	6-26-2001	Diphtheria vaccine
14	7-03-2001	Tetanus vaccine
15	7-10-2001	Hepatitis B vaccine
16	7-17-2001	Hepatitis B power treatment
17	7-24-2001	Salicylic acid
18	8-14-2001	Calcium salicylate
19	8-17-2001	Copper
20	8-21-2001	Albumin
21	8-28-2001	Gluten
22	9-04-2001	*Toxoplasma gondii*
23	9-11-2001	*Toxoplasma gondii* power treatment 1
24	9-20-2001	Salicylate power treatment
25	9-27-2001	Copper and vanadium
26	10-04-2001	Selenium, brain mapping
27	10-18-2001	Zinc
28	10-28-2001	Acetylcholine and neurotransmitters
29	11-1-2001	Brain Balance plus causal trellis
30	11-8-2001	Serotonin, methionine
31	11-15-2001	Acetic acid
32	11-20-2001	Heavy metals
33	11-26-2001	Chemicals
34	11-29-2001	*Toxoplasma gondii* power treatment 2

35	12-06-2001	Hypothalamus and mercury frequency data collection
36	12-13-2001	Monosodium glutamate
37	12-20-2001	*Toxoplasma gondii* power treatment 3
38	1-03-2002	*Toxoplasma gondii* power treatment 4
39	1-10-2002	Potato mix
40	1-17-2002	*Toxoplasma gondii* power treatment 5
41	2-7-2002	*Toxoplasma gondii* power treatment 6
43*	2-14-2002	1st stress hypothalamus
44*	2-18-2002	2nd stress hypothalamus—Hg sol, heavy metals
45*	2-21-2002	Amygdala, dura, brain, lymph, vaccines, solvents, herbicides, aluminum, cadmium, paint, heavy metals
46*	2-25-2002	3rd stressed brain-pharmaceuticals, mercury, cadmium, heavy metals, vaccines, MMR
47*	2-28-2002	2nd stress RBC—mercury, heavy metals, cadmium
48*	3-04-2002	3rd stress whole body, RBC—heavy metals, copper, mercury
49*	3-07-2002	1st degeneration hematopoietic zone DPT, vaccines
50*	3-11-2002	3rd stress thymus—helminth, copper, lead, cadmium, supplements, heavy metals
51	3-14-2002	*Toxoplasma gondii* and the helminth
52	3-18-2002	*Toxoplasma gondii* power treatment 7
53	3-21-2002	*Toxoplasma gondii* Sarah's personal energy
54	3-28-2002	*Toxoplasma gondii* power treatment 9
55	4-04-2002	*Toxoplasma gondii* power treatment 10
57	4-11-2002	*Toxoplasma gondii* amplification vial
58	4-15-2002	Central nervous system gram + bacteria, intestinal mucosa
59*	4-22-2002	2nd stress brain—*Toxoplasma gondii*
60*	4-25-2002	3 brain regions—*Toxoplasma gondii*, stressors, fruits, superficial mycoses, tetanus, rabies

* Indicates a treatment diagnosed using Field Control Therapy®.

61*	4-29-2002	2nd stress hypothalamus—xenobiotics, lead, heavy metals, solvents, lymph
62*	5-02-2002	2nd stress hypothalamus herbicides, mercury
63*	5-06-2002	3rd stress thymus, lymph—aluminum, mercury, pesticides, xenobiotics
64*	5-9-2002	3rd stress brain—bacteria, supplements, mercury, pharmaceuticals, poliomyelitis
65	5-13-2002	Parasite Mix II & *Toxoplasma gondii*
66	5-15-2002	*Staphylococcus* pleo and *Escherichia coli* pleo
67	5-16-2002	*Toxoplasma gondii* and Sarah's personal energy
68*	5-20-2002	2nd stress hypothalamus—bacteria, herbicides, heavy metals
69	5-27-2002	Zinc
70*	6-06-2002	2nd stress whole brain, lymph— heavy metals, helminths, vaccines, bacteria, aluminum, tobacco, xenobiotics, solvents
71	6-08-2002	Ren vessel
72*	6-10-2002	Stressed amygdala, occipital cerebral cortex—helminths, mercury, cadmium, heavy metals, lymph
73*	6-12-2002	1st stress thyroid—herbicides, cadmium, bacteria
74*	6-14-2002	1st degeneration RBCs—titanium, palladium, lithium, mercury, heavy metals
75*	6-17-2002	4th stress hemopoietic zone—mercury, helminths, virus, MMR, lymph
76*	6-21-2002	1st stress hemopoietic zone, pharmacology, streptococcus, vaccines, DPT, MMR, lymph
77*	6-24-2002	System discovery—whole body— trematodes (helminths) metals, food additives, superficial mycoses, MMR, herbicides
78*	6-26-2002	4th stress hemopoietic zone—heavy metals, ren vessel
79*	6-28-2002	1st degeneration hemopoietic zone, ren vessel—mercury, vaccines, virus

* Indicates a treatment diagnosed using Field Control Therapy®.

80*	7-01-2002	1st degeneration hematopoietic zone—mercury, paint, xenobiotics, vaccines, cadmium
81	7-03-2002	Right and left cerebral cortex, brain, nerves-neuropathogen, mercury, aluminum, cadmium, lymph
82*	7-08-2002	1st stress hypothalamus DNA-mercury, virus, xenobiotics, heavy metals, lead, virus
83	7-10-2002	Stinging insects—serotonin, dopamine, norepinephrine, corticosteroids, histidine
84*	7-12-2002	2nd stress corpus callosum-vaccines, mercury, heavy metals, cadmium, virus
85*	7-18-2002	3rd stress corpus callosum-vaccines, mercury, aluminum, heavy metals, solvents
86	7-22-2002	*Toxoplasma gondii*, neurotransmitters, lymph
87*	7-24-2002	3rd stress brain—xenobiotics, mercury, aluminum, paint, dissolved mercury
88	8-02-2002	*Toxoplasma gondii*, lymph
89*	8-23-2002	1st stress hematopoietic zone— lead, mercury, pesticides, herbicides, lymph, specific bandwidth range
90	8-27-2002	*Toxoplasma gondii*, biovial, parasites
91*	8-29-2002	2nd stress brain—herbicides, vaccines, cadmium, solvents, lead, mercury, DPT
92*	9-03-2002	3rd stress brain—heavy metals, herbicides, aluminum, lymph
93*	9-05-2002	4th stress brain, hypothalamus—xenobiotics mercury, pesticides, lead, cadmium, frequency range B, lymph
94	9-10-2002	*Toxoplasma gondii*, biovial, lymph
95	9-12-2002	Fatty acids, animal fat, vegetable fat, cell membranes, liver
96*	9-17-2002	3rd stress brain, hypothalamus, pituitary—paint, pesticides, herbicides, xenobiotics, heavy metals, large intestine toxins
97*	9-19-2002	3rd stress WBC, RBC—heavy metals, pharmaceuticals, xenobiotics, lymph

* Indicates a treatment diagnosed using Field Control Therapy®.

#	Date	Description
98	9-24-2002	Live vaccines-Merck Pharmaceutical MMR, Aventis Pasteur DPT, toxoids and acellular Pert vac, hemophilus B conj
99*	9-26-2002	3rd stress brain—previous immune samples
100*	10-01-2002	3rd stress brain—vaccines, xenobiotics, heavy metals, bacteria, cadmium, herbicides, solvents, lymph
101	10-03-2002	Central nervous system, cerebral cortex, neural vial, soluble fibrin monomer
102*	10-08-2002	1st stress liver, WBC—lead, pesticides, aluminum, streptococcus, protozoa, heavy metals, herbicides, dissolved mercury, xenobiotics, virus
103	10-10-2002	*Toxoplasma gondii*
104*	10-15-2002	3rd stress brain, cerebral cortex—large intestine toxins, lead, mercury, fibrin deposits, pesticides, minerals, thrombin, AA, TNFalpha
105*	10-17-2002	4th stress brain—pesticides xenobiotics, heavy metals, mercury, vaccines, virus, DPT, MMR, lymph
106*	10-22-2002	1st stress brain—cadmium, heavy metals, mercury, lymph
107*	10-24-02	3rd stress TB— liver—heavy metals, mercury, lead, herbicide, pesticides, cadmium, aluminum, solvents, pharmaceuticals, vaccines, xenobiotics, paint, lymph
108*	10-29-2002	3rd stress brain—Prot C, fibrin deposit, solvent, soluble fibrin, IL, TNFalpha, Prot S Lymph
109*	11-05-2002	2nd stress liver, gall bladder—mercury, helminths, solvents, xenobiotics, aluminum, paint, lead, virus
110	11-07-2002	*Toxoplasma gondii*, parasite II, new dog
111	11-12-2002	EPGF IC
112	11-14-2002	Neurotransmitters, CNS, cerebral cortex, meninges, lymph

* Indicates a treatment diagnosed using Field Control Therapy®.

113*	11-19-2002	1st hypothalamus—solvents, xenobiotics, heavy metals, pesticides, pharmaceuticals, paint, gluten, lymph
114*	11-21-2002	1st stress hypothalamus—solvents mercury, xenobiotics, gluten, lymph
115	11-26-2002	Neurotransmitters, CNS, cerebral cortex—aluminum, mercury, TNFalpha, dissolved fibrin, neurovial, biovial, lymph
116	11-29-2002	*Toxoplasma gondii*, parasite II
117*	12-03-2002	1st stress cerebral cortex—pesticides, herbicides, heavy metals, dissolved mercury, solvents, aluminum, lead, lymph drainage
118*	12-10-2002	1st stress hematopoietic zone—herbicides, pesticides, paint, lymph drainage
119*	12-12-2002	2nd stress hematopoietic zone—aluminum, solvents, paint, mercury, xenobiotics, cadmium, lymph
120	12-19-2002	*Toxoplasma gondii*
121*	1-07-2002	1st stress ACS*, Brain— *T. gondii*, heavy metals, cadmium, mercury, xenobiotics, pesticides, herbicides
122	1-09-2003	DNA, mercury vivus, dissolved mercury, cadmium, paint aluminum, heavy metals, herbicides
123	1-14-2003	ACS, cerebral cortex—cadmium, pesticides, solvents, xenobiotics aluminum
124	1-16-2003	ACS, Brain, cerebral cortex-lead, pesticides, herbicides, cadmium, aluminum, xenobiotics, mercury, DPT
125	1-21-2003	ACS—dissolved mercury, lead, heavy metals, pesticides, pharmaceuticals, solvents, xenobiotics, asbestos, cadmium, lymph drainage
126*	1-23-2003	5th stress brain, ACS— dissolved mercury, mercury, heavy metals, solvents, xenobiotics, MMR, lymph

* Indicates a treatment diagnosed using Field Control Therapy®.

127*	1-28-2003	1st stress brain, cerebral cortex, ACS, xenobiotics, heavy metals, solvents, mercury, cadmium
128	1-30-2003	ACS, cerebral cortex, xenobiotics, heavy metals, solvents, lead, herbicides, aluminum, dissolved mercury, cadmium
129	2-04-2003	*Toxoplasma gondii* power treatment
130	2-06-2003	Total brain, cerebral cortex, brain balance
131*	2-11-2003	1st stress hematopoietic zone, RBC—heavy metals, xenobiotics, cadmium, aluminum, fluorides, pesticides, herbicides, solvents
132*	2-20-2003	1st stress hematopoietic zone, RBC, CNT-mercury, heavy metals, xenobiotics, solvents, pesticides, herbicides, fluorides
133*	2-25-2003	1st stress hematopoietic zone—cadmium, aluminum, mercury, xenobiotics, solvents, pesticides, copper, herbicides,
134*	2-27-2003	1st stress, small intestine, pancreas, RBC, ACS—aluminum, xenobiotics, mercury, solvents, heavy metals, paint, MMR, virus, DPT
135*	3-04-2003	2nd stress small intestine, ACS—xenobiotics, solvents, paint, herbicides, pesticides, MMR, DPT, heavy metals, cadmium, aluminum, mercury, fluoride, dissolved mercury, large intestine toxins
136	3-06-2003	ACS, large intestine
137	3-11-2003	ACS, CNT, hematopoietic zone, RBC, dissolved mercury, cadmium, xenobiotics, pesticides, herbicides, aluminum
138*	3-13-2003	2nd stress, ACS, hematopoietic zone, CNT, RBC, WBC, heavy metals, aluminum, cadmium, xenobiotics, solvents, paint
139	3-18-2003	ACS, *Toxoplasma gondii*, parasite I
140	3-22-2003	ACS, Lyme disease
141*	3-25-2003	1st stress, brain—mercury, dissolved mercury, heavy metals, cadmium, solvents, xenobiotics, pesticides, herbicides

* Indicates a treatment diagnosed using Field Control Therapy®.

142*	3-27-2003	2nd stress cerebral cortex—mercury, xenobiotics, aluminum, solvents, lymph
143*	4-03-2003	3rd stress ACS, brain—dissolved mercury, mercury, cadmium, xenobiotics, solvents, paint, heavy metals, lymph drainage
144*	4-08-2003	2nd stress, ACS cerebral cortex, corpus callosum—dissolved mercury, solvents, xenobiotics, pesticides, herbicides, aluminum, fluorides, cadmium, lymph
145	4-11-2003	Brain—heavy metals, solvents, paint, mercury, aluminum, solvents, lymph
146	4-17-2003	ACS Brain—solvents, aluminum, fluorides, pesticides, herbicides
147	4-22-2003	ACS, *Toxoplasma gondii*
148	4-24-2003	ACS, *Toxoplasma gondii*, ocular tracking
149*	4-29-2003	2nd stress, ACS, cerebral cortex— dissolved mercury, heavy metals, cadmium, lead, solvents, xenobiotics, paint, aluminum, pesticides, lymph drainage
150*	5-06-2003	Cerebral Cortex 2nd stress level-Hg sol, Hg viv, HM, Cd, Pb, solvents, xenobiotics, paint, Al,
151*	5-08-2003	3rd stress, ACS, cerebral cortex—paint, mercury, DPT, pesticides
152	5-13-2003	Berry mix
153*	5-20-2003	Cerebral Cortex, 3rd stress level, HM, Hgsol, Hgviv Pb, Cd, solvents, xenobiotics, pesticides, herbicides, lymph
154	5-29-2003	*Ascaris lumbricoides, Necator americanus*
155	6-03-2003	*Toxoplasma gondii*
156	6-05-2003	Strawberries
157	6-10-2003	Vinegar
158	6-12-2003	Retina: aluminum, heavy metals, pesticides, herbicides, solvents, xenobiotics, lymph drainage
159	6-16-2003	Blueberry mix—fear of writing
160	6-23-2003	ACS, DNA, Hg sol, Hg viv, Al, Pb, Cd, xenobiotics, lymph drainage

* Indicates a treatment diagnosed using Field Control Therapy®.

161*	6-26-2003	ACS, 1st level Hg Pest, Pb, Cd, xenobiotics, HM, lymph drainage
162*	7-03-2003	ACS 1st level, Vis. Cortex, occipital lobe, speech ctr., retina, Hg sol, HM, xenobiotics, herbicides, Cd, Al, lymph
163	7-07-2003	Tomato, peppers, nightshades
164	7-10-2003	Solvents, heavy metals, lead, xenobiotics, aluminum, lymph
165	7-24-2003	Liver, histamine, histidine, sugar, calcitonin, serotonin, lymph
166	7-28-2003	Lyme disease
167	7-31-2003	Lyme disease
168	8-07-2003	Lyme disease
169	8-18-2003	Corn mix
170	8-21-2003	Brain, DNA, HM, Hg, xenobiotics, solvents, Cd, herbicides, aluminum, pesticides
171	12-04-2003	DNA/RNA, endocrine axis, neuro-transmitters, oxygen, Qi, histamines, BBF
172	12-08-2003	Walnuts and peanuts
173	12-11-2003	Milk mix
174	12-15-2003	peanuts, butter, and cream
175	12-18-2003	*Toxoplasma gondii*
176	12-23-2003	ACS
177	1-03-2004	ACS hypothalamus, pituitary, octopamine, dopamine, GABA, neurotransmitters
178	1-05-2004	ACS, acute V&B, PSP, TIT
179	1-15-2004	Amygdala, cerebral cortex, neurotoxins
180	1-12-2004	Cerebral cortex, amygdala, neurons, CNS, visual cortex, xenobiotics, fluoride, HM, Al, Pb, Hg sol, Hg viv, cadmium
181	1-19-2004	*Toxoplasma gondii*
182*	1-22-2004	ACS 1st level Pit, HM, Hg sol, Hg viv, cadmium
183	1-26-2004	*Toxoplasma gondii* power treatment
184	1-29-2004	*Toxoplasma gondii*
185.	2-02-2004	ACS, Brain, cerebral cortex, visual cortex, lymph drainage

* Indicates a treatment diagnosed using Field Control Therapy®.

186	2-09-2004	Brain, cerebral cortex, neurovial, hg sol, Hg viv, HM, solvents, xenobiotics, Cd, fluoride, Pb, lymph drainage
187	2-12-2004	Corpus callosum, Hg sol, Hg viv, Pb, Cd, Al, herbicides pesticides, lymph drainage
188	2-16-2004	Unknown
189	2-19-2004	Saliva
190	2-23-2004	Hypothalamus, adrenal cortex, pituitary, thyroid, T3, T4, dopamine, serotonin, xenobiotics, calcitonin, norepinephrine, ACTH, lymph
191	2-26-2004	Brain, taurine, carnitine, glutathione, isoleucine, lymph
192	3-01-2004	Hematopoietic zone, HM, Hg viv, solvents, herbicides, Cd, Cn, Al, xenobiotics, lymph drainage
193	3-04-2004	*Toxoplasma gondii*
194	3-15-2004	Brain, corpus callosum, paint, Pb, Hg viv, HM, Cd, Al, solvents, lymph
195	4-08-2004	*Toxoplasma gondii*
196	4-12-2004	Hematopoietic zone, RBCs, HM, Hg sol, Hg viv, herbicides, pesticides, Al, Fl, Cd, lymph
197	4-15-2004	Hypothalamus, CNS, reticular formation, Cd, HM, Hg viv, herbicides, xenobiotics, herbicides, lymph

Appendix E
How to Find a NAET or an FCT Practitioner

How to Find a NAET Practitioner

Nambudripad's Allergy Research Foundation (NARF) has a very well constructed website located at www.naet.com. Upon entering the site you will find a menu on the left. Select the bar that reads "AUTISM TREATMENT CENTER." This will take you to another window with a menu bar across the top. Select "Practitioner Locator." Now you can enter your zip code or country of origin, and a list of practitioners in your area will appear.
An essential document is the NAET Guide Book, which is also available through the NAET website or on Amazon.com. This book explains the technique step-by-step, as well as what the patient's responsibilities are.

Additional resources by Dr. Nambudripad include:

Freedom from Environmental Sensitivities
Say Good-bye to Illness
Say Good-bye to Children's Allergies
Say Good-bye to Your Allergies
Say Good-bye to Asthma
Say Good-bye to Allergy-Related Autism
Living Pain Free
NAET Autism Study 2004-2005 on DVD

How to Find an Field Control Therapist®

To locate an FCT® practitioner go to : *http://www.yurkovsky.com*. There is contact information on the website. Place a phone call or send an email requesting the location of an FCT® practitioner in your area.

Appendix F
Resources Used

Resources Used

Sites for books and DVDs:

http://www.naet.com/productcart/pc/viewCategories.asp?idCategory=9
http://healthlinkpartners.com/gplbookstore/index.php
http://www.fgshop.org
http://www.hwtears.com/hwt

Sites for nutrition:

www.wholefoodsmarket.com
(search for gluten-free, dairy-free)
www.ener-g.com/ (Good root products, excellent tapioca starch.)
www.indianharvest.com/ (good rice products; avoid the beans.)
www.lundberg.com/ (best grain products)

Sites for supplements:

www.drugstore.com/
www.myvillagegreen.com/
www.kirkmanlabs.com/ (this laboratory specializes in digestive enzymes for autistic kids)

Government sites:

www.fda.gov (search mercury and autism)
www.nimh.nih.gov
www.cdc.gov

Index

Symbols

3-Day Rule 78, 96

A

Acetic Acid 171
Acetylcholine 165
Acetylsalicylic acid 82
Additional Symptoms 77
ADD Symptoms 77
Adrenaline 86
Albumin 149
Aldehydes 85
Allergic Symptoms 77
Aluminum 200
Ambient energies 177
American Girl magazine 209
Amino Acids 102
Amino Acids I 135
Amino Acids II 136
Amygdala 187
Antioxidant OPCs 101
Aromatic aldehydes 80, 85, 86
Aspirin-sensitivity 82
Attention deficit 82
Autism Research Institute 98
Autism Source 111
Autism Symptoms 77
Autistic 56
Autistic enterocolitis 114
Azodicarbonamide (ADA) 82

B

Barley 84
Barley malt 83

B-Complex Vitamins 98, 104
Bioelectricity 107
Biofield 118
Bluebonnet 97
Brain Balance 166
Butylated hydroxyanisole (BHA) 82
Butylated hydroxytoluene (BHT) 82

C

Cadmium 200
Calcium Mix 125
Calcium salicylate 85
Calcium Salicylate 147
Carbon-carbon double bond 90
Carnitine 114
Carnitor 114
Casein 83
Casein peptides 113
Casomorphin 83, 84, 127
Cellular memory 113
Chelated minerals 100
Chelation process 100
Chemical chelation 143
Chi 107
Childhood Illness and the Allergy Connection 69
Chinese emotions 175
Chinese Medicine 119
Choline 98, 114
Citric acid 82
Coccidia 151
Cod Liver Oil 98
Coil 177
College Board Accuplacer Examination 209
Composition journal 66, 68
Contactants 172
Copper 147

Corn 84
Corn syrup 83
Corpus callosum 118
Country Life 97
Cross dominance 118
Cross Reactions 88
Cytokines 168

D

Dairy-free 73, 113
Dairy Sensitivity 83
Dairy stagnation 113
Dana Laake 111
Denatured 114
Detoxify 113
Dextrose 83
Diagnostic and Statistical Manual of Mental Disorders 75
Diphtheria 137, 139
Disodium guanylate (DSG) 82
Disodium inosinate (DSI) 82
DMG 98
DMSA 143
Docosahexaenoic acid (DHA) 99
Doctor's Data 112
Double-bonded carbon atoms 90
Duluth, Georgia 112
Dura Mater 187

E

Eggs 91
Eicosanoids 168
Electrical interference 179
Electrical noise 179
Electrostim 120
Energy medicine (EM) 107, 165
Epsom salts bath protocol 192

Epsom salts baths 154
Estrogen (from soy) 101
Ethane gas 206
Expense 72

F

FD&C Blue no. 2 82
FD&C Red no. 40 82
FD&C Yellow no. 5 82
Feingold, Ben F. MD 69
Fever 154
Field Control Therapy® 108, 154, 183, 197
Fluoride 201
Folic acid 98
Food Challenges 91
Food Elimination List 80, 87
Food Ingredient Labels 70
Free-range beef 91
Frequencies 179

G

Gamma-linolenic acid (GLA) 100
Genetically modified organisms 71
Gliadorphin 84
Glucose 83
Gluten 84, 150
Gluten-Free Flour Blend 85
Gluteomorphin 84
Goodheart, George DC 108
Grain-free 73
Great Plains Laboratory 112

H

Heavy Metals 172
Helminth 195, 196
Hematopoietic zone 184, 201

Hepatitis B 137, 141
Herbicides 200
Hidden Food Additives 91
High fructose corn syrup 83
Hold a memory 113
Home-schooling 191
Home-school umbrella group 192
Human biofield 118
Hydrogenated fats 89
Hydrolyzed corn syrup 83
Hyperactivity 82
Hypothalamus 173, 185

I

Immune-boosting properties 100
Immune system 155
Immunoglobulin E 53
Indigotine 92
Inflammation-fighting properties 100
Ingestants 172
Inhalants 172
Injectants 172
Inositol 98, 114
Insulin 88
Intestinal dysbiosis markers 113
Iron 98

J

Johns Hopkins 54
Johns Hopkins University Center for Gifted and Talented Children 209
Junior Olympics 209

K

Kaiser Permanente 69

Kamut 84
Kennedy Krieger Institute 192, 209
Killer cells 155
Kinesiology 108, 121

L

Lead 200
Lenexa, Kansas 112
Lindamood Auditory
    Conceptualization Test 192
Live-cell blood erythrocyte test 112
Luncheon meats 91

M

Maltodextrin 83
Maltose 83
Marrow Bone Stock 102, 103
Maryland Institute of Traditional
Maryland Oriental Medical
    Association (MOMA) 119
Masquelier's OPCs 101
Measles, mumps, and rubella
    (MMR) 118, 138
Mercury 114, 173
Meridian 110
Meridian system 107
Metabolic pathways 114
MetaMetrix Clinical Laboratory 112
Methionine 167
Millet 84
Minerals 100
Modified food starch 83
Monosodium Glutamate 174
Monosodium glutamate (MSG) 82
Mood swings 82
Muscle response testing (MRT) 108

Myelin sheath 99

N

NAET Research Institute 109
Nambudripad, Devi MD
    PhD LAc DC 109
Nambudripad's Allergy Elimination
    Technique (NAET) 108
National Center for Complementary
    and Alternative Medicine
    (NCCAM) 119
National Institutes of Health 119
Naturally Occurring 81
Neural Inflammation 168
Neural synapse receptor 82
Neuromins DHA 99, 100
Neuromuscular junctions 165
Neurotransmitters 88, 165
Nitric oxide synthase 167
N,N-dimethylglycine (DMG) 98
Non-GMO Project 71
Non-hydrogenated fats 89
Non-naturally Occurring 81
Norepinephrine 88, 167
Nutritional Supplements 73, 104, 170

O

Oats 84
Oligomeric proanthocyanidins
(OPC) 101
Omega-3 90, 99
Omega-6 90, 100
Oocytes 156
Optic Nerve 152
Organic Foods Store 72

P

PABA 98
Parasite II 156
Parasites 151
Parasitic protozoa 151
Parasitic spores 156
Peabody Picture Vocabulary Test 192
Pernicious energy 177
Pesticides 200
Phenolic Foods 87
Phenols 80, 85
Phenylethylamine 167
Power Treatment 142
Product Labels 80
Pyrimethamine 153

Q

Qi 107

R

Radioallergosorbent test (RAST) 53
Reactive stagnation 119
Red Blood Cell Elements 112
Red Blood Cells 188
Retina(s) 98, 152, 153, 203
Rice 84
Rice syrup 83
Rimland, Bernard MD 98
Rona, Zoltan MD 69
Royal Free Hospital 114
Rubella 114
Rye 84

S

Salicylate 80, 78, 85, 86, 87
Salicylate Power 159
Salicylic Acid 145
Salts and Chlorides 134

Saturated fat 89
Scalar energy 107
Selenium 161
Senomyx 82
Serotonin 102, 167
Severe bleeding 82
Solgar 97
Soluble fibrin monomer 168
Solvents 200
Soy 101
Spelt 84
Spleen Qi deficiency 119
Stagnation 113
Statistically significant 193
St. Charles, Illinois 112
Stressed level system (FCT) 183
Submolecular biology 107
Sucrose 83
Sugar in Labels 83
Sugar Mix 129
Sulfonamides 153
Sunflower seed oil 90

T

Tartrazine 82, 91
Tertiary butylhydroquinone (TBHQ) 82
Test of Language Competence 192
Test of Nonverbal Intelligence 192
Test of Word Finding 192
Tests strong 110
Tetanus 137, 140
T. gondii Power 154, 156, see also *Toxoplasma gondii*
The ADD Nutrition Solution 69
The Coil 177
"the lines" 156
Thimerosal 114
Thymus 195
TMG 98
Toxoplasma gondii (*T. gondii*) 151, 153, 154, 156, 203
Traditional Chinese medicine (TCM) 108
Trigger foods 91, 113
Tryptophan 102
Twin Labs 97
Tyrosine 113

U

University of Texas 72
Unlocking stressed organs 184
Uptake 97, 120
Urine Organix Profile 112

V

Vanadium 160
Vasoactive amines 168
Village Green Apothecary 97
Visual Cortex 152
Vital energy 107
Vitamin A 98, 131
Vitamin C 126
Vruit 124

W

Wakefield, Andrew MD 114, 137
Waxes 206
Wechsler Intelligence Scale 192
Wheat 84
Whole Foods Co-op 72
Why Is Your Child Hyperactive? 69

Winter itch 90
Woodcock-Johnson Tests 192

X

Xanthan gum 85
Xenobiotics 200

Y

Yurkovsky, Savely MD 108, 154, 183, 197

Z

Zimmerman, Marcia CN 69
Zinc 162

Advance Praise for Beating Autism
Dr. Devi's Review

Over a period of 30 years, I have had the opportunity to treat hundreds of children, from both sexes, who came to me with a label of autism. It was not an easy diagnosis that their helpless parents could handle. Some parents even disguised their family names and children's names for the fear that someone they knew would find out that their child is autistic. In 1980's, there was a great stigma attached to this diagnosis. I began my autism practice during at this time. I had to treat children for their sensitivities to foods, drinks, nutritional supplements, environmental sensitivity factors, and chemical factors as well as support the parents' emotions and sufferings. Most parents wanted a quick remedy, like swallowing a magic pill and the child would be cured of autism. It is not that easy. What can one do when the child's brain is perceiving everything in the child's world as a poison? The child's brain gets confused and frightened, sends wrong signals to the rest of the body, and leads to what we see in the child as autistic behaviors. So far no one has developed a magic potion to remedy such behaviors. Even though it takes hundreds of treatments in children with full spectrum autism, NAET has finally been able to put a stop to such devastating reactions and help children lead a normal lives. Dedicated parents who take the time to understand the NAET process, follow the NAET instructions, and help the child through the step-by-step elimination of various sensitivities to foods, nutrients, and environmental causes, hold the key to helping that child come out of the label of autism and join the normal children of the world. Holding back her emotions, without any hesitation, Anne M. Evans chose to travel the rocky road to bring her daughter Sarah back from the autistic world of uncertainty and confusion. The painful, but joyous, true story of her journey, and how that led to Sarah's full recovery from autism, is shared so beautifully in the book *Beating Autism*. This book is not only an inspiration for other mothers with children with Autism Spectrum Disorders (ASD), but will also serve as an informational guide for those who think they are at the end of the road with their child's health and progress and do not know where to turn. Great Book! A Must Read for everyone who wants to understand autism and how one can be freed from the clutches of this devastating malady- Autism.

Devi Nambudripad MD PhD LAc
Director Nambudripad's Allergy Research Foundation
Creator of Nambudripad's Allergy Elimination Technique (NAET)
www.naet.com

A Review by Laurence A Becker PhD

A major paradigm shift in autism occurred in 1964, when Dr. Bernard Rimland moved the discussion of autism from "refrigerator mothers," the primary psychological medical definition of the cause of autism, to a biomedical approach. Then another shift for me and many others in 2000, was Karyn Seroussi's Unraveling the Mystery of Autism and Pervasive Developmental Disorder. (My own education in autism had begun in 1978, when we were living in a tiny fishing village in DownEast, Maine, when my 14 year old daughter brought home a book that had been given to her by one of her classmates. The book was Son Rise by Barry Neal Kaufman . That was the first time I had ever heard the word autism.)

Now in 2015, I believe *Beating Autism: How Alternative Medicine Cured My Child*, has, for me, (and I am convinced for many others) provided yet another major paradigm shift! *Beating Autism* has pushed the biomedical approach to a new level. First, it identifies the pathogens (toxins and parasites) colonizing a child's heart, lungs, eyes, intestines, and brain; and, then it describes the accomplishment of removing them through 197 treatments, using integrated Chinese medicine and energy healing. Then, the reader is provided with documentation in the form of before and after medical tests, intelligence tests, photographs and copious notes from daily diaries of the treatment protocols.

Certainly this is one of the most compelling and comprehensive accounts of autism that I have read in the last 40 years!

I believe the book needs a WARNING label:

Beware! Do not attempt to read this book unless you are willing to entertain a major scientific learning curve AND are prepared to acknowledge a major paradigm shift in the cause and cure of autism!

I have heard it said by many in the Western medical community, "We do not know the cause of autism, but we know there is no cure." At last comes along a mother who dares to delve deeply into biology, immunology, traditional and integrated Chinese medicine both to discover the cause of her daughter's autism and to proceed to cure it.

Be prepared to witness a mother's amazement and joy of participating in the "miracle" of discovery and healing. It is a journey you will never forget and will forever be changed by experiencing it with the author, her husband, and their beautiful, brilliant, and healed daughter, Sarah.

Laurence A. Becker, PhD, educator/aqueduct
CREATIVE LEARNING ENVIRONMENTS

KIRKUS REVIEWS

A mother turns to Chinese medicine and alternative therapies to heal her autistic child.

Evans' daughter, Sarah, was a bright, happy child until the age of 4, when she began exhibiting some unusual symptoms, including an awkward gait, repetitive speech patterns, and trouble socializing with other children. Her behavioral issues were compounded by disturbing physical symptoms, including food sensitivities, hives, vomiting, and bug bites that refused to heal. Trips to numerous doctors yielded no clear answers. The official diagnosis from her pediatrician was "delayed development," although Evans recounts that "he told me in words that she was autistic." Desperate for answers, the author embarked on a quest to cure her child. Eventually, a friend's recommendation led her to Dr. Ross J. Stark, who practiced traditional Chinese medicine as well as an unusual alternative therapy called Nambudripad's Allergy Elimination Technique, developed by a chiropractor and acupuncturist named Devi Nambudripad in the 1980s. Once Sarah began the NAET treatments, Evans writes, her condition improved dramatically. The child's visits to Dr. Stark, coupled with dietary changes, seemed to reduce her dyslexia symptoms, improve her ability to focus, and enhance her coordination. The author tells of her daughter's therapy in exhaustive detail, explaining the meticulous process of clearing Sarah's body of the "blockages in her system that did not allow various nutrients to flow freely." Although Evans had already removed many problematic foods from Sarah's diet months earlier, she says, "they would still be present in her system since the body carries a memory of everything that passes through it"; the alternative therapies, she notes, recalibrated Sarah's digestive system and eventually allowed her to return some offending foods to her diet. Evans' account of her daughter's transformation is certainly inspiring....The author's commitment to doing whatever it took to ease her daughter's symptoms will appeal to other parents looking for solutions to their own children's health problems.

Skeptics will raise their eyebrows, but open-minded parents will find encouragement in Evans' story.

Kirkus Reviews

About the Author

Anne M. Evans received her undergraduate degree in microbiology from the University of Texas at Austin 1986 and her graduate degree in Biomedical Communications from the University of Texas Southwestern Medical Center in Dallas in 1989. She was publications and marketing manager for two global biotech firms. She was married to Norman Evans, an electrical engineer, in 1993 and gave birth to Sarah 1995. Her publications include: *Cryofixation, Cryolabeling, and Cryotransfer*, and *Immunogold Labeling*. She collaborated on the Pediatric Handbook for the University of Texas Systems Medical Schools.

CPSIA information can be obtained
at www.ICGtesting.com
Printed in the USA
BVOW11s0929160316

440539BV00009B/248/P